Romans and Britons
in
North-West England

Romans and Britons in North-West England

David Shotter

Substantially Revised and Expanded Edition

Centre for North-West Regional Studies
University of Lancaster
2004
Series Editor: Jean Turnbull

Romans and Britons in North-West England, 3rd Edition

This volume is the 51st in a series published by the
Centre for North-West Regional Studies at the University of Lancaster

Text copyright © David Shotter 1993, 1997, 2004

First Edition, 1993
Second Revised Edition, 1997
Third Substantially Revised and Expanded Edition, 2004

Designed, typeset, printed and bound by
JW Arrowsmith Ltd, Bristol

British Library Cataloguing-in-Publication Data
A CIP catalogue record for this book is available from the British Library

ISBN 1-86220-152-8

Contents

Acknowledgements

In retirement, as an Honorary Research Fellow of the Centre for North-West Regional Studies at Lancaster University, I have been fortunate to enjoy the support and encouragement in the present project of Jacqueline Whiteside, Jean Turnbull and Christine Wilkinson. I am also – as always – indebted to my wife, Anne, for her production of the manuscript and for taking many of the photographs that are included in the book.

I am also grateful to Chris Beacock for redrawing the maps which appear as figures 1.1, 2.1, 2.2, 3.1, 4.1, 5.1, 6.1, 6.2, 6.5; and to the following for permission to publish site-drawings and/or photographs of sites or artefacts: Birdoswald Roman Fort (7.6), Bradford Museums, Galleries and Heritage (Cliffe Castle Museum) (2.2), Brougham Castle Museum (1.3), Cambridge University Collection of Air Photographs, Unit for Landscape Modelling (6.32), Cumberland and Westmorland Ant. and Arch. Society (5.2), Grosvenor Museum/Chester City Council (3.12), the late Professor G. D. B. Jones (2.4, 4.2, 4.3, 5.4, 5.13, 5.16, 5.18, 6.2), Lancashire County Council (1.1), Lancashire Sites and Monuments Record (Figs 6.3, 6.4, 6.5 and Plates 6.34, 6.35, 6.36), Lancaster City Museums (4.19, 6.1, 6.3, 6.24, 6.27), Oxford Archaeological Unit Ltd. (Fig 4.2, Plates 3.15, 3.18, 6.13, 6.25, 6.26), Ribchester Museum Trust (3.13, 3.14, 6.12), Royal Museum of Scotland (1.2), The Salt Museum, Northwich (6.23), Messrs. Sanderson and Dixon (4.10), Senhouse Museum Trust (5.3, 5.17, 6.16), Joe Thompson (4.18), Tullie House Museum and Art Gallery, Carlisle (6.4, 6.14, 6.21, 6.31), Tyne and Wear Museums (5.1, 5.24, 5.25), The Vindolanda Trust (4.6, 5.26, 5.27, 6.15, 6.22).

List of Maps

Maps

List of Photographic Plates

Plates

Preface

'What did the Romans do for us?' is a question that, in recent times, has been posed by Adam Hart-Davis in his series on BBC2 Television, and by the 'People's Front of Judaea' in *Monty Python's Life of Brian*. The question itself echoes a gulf which appears to exist between the harsh condemnation of Romanisation put by Tacitus into the mouth of the Caledonian chieftain, Calgacus, before his fateful battle with the Romans under Agricola – ('They create a desolation and they call it peace') – and Tacitus' own observation regarding the readiness of Britons to adopt the new culture that had been put before them.

Nowadays, historians and archaeologists are far more convinced by the relevance to Britain of Dio Cassius' assertion that in Germany the tribesmen found themselves involved in the Roman 'market-economy' and that they thereby 'became different without knowing it'. Little conviction attaches now to the more traditional picture of the 'sullen Briton' waiting, occasionally rebelliously, for three-and-a-half centuries for his Mediterranean tormentors to 'go home'.

What we mean by 'Romanisation' is a central question in this book: over the years, it has, thanks to the discovery of evidently-thriving towns and villas, become easier to see the Britons of the south ('the lowland zone') accepting and adapting Roman culture, often eagerly, to suit their own imperatives. The north west, on the other hand, with its near-absence of villas and large towns, has found it harder to 'qualify' for Romanisation. However, we can now see, in rather different circumstances, that, although undoubtedly some must have remained marginal to the influence of Roman ideas, many after their own fashion were affected by the presence of Rome; they were changed as much as was their landscape. This conclusion has been drawn from the analysis of many Roman and Romano-British sites, although the material contained within such sources as the writing-tablets from Vindolanda and Carlisle leaves the issue in little doubt. In the north, as in the south, the British – or 'wretched little Brits', as they were termed at first – became part of a cosmopolitan, Romanised society. The rebellions, so often seen as a backdrop to Roman occupation, became increasingly elusive – once, that is, initial difficulties were overcome and until the later years when Britain became part of the *internal* political wranglings that disfigured so much of the Roman empire from the third century.

Thus, the Romanised northern Britons occupy a central part of this book; but scholarship has not remained static on other matters: the study of the military conquest and consolidation of the north, so long regarded as an essentially completed 'story', has in recent years shown that there is still much to learn, not only of the detail, but also of the major issues.

The realisation that the north west was opened up by Roman governors earlier than Agricola is having profound consequences. Of similarly great significance is the demonstration in the excavations at Birdoswald, in the 1980s and 1990s, that the traditional picture of a Britain deserted by Roman troops and Roman culture in the later-fourth century could not be further from the truth.

Once again, as in 1984 when a form of this book first appeared, this is an 'interim statement' of what we believe now; potentially there must be sufficient material awaiting discovery and analysis in the north west to make this book redundant as quickly as events have done in the cases of its predecessors of 1993 and 1997.

We are discovering more of what the Romans did for us – and what we did for them: Romans and Britons in north-west England clearly had a dynamic which brought them together. This book is, again, like its predecessors, a contribution to the larger discussion of what the Roman occupation of the north west was really about.

This book is dedicated to the memories of two friends – Professor Barri Jones and Dr. Tim Potter – with whom many ideas contributed herein have been discussed in the past, and would have continued to be. The Roman Archaeology of north-west England is, sadly, the poorer without their presence; that it is where it is, however, is due in no small measure to their efforts and commitment.

Lancaster, 2004.

CHAPTER ONE

Before Rome

Over recent decades, views on the condition of northern England before the Roman occupation have changed considerably: what was once seen as an inhospitable landscape dominated by dense forests is now appreciated as one which, in the last millennium B.C., saw extensive clearance-episodes resulting in the development of local economies – agricultural and industrial – which were, in late prehistory, more vibrant than was once thought.[1] In its turn, this suggests the likelihood that some tribal societies, at least, were, on the eve of the Roman invasion, more hierarchical and, indeed, organised in their activities.

Of course, discussion of the pre-Roman background is severely hampered by the absence of *contemporary* documentary records; further, classical authors, who are notoriously vague over matters of chronology and location and who are, in any case, given to stereotyping in their treatment of 'barbarians',[2] have left us a collection of tribal names, but little else to facilitate the unravelling of the political, social and economic structures of the British who inhabited the north of England in the pre-Roman period. Nor should we forget that, during their occupation, Rome may have made adjustments to the locations, and indeed the names, of groups which they encountered.

Again, centuries of subsequent agricultural activity have inflicted severe damage on often-ephemeral ancient landscapes; nonetheless, fragments of such ancient landscapes do survive to the present day, particularly, for example, in parts of the valley of the river Lune.[3] Aerial reconnaissance, aimed at revealing the locations of sites, is often patchy in extent and is not especially useful in certain soil-conditions, such as those experienced in much of Lancashire.[4] In any case, few known sites have benefited from modern excavation aimed at the clarification of chronologies, development and patterns of usage. However, as more work is done, differences in settlement-patterns become more apparent,[5] as do the complexities of individual sites.

We should, however, turn first to the identities of the tribes themselves, remembering that the evidence upon which such a discussion is based derives very largely from sources of the Roman period. Some of these are literary works, others documentary; in almost all cases, however, such material has been transmitted to us through successive generations of manuscript-reproduction into the medieval period. It is hardly surprising if errors accumulate in the hands of scribes copying names which probably meant little or nothing to them.

It is evident that, in late prehistory, the principal tribe occupying territory in northern England was that known to us as the Brigantes: the name appears to refer either to 'upland locations' or to 'overlordship'.[6] The Roman historian, Cornelius Tacitus, writing at the end of the first century A.D., described this tribe as the 'most populous in Britain'.[7] Half a century later, the Alexandrian geographer, Claudius Ptolemaeus (Ptolemy),[8] who probably derived much of his information about northern Britain from military sources of the later-first and early-second centuries A.D., indicates that Brigantian territory 'stretched from sea to sea'. Such references as these have led, not surprisingly, to the assumption that Brigantian territory consisted of everything within a line drawn from the Dee to the Humber in the south to Hadrian's Wall in the north.[9] It has been further conjectured, on the basis of the discovery at Birrens (Dumfriesshire) of a relief-carving of the tutelary deity, *Brigantia*, depicted in Romanised form as *Minerva Victrix*, that the tribe's territory may have stretched well to the north of Hadrian's Wall.[10]

Such an assessment of the apparent extent of tribal territory gives rise to a number of questions: for example, were other tribal territories, known to us by name only, subsumed into a 'Greater Brigantia'?[11] If so, how were control and communication exercised in such extensive and

Plate 1.1: Leck Beck and Eller Beck: Surviving ancient landscape, containing features of the Bronze and Iron Ages and of the Romano-British period: Reproduced by courtesy of the Lancashire County Council

Plate 1.2: Birrens, Dumfriesshire: The goddess Brigantia in the form of Minerva Victrix (early-third century A.D.): Reproduced by courtesy of the Royal Museum of Scotland

difficult terrain? We should, in any case, bear in mind that when the Romans organised the Brigantes into an administrative unit, known as a *civitas*, the territory seems to have lain in and to the east of the Pennines, with a 'capital' established at Aldborough (*Isurium Brigantum*). To advance our understanding of Brigantian territory, we need to examine the evidence for other tribal groups whose names appear to be associated with northern England.

The tribe of the Parisi[12] was located on the east coast of Yorkshire, and appears to have been culturally distinct from the Brigantes. The tribal territory ran northwards either from the river Humber, or perhaps from a point to the south of it, and thus encompassing the estuary. The northward extent is unclear, though it is generally assumed that the Roman road-line from Brough-on-Humber (*Petuaria*: the Romanised *civitas*-centre), through Malton, to the coast may have marked a boundary. It is not, however, inconceivable that the legionary fortress at York was placed in such a way as to facilitate the policing of the separation of the Parisi from the Brigantes.

The Carvetii are known in the late Roman period;[13] the territory normally assigned to them includes the Solway Plain, the Eden valley and (possibly) part of the Lune valley.[14] It is thought likely that their territory in Roman times extended to the north of Hadrian's Wall; if Carlisle is taken to have been their Romanised *civitas*-centre, it would appear rather risky to have left such a prestigious site so close to the provincial boundary. Clearly, this creates a difficulty in that, as we have seen, the territory to the north of the Wall could be assigned equally well to the Carvetii or to the Brigantes. However, the 'claim' of the latter rests on the interpretation of the *Brigantia*-carving from Birrens. The dedicator, Amandus, describes himself as *arc(h)itectus*, indicating that he was probably attached to legion VI *Victrix* at York; this probably explains his connection with the cult, particularly since the goddess is depicted wearing a 'mural crown' which would signify a reference more appropriate to York than to Birrens. The cult of *Brigantia*, organised by Septimius Severus after the division of Britain into two provinces, appears most frequently east of the Pennines.

Figure 1.1: Possible locations of British tribes at the time of the Roman conquest

We should not, however, overlook the possibility that the *civitas Carvetiorum* represents a Roman tribal creation out of Brigantian territory; an obvious parallel in southern Britain would be the creation of the Regnenses, the Atrebates and the Belgae out of what appears to have been the territory of the pre-Roman Atrebates. Although the circumstances of such a creation in the north west may elude us, some weight is added to the idea by the likely connection with the area of the

Plate 1.3: Brougham, Cumbria: Milestone erected by the *Civitas Carvetiorum* (mid-third century A.D.): Reproduced by courtesy of Brougham Castle Museum

The inscription reads 'For the Emperor, Caesar, Marcus Cassianus Latinius Postumus Augustus, Pious and Fortunate, the *civitas* of the CAR(vetii)".

first-century leader, Venutius, who is described unequivocally by Tacitus as a Brigantian.[15] Further, the vicinity of Clifton Dykes, a presumed pre-Roman centre, is seen as a possible cult-centre for the Brigantian horned deity, Belatucadrus.[16] This, and the existence of other hillforts (as at Carrock Fell), combine to suggest that what the Romans developed as the *civitas Carvetiorum* may, in the pre-Roman period, have constituted a semi-independent 'sub-group' of the Brigantes.

These three – the Parisi, the Brigantes and the Carvetii – appear to have been marked out as the most loyal and economically-promising areas of northern England, as is shown by their formation into *civitates*. We should not, however, ignore the possibility that other groups, too, in the later Roman period may have attained such a status.[17]

The *Geographia* of Ptolemy[18] is the source of further tribal names, although it is not easy to assign territorial locations to many of them. The Gabrantovices are an otherwise-unknown group who *may* have been a coastal tribe in the north east, perhaps lying between the Parisi and the mouth of the Tyne. The Lopocares have been placed by some in the vicinity of Corbridge;[19] because Corbridge appears in the *Antonine Itinerary* as *Corstopitum*, it has been suggested that *Lopocares* may represent a corruption of some such name as *Sopites*. However, Ptolemy's name appears to receive confirmation from the *Ravenna Cosmography*, which has Corbridge as *Corie Lopocarium*. Further, the combination of a place-name with a tribal name suggests that Corbridge attained the status of a *civitas*-capital, thus supporting Mann's contention regarding further *civitas*-creations in northern Britain. On the other hand, it has to be said that the association of Corbridge with the Lopocares is not without its difficulties: some feel that *Coria* – the name, as it appears in documents from Vindolanda[20] – lay in the territory of the pro-Roman Votadini.

A further complication arises from a dedication made by a prefect of cavalry, following a successful clash with a band of the Corionototae.[21] It is tempting to see this name as a corrupted form from *Coria* and a tribal name, itself corrupted from *Lopocares* and/or *Votadini*; otherwise, the Corionototae must be regarded as a further tribe to be located in the Corbridge-area. Yet another tribal name, cited on a single inscription (which was found near Vindolanda), is that of the Tectoverdi (or Textoverdi).[22]

Such evidence as this appears, therefore, to suggest a complex tribal picture in this part of northern and north-eastern England, possibly of sub-groups of larger and better-known tribes. It may also provide substance to the reference in Tacitus[23] to the existence of a plurality of groups, presumably small, who acted independently of others and who may in time have become involved in tribal re-organisation – perhaps even creation – in the Roman period itself. We may note, for example, that four of the five tribes, who in 54 B.C. sent embassies to Julius Caesar,[24] do not appear to have survived as distinct entities into the Roman period of occupation.

It can thus be seen that the tribal geography, both before and during the Roman occupation, presents a picture hedged around with uncertainties, but one which was evidently viewed by Rome in a flexible fashion. To this, we should add groups which emerged in the Roman period, possibly with occupational and/or religious associations; such groups include the *venatores Bannienses* (from Birdoswald) and the *vicani Vindolandenses* (from Vindolanda);[25] these names may well have been simply locational, without implying the exercise of any territorial control at all.

The picture is completed by two further groups, both of whom, for different reasons, may be regarded as controversial – the Setantii and the Anavionenses. Again, neither of these can with any confidence be assigned a territorial location. Ptolemy[26] refers to a site named *Portus Setantiorum* ('Harbour of the Setantii'), which was evidently located in north-west England. There has been a long-held local tradition that this was a site, now lost to coastal erosion, placed near the mouth of the river Wyre (in Lancashire). The evidence for this, however, appears tenuous, particularly if the hinterland for such a location – the Lancashire Fylde – was then of dubious viability.[27]

Plate 1.4: Burnswark, Dumfriesshire: Hillfort, possibly of the Carvetii

There are other possibilities: for example, the name, *Seteia*, appears to have been attached to the river Mersey, which is believed to have formed the boundary between the Cornovii (to the south)[28] and another tribe to the north, possibly the elusive Setantii. This area, between the Mersey and Ribble, has traditionally been dismissed as of little importance in either the pre-Roman or Roman periods. It is true that it may have been economically, and thus politically, marginal[29] to activities elsewhere in north-west England, but recent work has suggested that it should not be ignored: although, because of prevailing soil-conditions, sites are difficult to recognise through aerial reconnaissance, field-work and excavation have demonstrated that they are to be found, and display continuity from the pre-Roman to the Roman period.[30]

An alternative – or perhaps supplementary – argument has been that we should look, in our search for the Setantii, to the northern side of Morecambe Bay – that is, in what is now southern Cumbria.[31] In this case, the *Portus* could conceivably have been located on the southern end of Windermere, or might have been a site, since lost, on the southern Cumbrian coast.[32] The potential significance of the area in pre-Roman times is perhaps indicated by the presence of hillfort (*oppidum*) sites – Skelmore Heads, Warton Crag, Castlehead (Allithwaite), the Helme (Natland) and Millom.[33] In contrast to many of the hillfort-sites in the region,[34] those mentioned here, for which an established chronology exists, appear compatible with usage in the late pre-Roman Iron Age.

The last group for whom evidence survives is the Anavionenses, who are mentioned on the career-inscription of an equestrian officer, Titus Haterius Nepos, who held the post of *censitor Brittonum Anavionensium* at a date estimated by Birley to have been *c.* A.D. 100.[35] Such an appointment would indicate that at that time, at least, the Anavionenses lay *within* the province of *Britannia*. It has recently been suggested[36] that the Flavian withdrawal from Scotland in the late-80s was radical – to a new frontier based upon the Stanegate road; however, this hypothesis allows for a considerable area to the north of the line of the Tyne to Solway to have been maintained at least into the earliest years of the second century – perhaps bounded by a line running approximately from Newstead to Dalswinton. Thus, if the Anavionenses are to be associated with the river Annan (*Anava*), then much of their likely territory, including a possible centre at Lochmaben (*Locus Maponi?*), would have remained formally within the province until after A.D. 100. It is, however, possible that the name, *Anavionenses*, on the analogy of *Banniensis* and *Vindolandenses*, belonged to a group associated with a known Roman site – perhaps Brough-on-Noe (*Anavio*), in Derbyshire.

The *political* geography of these tribes at the time of the Roman conquest, particularly as they related to the two Brigantian leaders, Cartimandua and Venutius, will be explored below (in chapter 2); suffice

Plate 1.5: Warton Crag, Lancashire: Hillfort, possibly of the Setantii

to say for the present purpose that, to attract Roman attention, both leaders must have commanded considerable wealth and power. As we shall see, this points to respective 'power-bases' to the east of the Pennines and in north-west England, areas which, in the Romano-British period, had considerable agricultural potential. The frequency with which Roman sites were built upon land that was already subject to the plough suggests that the situation was not so different in the late pre-Roman Iron Age.[37]

Views of the late Iron Age in the north west have changed radically in recent years:[38] no longer was the constant warfare, which was thought to be the implication of the region's large hillforts, the consuming activity of life. Such hillforts had, in most cases, fallen out of use as the centres of a dominating political power; some were becoming the hubs of economic activity. Indeed, the north west, far from being a backward region of Britain in the later Iron Age, can be seen as progressive and entrepreneurial. A hierarchy of settlement-types presumably mirrored the hierarchy of wealth in society, just as it would in Roman Britain also.

Only slowly, however, is the existence and potential of sites recognised: much has obviously disappeared under the plough or is difficult to retrieve for other reasons. The majority of known rural sites cannot easily be distinguished into periods on the basis of such identification-techniques as aerial photography. There is, however, no reason to believe that the late pre-Roman Iron Age is not represented amongst them. Further, it is reasonable to suppose that these include both agricultural sites and sites concerned with the extraction and working of minerals.

We must conclude also, on the basis of 'wealthy', multi-phase sites, such as Meols (on the Wirral),[39] that trade was carried on by sea into and out of the north west,[40] as well as overland. The situation must have been

Plate 1.6:
Ingleborough,
Yorkshire: Hillfort of
the Brigantes

similar to the east of the Pennines; this at any rate would appear to be the conclusion to be drawn from the wealth of material from Britain and further afield that has been recognised at Stanwick in the late pre-Roman Iron Age.[41]

The late Iron Age in the north west was probably not viewable as of uniform 'success'; it is clear that areas such as the Solway Plain, the Eden and Lune valleys and perhaps southern Cumbria and Cheshire were in varying degrees thriving. The territory covered by much of modern Lancashire, on the other hand, may have been more marginal. The north west had resources and raw materials that were valuable to Rome and which were already being exploited: why else did Rome, in A.D. 43, come to terms with Cartimandua and Venutius unless they both commanded resources and, through their wealth, exercised control? This provided the sound basis of a northern client-kingdom which was to ensure the effective, if temporary, neutrality of the territory on the right flank of Rome's crucial line of advance westwards through the north midlands.

Notes

1. See in general Higham, 1986, especially pp. 117ff. Also Matthews, 2001; Wells, 2003.
2. See Ferris, 2000.
3. See Hazelgrove, 1996, 61ff; also Higham and Jones, 1975; Higham, 1980 and 1982; Lowndes, 1963 and 1964.
4. See Bewley, 1994; Middleton, Wells and Huckerby, 1995; Nevell, 1999 and 2001.
5. See Cowell and Philpott, 2000.

6. Rivet and Smith, 1979, 278ff.

7. *Life of Agricola* 17, 1; it is worth remembering that Tacitus *may* have been able to draw on personal experience for this, as well, of course, as on the memories of his father-in-law, the Roman governor, Gnaeus Julius Agricola (See Birley A.R., 2000).

8. *Geographia* II. 3.

9. For a discussion of tribal territory, see Hartley and Fitts, 1988.

10. *RIB* 2091; see Joliffe, 1941 and Higham and Jones, 1985, 12–13.

11. The 'territorial' name 'Brigantia' is used here simply for convenience of reference: it has no ancient authority.

12. Ramm, 1978.

13. Higham and Jones, 1985; two inscriptions carry the name – *RIB* 933 (a tombstone from Old Penrith) and *Journ. Rom. Stud.* 55 (1965), 224 (a milestone from Frenchfield, north of Brougham); the latter 'proves' the *civitas*-status of the Carvetii in the mid-third century.

14. The milestone from Middleton-in-Lonsdale (*RIB* 2283), which gives a distance of fifty-three miles from an unnamed location, is widely thought to refer to Carlisle; from this it has been inferred that the stone marked the southern boundary of the territory of the Carvetii (Stevens, 1937, 200); Birley (1953a), however, took the significance of Carlisle to have been a temporary role (*c.* A.D. 193–213) as the chief city of the newly-separated province of *Britannia Inferior.*

15. *Annals* XII. 40, 3.

16. Higham and Jones, 1985, 11.

17. See Mann, 1974, 38–9.

18. *Geographia* II. 3.

19. Rivet and Smith, 1979, 322ff.

20. A.R. Birley, pp. 18–72 (esp. p.23) in Birley, Birley and Birley, 1993.

21. *RIB* 1142; this inscription, which is now lost, was found originally in the crypt of Hexham Abbey – thus strengthening the likelihood of a local base for the Corionototae. For the name, see Rivet and Smith, 1979, 322.

22. *RIB* 1695; Rivet and Smith, 1979, 470ff. It is generally assumed that the *curia*, mentioned in the inscription, is not the equivalent of *Corio*, but refers to a tribal sub-division (perhaps, in this case, of the Brigantes).

23. *Life of Agricola* 20, 3.

24. *On the Gallic War* V. 21, 1.

25. *RIB* 1905 (Birdoswald) and 1700 (Vindolanda).

26. *Geographia* II. 3, 2.

27. Middleton, Wells and Huckerby, 1995, 206–7; Lightbown, 1996.

28. Webster, 1991.

29. Nevell, 1999 and 2001.

30. Cowell and Philpott, 2000.

31. Higham, 1986, 146.

32. Jones G.D.B., 1980; Shotter, 1995b.

33. Powell, 1963; Forde-Johnston, 1962; also *RCHM (Westmorland)*, London, 1936, 181–2.

34. Matthews, 2001, 8.

35. Birley A.R., 1981, 302f and 2001; *ILS* 1338.

36. For references, see below, in chapter 4.

37. E.g. see McCarthy, 2002, 40ff.
38. See especially, Matthews, 2001.
39. Thompson, 1965, 97ff; Matthews, 2001, 17ff; the substantial collection of artefactual material is currently undergoing fresh analysis, the results are expected to be ready for publication in 2005 (Dr. R.A. Philpott, *pers. comm.*).
40. See Raftery, 1994.
41. Turnbull, 1984.

CHAPTER TWO

Britain and Rome

Britain had been known to the Classical world for centuries before the Romans formed it into a province in the first century A.D. However, although written accounts existed – such as that of the traveller, Pytheas of Massilia (Marseilles), of the late-fourth century B.C. – many Romans evidently remained unsure whether Britain was part of the real or mythical world or where it was in relation to the sea (*Oceanus*) which was thought to encompass the 'inhabited world'.

It was, therefore, seen by many as a triumph of extraordinary proportion when, in 55 and 54 B.C., Gaius Julius Caesar brought troops to Britain during his term as proconsul of Gaul (58–50 B.C.). Caesar[1] was a sufficiently astute politician to appreciate the personal glory that would attach to such an enterprise and the potential of this for the enhancement of his standing in Rome, particularly in relation to his two chief rivals, Gnaeus Pompeius Magnus (Pompey) and Marcus Licinius Crassus. He came to know during his proconsulship the connections which made Britain and its tribes relevant to the conquest and Romanisation of Gaul.

Caesar's objectives in Britain are unclear; nor does he make much impact on the archaeological record. His own account – probably deliberately – leaves many questions unanswered. It may be surmised, however, that he wished to introduce into the south east a political and military equilibrium which would reduce the difficulties that the British might cause him in Gaul. His arrangements suggest that he regarded Britain as a 'potential province', but one which would require much more attention. He had, however, by bitter experience learned of the treacherous weather and tidal conditions that contributed to two disasters to his fleet.

The remainder of Caesar's life (until his assassination in 44 B.C.) left no room for a return to Britain; after a period of civil war which followed Caesar's death, it was left to his adopted son, the first emperor of Rome, Augustus Caesar, to develop further a Roman policy for Britain.

The most significant feature of Caesar's 'diplomatic' settlement was his attempt to curtail the expansionism of the Catuvellauni and their leader, Cassivellaunus, by re-establishing the territorial integrity of their eastern neighbours, the Trinovantes; the Trinovantian leader with whom Caesar dealt was one, Mandubracius. The precise course of events in the ensuing years is none too clear, though it will have been complicated by groups arriving in Britain, seeking refuge from the advancing tide of Romanisation in Gaul which followed Caesar's final victory there in 51–50 B.C. Caesar evidently imposed tribute, but it was not paid for long.[2]

That Britain was unfinished business for Augustus and that he intended to rectify this is made clear by the reference in one of the so-called 'Roman Odes' of Quintus Horatius Flaccus (Horace) who was close to the new emperor: Augustus, he wrote, would be considered a god upon earth when he had added the Parthians and the Britons to the Empire.[3] The third-century historian, Dio Cassius, indicates that Augustus three times considered launching expeditions to Britain;[4] that he never did so was due partly to his pre-occupation with other problems and partly to the fact that he managed to foster diplomatic arrangements which, temporarily at least, checked the development of serious problems in Britain.

Gradually, political conditions changed in Britain: the Atrebates (of Sussex and Hampshire) emerged as philo-Roman, especially under their leader, Verica. There is powerful archaeological evidence of their trading with the Mediterranean world in terms of both foodstuffs and durables: it may have been this development which brought to an end what appears to have been a flourishing trade between the Atrebates and the Dobunni.[5] At the same time, we have evidence of major connections between the Atrebates and Rome;[6] the Atrebatic coin carrying the motif of the vine-leaf can probably be taken as symbolic of a significant cultural shift south of the river Thames. By the A.D. 30s, Verica was certainly a 'client-monarch' in the Roman interest. Recent work in Silchester, a principal Atrebatic site, has demonstrated that the degree of contact with Rome was such that it would not be unreasonable to regard the centre as becoming Romanised during the *pre*-conquest period.

North of the Thames, the separation of the Catuvellauni and the Trinovantes, engineered by Caesar, evidently broke down in the early Augustan period: the tribes once again came under a single authority – that of Cunobelinus who ruled from Colchester (*Camulodunum*). It remains uncertain, however, whether this man, who styled himself 'son of Tasciovanus', was actually of Catuvellaunian or Trinovantian origin. The fate of Mandubracius and his family remains unclear, though it is possible that, in any upheaval, they were driven out, perhaps 'relocating' in the north; it is tempting to see a connection of names with the later Brigantian leader, Cart*imandua*.

That Cunobelinus was a 'tribal nationalist' seems likely: it is equally likely, however, that he was a realist. Whilst his famous 'ear-of-barley' coin appears to make a statement which was as much political as economic, his coinage also indicates that he was designated *REX* ('king'), presumably indicating that he enjoyed the status of a client of Rome. Certainly, trade with the Roman Empire appears to have flourished, and Strabo[7] (writing at about the time of Augustus' death in A.D. 14) lists grain as amongst British exports. The mention also of slaves in Strabo's 'list' suggests that human beings may have been used to pay for goods from the Roman world. It also appears that, in the absence of actively dangerous anti-Roman feeling in Britain, Augustus was content to enjoy the advantages that accrued from trade. Nor do we need to assume that such activity was limited to the south east; it may well have extended up the eastern coast, possibly embracing tribes as far north as the Votadini and Venicones in what is now Scotland. It was presumably a tribal leader with territory on the east coast – perhaps Cunobelinus himself – who in A.D. 16 returned to Rome unharmed some troops who had been washed across the North Sea during an episode of fierce weather.[8]

Augustus' successor, Tiberius Caesar, chose not to depart from the general tendencies of Augustan imperial policy, though relations between Rome and British tribes cannot be expected to have remained static. Rome's friends grew older, and behind them waited a new generation of younger leaders, perhaps entertaining a view of the world in which they lived which was altogether more 'black-and-white' than those of their elders. A 'catalyst' to such people may have been provided by the Druidic priests of whom Caesar had written.[9] Although we can hardly now expect to be able to reconstruct a picture of their 'network', one major centre was certainly on Anglesey and it may not be insignificant that it was in that direction that the British leader, Caratacus (son of Cunobelinus), was evidently heading when finally brought to battle by Roman troops in A.D. 50–51.[10]

Earlier, in A.D. 21–22,[11] Rome had put down a rebellion on the Rhine, which was headed by a Romanised Gaul, named Julius *Sacrovir*, the name probably marks him out as a Druid. In the aftermath, whilst some Druids were put to death, others were driven out; Britain may well have provided a natural haven for such dissidents. As philosophers and teachers, it would be likely that they would have engaged with a younger generation of British leaders, perhaps irritated by the stance adopted towards Rome by their elders. If such were the case, then this next generation of Britons will probably have proved less easy for Rome to manipulate.

An indication of this is perhaps provided by the decision in A.D. 40 of the emperor, Gaius (Caligula: A.D. 37–41), to bring troops to the Gallic coast. His intentions are not now clear to us, obfuscated as they have been by a welter of Roman propaganda hostile to Gaius; Roman sources present it as a farce, symptomatic of that emperor's supposed insanity. But it should be noted that during the later 20s and 30s, the Roman ability to dominate events in Britain had evidently diminished: the kingdom of Cunobelinus had taken over that of the Cantiaci (Kent), and was bringing pressure to bear on Verica and the Atrebates; there had been disturbances involving traders from the Roman Empire. Evidently, on their father's death, Caratacus and his brother, Togodumnus, had driven Adminius (or Amminius), their 'pro-Roman' brother, from the kingdom; his appearance in Gaul appears to have coincided with the arrival there of Gaius. It may well be that some of the activities on Gaius' part, which were characterised in Rome as signs of his madness, were in fact symbolic gestures in support of Adminius and intended as warnings to his brothers.[12] After all, in the face of the destabilising of 'client-kingdoms', Rome had a great deal to lose.

Gaius was assassinated in A.D. 41, but his British policy appears to have been taken fully on board by his uncle and successor, Claudius (A.D. 41–54). Indeed, Claudius' invasion of A.D. 43 may have been the 'natural response' to the evident failure of Caligula's ultimatum. The details of the Claudian invasion need not concern us here, except to note that the inscription from the triumphal arch, erected by the emperor in Rome,[13] indicates that eleven British tribal leaders submitted to Claudius. Predictably, the chief resistance to Rome over the ensuing seven years came from Caratacus,[14] with signs of bitter encounters at sites such as Hod Hill and Maiden Castle (in Dorset). In view of the submissions, however, we should perhaps not overstress the amount of hostility encountered by Rome.

Equally significant, however, was Claudius' following of the famous 'advice' contained in Virgil's epic poem, the *Aeneid*, when he 'told' the Romans that their objective was to 'war down the proud *and offer the blessings of peace to those who submitted*'.[15] As well as sending military groups from the initial base (Colchester) to the north, north west and south west, Claudius entered into agreements with four British tribal leaders – Cogidubnus (of the southern portion of the Atrebates, now termed Regnenses), Prasutagus (of the Iceni) and Cartimandua and Venutius (of the Brigantes); these were to act as client-rulers in Rome's name until it was decided to bring their territories formally into the provincial organisation.

Obviously, the agreement with Cartimandua and Venutius concerns us most closely in the present context. Although the text of Tacitus' *Annals* is lost for the invasion itself and its immediate aftermath, we can make out the essence of the agreement. Clearly, the chief objective must have been to have a

Plate 2.1: Rome: fragment of an inscription erected by Claudius to commemorate the submission of British kings in A.D. 43

friendly, or at least a neutral, presence on the northern flank of the western advance through the midlands and into Wales. The two Brigantians will have undertaken to support the Roman interest in return, presumably, for being able to call on Roman help, if required. Little is known of either leader, though it may have been an incentive to Claudius to proceed diplomatically, if Cartimandua was indeed, as suggested above, descended from an ousted Trinovantian royal house: to renew an association which dated back to the time of Julius Caesar will have appealed to an emperor who held Caesar in such high esteem. The fact that Claudius seems to have insisted on a marriage between the two Brigantians may indicate that the two were leaders of rival factions in the tribe, and that perhaps Venutius was less completely trusted than his wife. Tacitus[16] seems to suggest that Venutius' loyalty to Rome depended on the marriage.

It has never been easy to locate the individual interests of the two Brigantians, although it is usually assumed that the chief concerns of Cartimandua lay in and to the east of the Pennines,[17] with her wealth (and thus her power) depending on the exploitation of the agricultural potential of the Vale of York and possibly casting a 'jealous eye' in the direction of the land of the Parisi (on the east coast). Her chief centre(s) have proved elusive, and some 'candidates' (such as Almondbury) have proved to be chronologically inappropriate; nor is there any sign of significant pre-Roman activity at York. A strong possibility, however, is the substantial *oppidum* at Stanwick, which lies adjacent both to York and to the later Romanised administrative centre (*civitas*-capital) at Aldborough. It has been shown that this site was expanding rapidly in the late pre-Roman period and that it was evidently trading with the Romanised world:[18] this would suit the apparent sympathies of Cartimandua. A further centre has been canvassed in the neighbourhood of Leeds, at Barwick-in-Elmet.[19]

Venutius is harder to place,[20] though he is usually seen as belonging to the western part of the tribal area. Clearly, to have been 'part of the deal' between the Romans and Cartimandua, he must have enjoyed wealth and power, both of which presumably depended ultimately on agricultural prosperity. Recent research[21] has tended to indicate that such conditions are unlikely to have existed in the south of the region – that is, between the river Mersey (presumably the northern border of the Cornovii) and the Ribble, or even the Lune. From the Lune estuary northwards, however, conditions appear to have become more favourable.[22] The area around Penrith probably provided some of the best agricultural land in the north west, especially in the area of the confluence of the rivers Eden and Eamont; indeed, this is most likely to have been included in the territory which, in the third century, was 'handed over' to the *civitas Carvetiorum*.[23] If the Brigantes, the most populous tribe in Britain, whose territory stretched from sea to sea, were

Plate 2.2: Silsden, Yorkshire: Two coins from a Celtic gold hoard (Photograph: Wallbank). The coins, which are now housed in Cliffe Castle Museum at Keighley, Bradford Museums, Galleries and Heritage, are issues of Cunobelinus: above, winged horse with CVNO(belinus), and below, an ear of barley with CAMV(lodunum).

indeed some kind of 'federation', then Venutius emerges plausibly as the leader of a group which was second in power only to the main tribe itself which was situated east of the Pennines. The Romanised centre of the Carvetii was established at Carlisle, though there is evidence that, at the time of the Roman invasion, Venutius' centre was probably located in the Brougham area, perhaps at Clifton Dykes. Amongst other considerations, this seems to have been a centre of the horned god, Belatucadrus.[24]

The establishment of a pro-Roman alliance between Cartimandua and Venutius, based upon a marriage-arrangement, was one thing; maintaining its stability was evidently quite another. Nor, if their centres – Stanwick and Clifton Dykes – have been correctly recognised, were the two leaders far apart if they turned to quarrelling. Unfortunately, our principal source (Tacitus) is less than specific regarding the details of the relationship; the locations and chronology of the 'descent' from marriage to divorce are not made clear, apart from the inference that may be drawn that there were a number of incidents in the 50s and 60s, some of which required Roman military intervention.[25]

The overriding cause of these may have been natural rivalry between two strong-minded leaders, but there may also have been specific points of friction. The recent discovery at Silsden (Yorkshire)[26] of a hoard of Celtic gold coins, most of which originated in the kingdom of Cunobelinus, suggests the possibility that one such 'bone of contention' arose out of the fate of Caratacus. Silsden, it should be noted, is not far from the likely Cartimanduan centre at Barwick-in-Elmet. It is known that, as Roman troops closed in on him, Caratacus made an unsuccessful plea to Cartimandua for sanctuary.[27] The gold may represent an attempt to bribe Cartimandua to accede to Caratacus' request and, in any case, highlights the likely tensions that were exposed between Cartimandua and Venutius. He, described by Tacitus (pointedly, perhaps) as second only to Caratacus as a strategist,[28] may have been prepared to refrain from general involvement on Caratacus' side, but 'selling him out' to the Romans may have been a step too far for him, and one in which he could not readily carry his fellow-nobles with him. Caratacus' fate, after his defeat probably at Llanymynech Mountain on the borders of Wales and Shropshire,[29] was capture and he provided the principal adornment of Claudius' victory-celebrations in Rome.

A further point of tension is likely to have been caused by the rebellion of Boudica in A.D. 60. This bitter dispute was caused by the excessively high-handed behaviour of the financial Procurator in the province, Catus Decianus, when he acted, presumably on the orders of Nero, to integrate the former client-kingdom of the Iceni into the provincial administration, following the death of its client-king, Prasutagus.[30] The treatment of Boudica will have bruised sensibilities beyond East Anglia itself, and certainly caused the Trinovantes, who were still smarting over

Plate 2.3: Copies of
aes-issues of Claudiu

Roman behaviour in and around Colchester, to make common cause with the Iceni. It is likely that there was also Druidic involvement in the episode: all of this will have served to heighten the tensions between Cartimandua and Venutius. It is likely that the line later formalised by the Romans as Watling Street may have formed an important route of communication between west and east in the pre-Roman period also. Further, Roman mishandling of the rebellion itself left tensions on their side, too: it is, for example, likely that the 'frosty' relationship that was to emerge between Agricola and Tacitus on the one hand and Petillius Cerialis on the other had some at least of its origins in this episode.[31]

These, then, may be reasonably advanced as possible points of tension between the Brigantian leaders; Tacitus, however, beyond indicating that there were quarrels, even skirmishes, between them, gives no information that would allow us to characterise, or even date, them. So, what can archaeological evidence do to 'retrieve' this state of affairs? In the first place, there is no evidence for the establishment of any *permanent* military site in the north west, north of the river Mersey, before the 70s. Through the 50s, Roman military activity was concentrated on to Wales and the north midlands; it can be seen that slowly the Roman 'front-line' was moving northwards, so that by *c.* A.D. 60 it lay along a line from Wroxeter, the base of legion XX, to Little Chester (Derby), sites which were to provide the 'jumping-off' points for advances further north.[32] It seems reasonable to suppose that military sites to the north of this 'line' may represent movements connected with instability in the Brigantian kingdom.

Thus, Whitchurch,[33] whilst it may initially have been seen as leading to a crossing of the river Dee at Farndon,[34] became the starting point of a secondary route from Farndon to the Dee-estuary at what was to become a major military site at Chester.[35] Indeed, the Dee-estuary may well have been the location alluded to by Tacitus[36] in connection with ship-repairs during the governorship of Suetonius Paullinus; its maritime proximity to Anglesey needs no emphasis. Further, Little Chester would appear to

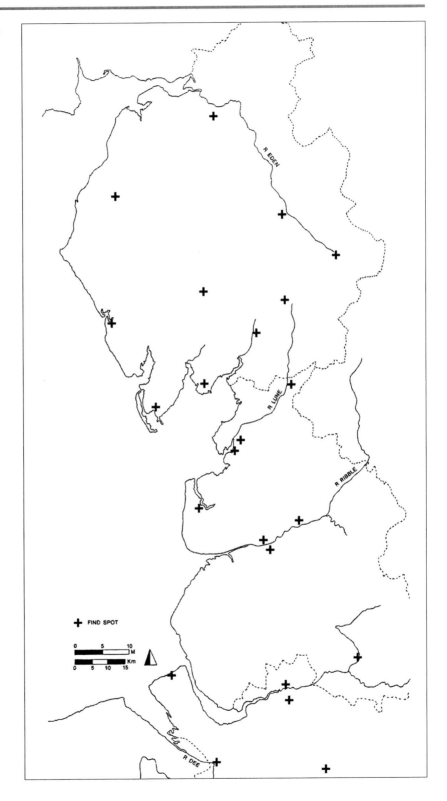

Figure 2.1: Findspots of pre-Neronian *aes* coins

have provided a base for overland-routes through Chesterton and Middlewich[37] (giving access to the north-west coast) and through Templeborough and Rossington Bridge,[38] which would have brought troops close to the Iron-Age centre at Barwick-in-Elmet. It should be noted that Chester's location, whilst ideal for maritime operations, was not suitable as a base for overland-*conquest*. Thus, while there may have been a 'pre-fortress' phase in the late 60s and early 70s, Chester's role developed much more clearly as a base for *occupation*, once conquest in the north west was complete; indeed, the road from Chester, through Northwich, Manchester and Ribchester, as well as over the Pennines, via Castleshaw, to York, should be seen as secondary to the routes associated with conquest.

We may, therefore, envisage that Roman commanders in Britain were developing a strategy to contain both north Wales and north-west England in the years prior to full conquest. Archaeological evidence is relatively limited, although finds of early coins – especially *aes*-issues of Julio-Claudian emperors, and in particular contemporary copies of the *aes*-issues of Claudius – may provide the best indications:[39] the locational distribution of these suggests that the chief tactic in the containing of outbreaks of trouble between Cartimandua and Venutius was the employment of combined operations by land and sea – a tactic clearly used in other episodes of the conquest of Britain, and to the effectiveness of which Tacitus explicitly refers in his account of Agricola's later campaigns in northern Scotland.[40]

These campaigns, as already noted, left no permanent sites north of the Mersey; evidence of them will have consisted of temporary camps for the campaigning army, although sites of this nature have proved extremely vulnerable to plough-damage and are thus hard to locate except in highland areas. However, the existence of such sites at Kirkham[41] (on the north bank of the Ribble-estuary), taken in conjunction with the distribution of relevant artefactual evidence, suggests that rendezvous were made in the large estuaries of the north west between troops conveyed by sea and those who had marched overland, and that together they carried out 'search-and-destroy' missions, moving along the river-valleys, before returning to their bases further south.

This approach probably contained the area, despite sharply deteriorating relations between Venutius and Cartimandua, until the latter years of Nero's reign brought new problems for Britain. It is evident that, after the revolt of Boudica, the military emphasis in Britain had declined: governors were appointed whose role appears principally to have been not 'to make waves' in the wake of the recent upheaval;[42] in particular, Marcus Trebellius Maximus (A.D. 63–69) appears to have been an elderly man with little inclination for launching military

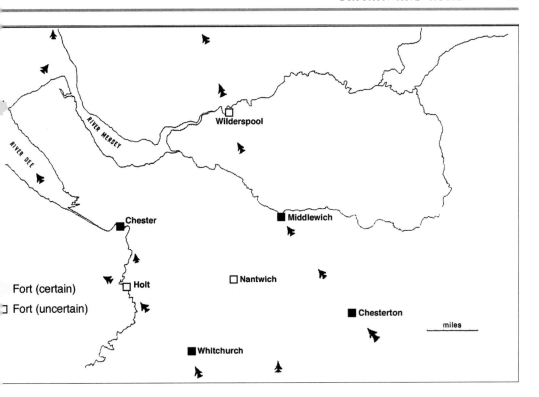

gure 2.2: Probable
itial routes of
oman military
enetration into
orth-west England

initiatives. In A.D. 67, Nero's plans elsewhere in the empire led to the removal of one of Britain's four legions (XIV *Gemina Martia Victrix*).

Within a year of this, the Roman world was in tumult, with the toppling of Nero in the early summer of 68 followed by a succession of short-lived Emperors (Galba, Otho and Vitellius) until Vespasian established himself and a new ruling dynasty (the Flavians) in the last days of A.D. 69. It is clear that this was not a good period in the history of Roman Britain: an on-going dispute between the governor and the *legatus* of legion XX (Roscius Coelius) provided one distraction, whilst, in 69, troops – perhaps up to eight thousand – were taken to the European mainland in support of the cause of Aulus Vitellius. Not only this, but legion XIV was, during 69, temporarily returned to Britain, its dissatisfaction with the course of events in Europe leaving it prey to the approaches of Vespasian's agents. Further, these same agents were evidently tampering with the political stance of II *Augusta*, the legion that had been commanded by Vespasian in the invasion of A.D. 43. In addition, Trebellius Maximus fled the province in the spring of 69 to be replaced by the Vitellian, Marcus Vettius Bolanus; the favour that he was to enjoy under the Flavian emperors suggests that he did not remain loyal to Vitellius for too long.

With this cauldron of uncertainty on the Roman side, it is not surprising that Rome's enemies saw a golden opportunity in which to

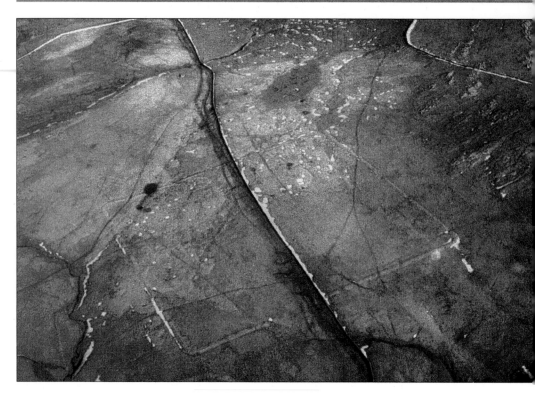

press their cause. Venutius again attacked his former wife, Cartimandua: although Tacitus[43] is, as usual, extremely sparing of detail, we may surmise that Venutius took his troops eastward over Stainmore, ousting Cartimandua from her stronghold at Stanwick and perhaps driving her south towards Barwick-in-Elmet. That she was rescued by Rome is clear – perhaps by means of a pincer-movement from Rossington Bridge and via the Ribble-Aire corridor; from that point, Cartimandua disappears from history. Tacitus tersely observed: 'Venutius got the kingdom, whilst we were left with a war to fight'.

Again, posterity is left by Tacitus in a quandary as to the run of events. We are told that the young Agricola[44] was sent out to replace Roscius Coelius as *legatus* of the troubled legion XX to bring it over to Vespasian's side; at the same time, the governor, Vettius Bolanus, is dismissed by Tacitus as 'too mild a man for a dangerous province'.[45] We are left with the impression, therefore, that nothing was done about Venutius' rebellion until Bolanus' replacement by Petillius Cerialis in A.D.71, by which time the new ruling dynasty had 'got its act together'. But is this credible? Even if Venutius wanted no more than Roman recognition of his primacy of the Brigantes, Rome could hardly ignore for long the removal of one of its client-monarchs. It was faced, in other words, with a repetition of the same problem that, thirty years previously, had prompted the invasion of Britain. The mere fact that Bolanus remained

Plate 2.4: Mastiles Lane, Malham Moo Campaign-camp (Photograph: G.D.B. Jones)

in post until 71 must suggest that his actions were regarded, at the least, as satisfactory.

Tacitus provides no indication whatever of the course of events during the years, A.D. 69–71. However, other sources of information are less reticent: recently,[46] it has been suggested on the basis of finds made at Lambay Island (off the coast of Co. Dublin) that some, at least, of Venutius' followers may have been driven from Britain to take refuge across the Irish Sea. Again, the Flavian poet, Papinius Statius, writing in the reign of Domitian, presents Bolanus' son, Vettius Crispinus, with achievements of his father's career as examples to follow:[47] the poet indicates that Bolanus penetrated Caledonia which, to Romans, lay *beyond* the line of the Forth and the Clyde; there, he constructed roads, forts and watchtowers and stripped a British king of his armour. How much precision we can attach to this is unclear, although half-a-century ago Eric Birley warned us that it would have been difficult for Statius, so soon after the event, to have fabricated it completely.[48] We cannot, of course, be certain of the identity of the British king, but it certainly could have been Venutius or one of his allies; further, unless the reference to military building is to be regarded as stereotypical, it would not be impossible to connect Statius' description with the construction of the Gask Ridge *limes* in Scotland, which eventually stretched from the Forth to the Tay and which separated the coastal Venicones (perhaps friends of Rome) from their inland highland neighbours.[49] Such an interpretation seems less unreasonable than it might have done in the past, and is, in any case, made easier with the realisation that the structures which make up the Gask Ridge *limes* saw a plurality of construction phases. In the course of all this, it seems likely that Venutius was either killed – or, at least, rendered harmless.

It remains to address the question of Tacitus' decidedly unenthusiastic attitude towards Vettius Bolanus[50] in the *Life of Agricola*: it should first be noted that Tacitus' attitude was evidently not matched by that of Vespasian who, in 73 or 74, rewarded Bolanus with elevation to the patriciate. Nor, evidently, was Bolanus 'guilty' of prolonged loyalty to Vitellius; the contrast between his treatment and that of the Vitellian legionary *legatus*, Roscius Coelius, who had to wait until A.D. 81 for a consulship, demonstrates this. Both Vettius Bolanus and Petillius Cerialis were governors of the province whilst Agricola was *legatus* of legion XX; this relationship could, in both cases, have provoked tensions, particularly if Agricola's legion spearheaded the considerable achievements of A.D. 69–74; Tacitus' references to Agricola's modesty and self-effacement[51] at these times may conceal dissatisfaction on the part of the *legatus*. Again, as we shall see (in chapter 3), policy in Britain was probably under close imperial scrutiny in the early years of Domitian's reign; it is not unreasonable to suppose that both Cerialis (perhaps as consul in A.D. 83) and Bolanus (as a senior *consularis* and former governor of Britain) were involved in advising the emperor in the making of crucial decisions. Quite aside from this, Domitian's reign was not an easy period for some members of the senatorial order;[52] Tacitus' attitude to both Bolanus and Cerialis could have been adversely affected by disputes of which details do not survive, although the tensions are abundantly obvious in the historian's account of the latter years of Agricola's life.

Finally, we should bear in mind that our chief source for events in Roman Britain during the Flavian period is akin to a written funeral eulogy of Gnaeus Julius Agricola; the author's 'duty' of placing his subject firmly at the centre of events may well have led to inaccuracies of fact or emphasis which it is often impossible now for posterity to rectify. Whilst the artefactual evidence of archaeology is able to provide some corrective, ultimately Vettius Bolanus and Petillius Cerialis may remain the victims of the literary *genre* in which Cornelius Tacitus chose to write.

Notes

1. For Caesar's life and career, see Meier, 1995; the British campaigns are discussed on pp.280–2 and 292–3. For Caesar's own account, see *On the Gallic War* IV.20–38; V. 8–23.

2. Strabo *Geographia* II.5,8.

3. Horace *Odes* III.5,1–4.

4. Dio Cassius, *History of Rome* 49.38,2 (34 B.C.); 53.22,5 (27 B.C.); 53.25,2 (26 B.C.).

5. Van Arsdell, 1989; 1994, 28; some of the Dobunni may have been clients of the Catuvellauni.

6. Soffe and Henig, 1999.

7. Strabo *Geographia* IV.5,2.

8. Tacitus *Annals* II.23–24 (esp. 24,5).

9. Caesar *On the Gallic War* VI.13–14; Ross and Robins, 1989; an indication of Druidic power may be seen in the almost-certainly ritualistic killing of 'Lindow Man'.

10. Tacitus *Annals* XII.33–35.

11. Tacitus *Annals* III.40–47.

12. Barrett, 1989, 135–139.

13. *ILS* 216.

14. Webster, 1980; 1981.

15. Virgil *Aeneid* VI.851–3 (the italics in the quotation are mine).

16. Tacitus *Annals* XII.40,3.

17. Richmond, 1954.

18. Turnbull, 1984.

19. Ramm, 1978, 26 and 141; Hartley and Fitts, 1988, 7 and 18.

20. See Higham and Jones, 1985, 10f.

21. Cowell and Philpott, 2000, 175ff; Nevell, 1999 and 2001.

22. Higham and Jones, 1975.
23. *Journ. Rom. St.* 55 (1965), 224.
24. Webster, 1986, 74.
25. Braund, 1984; Hanson and Campbell, 1986; Shotter, 1994.
26. See *Britannia* 30 (1999), 342.
27. Tacitus *Annals* XII.36–37. The Silsden Hoard is to be published in 2004 in an article entitled *The Silsden Hoard: Discovery, Investigation and New Interpretations* by Gavin Edwards and Megan Dennis (Gavin Edwards, *pers. comm.*).
28. Tacitus *Annals* XII.40,2.
29. Jones and Mattingly, 1990, 61 and 67; Jones, 1990a, 57ff.
30. Tacitus *Annals* XIV.29–39; Webster, 1978.
31. Birley A.R., 1973; Shotter, 2000b, 39.
32. Webster, 1971; Carrington, 1985.
33. Jones and Webster, 1968.
34. Jones, 1991; for the road, see *Britannia* 11 (1980), 365; Waddelove A. C., 1986; Waddelove A. C. and E, 1983, 21; *Britannia* 22 (1991), 222. I am most grateful to Mr. Edmund Waddelove for his observations on the evolution of the road-system in the area (*pers. comm.*).
35. Shotter, 2002a; Mason, 2001, 31ff.
36. Tacitus *Annals* XIV.29,3.
37. For the military site, see *Britannia* 21 (1990), 331 and 26 (1995), 348; Strickland, 2001, 20ff; Shotter, 1999a; 2000b, 37.
38. Carrington, 1985, 10; Webster, 1981, 93ff.
39. Shotter, 1994.
40. *Life of Agricola* 25; Hanson, 1987, 175. See also Mason, 2003.
41. Howard-Davis and Buxton, 2000.
42. Shotter, 2002b.
43. Tacitus *Histories* III.45.
44. *Life of Agricola* 7,3.
45. *Life of Agricola* 8,1.
46. Raftery, 1994, 200–203.
47. *Silvae* V.2, esp. 140–149.
48. Birley E. B., 1953b, 11ff. It is worth noting that it is the clear implication of a passage in the *Natural History* of the Elder Pliny (4.103) that Roman troops had penetrated Caledonia prior to the governorship of Agricola.
49. Woolliscroft, 2002.
50. Birley A.R., 1981, 62–65.
51. *Life of Agricola* 8, 3.
52. For example, *Life of Agricola* 45; Southern, 1997.

CHAPTER THREE

The Conquest

As we have seen, although the conquest of the north of England did not begin in earnest until the 70s, the 'front-line' had been edging northwards through the 50s and 60s, and Roman troops will have gained some previous familiarity with the area through the military operations which had been required to maintain an acceptable degree of peace and stability in the north. Our understanding of the conquest itself has been heavily dependent upon the material contained in Tacitus' biography of his father-in-law, Gnaeus Julius Agricola, who was governor of the province between A.D. 77 and 83,[1] and who played a major role in the annexation of northern Britain.

Tacitus' account, however, as has long been recognised, is not without its difficulties: the *Life of Agricola* was published in A.D. 98, five years after Agricola's death and at a time when Trajan had just succeeded Nerva as emperor – an episode heavily cloaked in constitutional proprieties, but one which may have revived uncomfortable memories of the turbulent events which had precipitated and followed Nero's fall thirty years previously. The *Life of Agricola* is not a biography in a modern sense; rather, it is a written version of the type of eulogy which might have been pronounced at Agricola's funeral, from which Tacitus was probably absent on official business.[2] The subject was obviously a man for whom Tacitus entertained deep respect and admiration. Inevitably, therefore, other characters occupy places in the background only, although some – especially the emperor, Domitian – suffer an implied or explicit contrast with the work's 'hero'. In short, therefore, the *Life of Agricola* is a work written not for the benefit of historians, but one which they have no option but to use and attempt to interpret.[3]

In the *Life of Agricola*, the prominence afforded to the subject's governorship of Britain long prompted the assumption that the conquest of the north was almost entirely Agricola's achievement; published maps abound which indicate virtually every military site between the north midlands and the Moray Firth as an Agricolan establishment. Consequently, relatively little detailed attention was given to the contributions made by Agricola's predecessors and successors.[4] In short, as the late Barri Jones wrote many years ago,[5] ' "Agricolan" is an overworked adjective'. A principal objective, therefore, of the present

Figure 3.1: Probable
early-Flavian military
sites in north-west
England

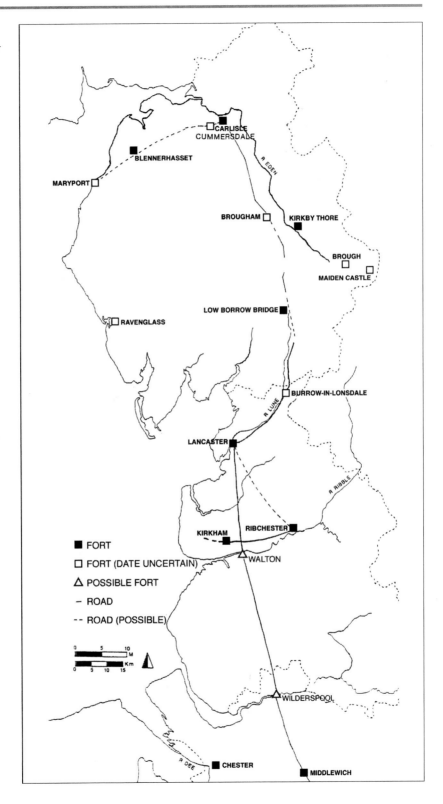

Plate 3.1: Carlisle: Flavian coins from the Roman fort

chapter is to re-examine accepted hypotheses, with a view to achieving an interpretation which is in accordance with the totality of the surviving evidence.

We have seen that Roman troops had been introduced into the north west during the 50s and 60s to keep the peace; as far as we know at present, however, these operations did not lead to the establishment of many *permanent* military sites, and certainly not north of the river Mersey. It is possible, however, that permanent forts had been established as far north as, for example, Middlewich and Chester.[6] However, the take-over of the Brigantes in A.D. 69 by Venutius completely transformed the situation; the task of bringing him personally to book must almost certainly have been well-advanced, if not completed, in the governorship of Vettius Bolanus.[7] Although Tacitus is dismissive of Bolanus' achievements, it does not seem reasonable to suppose that initial moves against the Brigantes could have been delayed until the arrival of Cerialis in A.D.71.[8] In view of the fact that Agricola was *legatus* of legion XX from A.D.70, it does not appear reasonable to suppose that Tacitus could have been ignorant of these moves.

In the current state of our evidence, it is not possible easily to separate in detail the work of Bolanus and Cerialis, although advances in dating-techniques[9] have made it far easier to distinguish between their work and that of later Flavian governors (including Agricola). Tacitus is not enlightening on the subject of Bolanus' actions, but others, as we have seen, suggest the possibility of his penetration of Caledonia. Tacitus is similarly unforthcoming on the achievements of Cerialis' governorship, though he was not generally a man to earn the historian's approbation.[10] In the *Life of Agricola*, Tacitus' notice of Cerialis is grudging;[11] although to be included amongst the 'great generals' (*magni duces*) of the Flavian period, Cerialis' activities in Britain are hardly cited in such a way as to encourage the reader to dwell on them: 'Petillius Cerialis straightaway struck terror into the hearts of the Brigantes. There were many battles, some of them not uncostly, as Cerialis embraced the greater part of Brigantian territory with victory or, at least, warfare'.

Tacitus does inform us *how* the attack on the Brigantes was managed: Cerialis evidently shared command and the available troops with Agricola;[12] we may perhaps assume that Cerialis made his advance east of the Pennines, spearheading it with his old legion from A.D. 60 – IX *Hispana*. Agricola led legion XX *Valeria Victrix* on the western side of the country. It is also likely that there was a maritime element to this episode of campaigning, as Cerialis had brought to Britain with him in 71 a new legion (II *Adiutrix*), which had recently been recruited from sailors of the Ravenna-fleet. From coastal bases, such as Chester,[13] the soldiers of the II *Adiutrix* perhaps effected rendezvous with land-based troops in the principal river-estuaries – a tactic which, according to Tacitus,[14] was found extremely demoralising by the British.

Although these early campaigns cannot be reconstructed in any detail, the evidence of coin-loss in north-west England – particularly of *aes*-coins of the Julio-Claudian era and of the early years of Vespasian's reign – provides the ground for an hypothesis.[15] It was at one time taken as axiomatic that Chester provided the starting-point for these campaigns and that their route ran via Northwich, Manchester and, from there, eastwards in the direction of Castleshaw and (eventually) York, and northwards towards Ribchester and Burrow-in-Lonsdale.[16] However, recent re-appraisal of the role of Chester suggests that, whilst the 'naval arm' of the early-Flavian military advance started from there, it was poorly placed as the base for overland *conquest* in the north west. It seems

Plate 3.2: Lancaster: Castle Hill, remains of the Flavian turf rampart

more likely that, on this occasion, troops came from their bases in the north midlands following the 'King Street route' into the north west,[17] as far as Lancaster. Such a route would have early on provided the Roman army with access to the salt-deposits of Cheshire, which will have been vital to their purposes.

It should be stressed, however, that whilst this represents a reasonable model of early conquest, it cannot yet be regarded as certain, since no *structural* evidence of early-Flavian military sites has been recovered from either Wilderspool or Walton-le-Dale. Excavation on Castle Hill at Lancaster, however, has produced artefactual and structural evidence which make a Cerialian foundation very likely.[18] Elements of a turf rampart have been located on the east, north and west sides of the fort, together with the site of the east gate, which shows that Church Street represented a principal access-route.

Plate 3.3: Ribchester: Three phases of timber 'strapping' (o 'corduroy') laid as a foundation for the turf rampart

With regard to sea-borne landings, the Ribble estuary seems a strong possibility: the complexity of sites/phases recorded at Kirkham[19] and at Ribchester support activity from an early date; indeed, the well-preserved campaign-camp at Mastiles Lane (Malham Moor) points to the use of the Ribble as a route of penetration well inland.[20] We shall return to the likely importance of the Lune; suffice to say that it offered a route for deep northward penetration. The coast of Cumbria presents more problems: it seems clear, for example, that Watercrook (on the Kent) was not an early establishment, although there is some evidence to suggest that there may have been an early military site at Hincaster.[21] Artefactual evidence suggests the possibility of early activity of some kind at Ravenglass,[22] whilst the presence at Blennerhasset[23] of what appears to have been one of the earliest military sites in Cumbria serves to point to the possibility of similarly early activity at Beckfoot or Maryport. On the whole, however, it seems that the Lake District was not tackled militarily in a comprehensive way until the later years of the first century. The intersection of routes running from south to north and from west to east will have had the effect of dividing western Brigantian territory into smaller areas, and may represent a tactic ascribed by Tacitus to Agricola during his governorship – namely 'divide and rule'.[24] The historian's mention of 'estuaries and woods' seems most likely to place the location in the north west. Nor should we overlook the fact that the road from Carlisle to the west coast through Blennerhasset, which bears the signs of early establishment, may have been intended to offer protection to the grain-growing coastal farmers by separating them from their inland neighbours – a procedure perhaps paralleled east of the Pennines by the 'protection' of the Parisi.[25] Chronological evidence from relevant sites places both of these moves firmly in the governorship of Cerialis, though we should keep in our minds that Agricola will have been involved as commander of legion XX.

As already suggested, the Lune and Eden river-valleys offered the chance for effective penetration northwards. Indeed, the route itself is still very clearly apparent – the fine Hadrianic milestone (*RIB* 2272) found at Caton, and surviving traces through Barbondale, Upper Lunesdale (particularly in the form of Fairmile which remains in use today as a minor road) and along the modern A6 between Penrith and Carlisle.[26] Little is known about the history of the fort at Burrow-in-Lonsdale, although it does appear that beneath the visible fort at Low Borrow Bridge lies an earlier – and smaller – establishment.[27] The Roman fort at Brougham, on a site now dominated by the remains of the medieval castle,[28] is visible as an earthwork, although there is little indication of dating. However, in view of its position – close to the possible 'Carvetian' centre at Clifton Dykes, and at the junction of the road from the south and that crossing Stainmore and in the middle of the fine agricultural land that characterises the confluence of the Eden and

Plate 3.4: Low Borrow Bridge: Roman fort

Plate 3.5: Brougham: Roman fort, surviving as an earthwork adjacent to the medieval castle

Eamont rivers – it is difficult not to believe that it must have had an important role from an early date.

It is not clear how far north the 'eastern wing' of the advance proceeded, though it may have been at least as far as Corbridge;[29] however, it seems likely that some of the troops engaged in this crossed Stainmore to join their colleagues at Brougham.[30] Dating-evidence for the forts over Stainmore[31] – Greta Bridge, Bowes, Maiden Castle, Brough-under-Stainmore and Kirkby Thore – is scanty, although they have generally been assumed to have been of Agricolan date. It is likely, however, that the route itself is of earlier origin; as we have seen, it may well have been Vettius Bolanus who drove Venutius from Stanwick, and the campaign-camps over Stainmore – Rey Cross, Crackenthorpe, Kirkby Thore and Plumpton Head – may also date either to Bolanus' or to Cerialis' governorship.[32] The shapes of these camps are by no means as regular as the familiar 'playing-card shape' of permanent forts; whilst Rey Cross is rectilinear, Plumpton Head assumes an irregular trapezoidal shape.

The finest of them is undeniably Rey Cross, its earthworks preserved as the land is virtually unploughable. A near-complete rampart-circuit survives, together with entrances defended by outer covering mounds (*tutuli*). Camps[33] varied considerably in extent depending on the size of the campaigning army, but essentially provided protected space for the troops' leather tents. Although it was normal, even if a camp was to be used only for a single night, for a full rampart-and-ditch protection to be constructed, alternative defences (caltrops) might be used, consisting of stakes bound together in 'tripods', forming a defence akin to modern barbed wire. A complete example of such a stake (*pilum murale*) was recovered during excavations at Kirkham.[34] It is evident that each soldier carried three of these in his normal equipment. Recent excavations at Rey Cross have revealed 'post-holes' which may have resulted from the use of tent-pegs; examples of such pegs were found in excavations at Kirkham.

Alongside the temporary camps and permanent forts across Stainmore, there are also signal- or watch-towers, three on Stainmore itself, if we include Maiden Castle. Bowes Moor and Roper Castle are closely comparable as oblong earthworks. In recent years, it has been shown that there are other small sites on the western approaches to Stainmore in the form of earthworks made up of a 'platform' with a four-post tower protected by two circular ditches. Sites of this kind observed and part-tested are Punchbowl Hotel, Augill Bridge, Appleby Golf Course and Johnson's Plain.[35] It has been suggested that the close proximity of these sites, one to another, may have been due to the fact that visibility in the area was frequently poor. There is at present no conclusive evidence by which to date these 'western Stainmore' sites, although it is hard to believe that their inception was later than the first century. However, excavations at the rectilinear site at Bowes Moor have produced pottery of the fourth century. This, and some later pottery from Rey Cross, indicates that caution has to be exercised in assessing the chronological relationships of the Stainmore sites.

From Brougham[36] Roman troops proceeded northwards, following the line of the present A6–road; the area is complex in its Roman archaeology. A little to the north of the town of Penrith lies the Roman fort and extramural settlement at Old Penrith. A relatively extensive excavation in the 1970s suggested that this site is not earlier than the later years of the first century, though it should be borne in mind that the

Plate 3.6: Rey Cross: Campaign-camp (from the interior), showing the eastern rampart pierced by an entrance which was 'covered' by a *tutulus*-mound

excavation was more concerned with the extramural settlement than with the fort itself.[37] At least three other sites have been identified in the vicinity; one of these is probably a campaign-camp whilst the natures and dating of the other two remain uncertain.[38] In addition, there are further campaign-camps and an industrial site at Scalesceugh which appears to have operated between the first and the fourth centuries.[39]

Plate 3.7: Stainmore (Punchbowl Hotel): Watchtower showing as a circular earthwork

Until the 1970s, Roman Carlisle was known by a considerable amount of artefactual material, and some structural evidence; a virtually continuous programme of excavation since the early 1970s has, however, transformed our perception of the site – not all of it directly connected to Carlisle's *military* role.[40] It had long been suspected by some[41] that Roman armies had reached at least this far north during Cerialis' governorship. It was not, however, until the 1980s that the advent of dendrochronological analysis for Roman sites brought indisputable confirmation of this. Extensive excavations in the 1970s, 1980s and 1990s in the area of Annetwell Street, Abbey Street and Castle Street revealed elements, exceptionally well preserved, of a turf-and-timber fort, including the complex of the southern gateway. This showed that, as so often happens, the medieval castle must have been built within the fort-area where

Plate 3.8: Carlisle: Southern timber gateway of the Roman fort (from the interior)

Plate 3.9: Carlisle: Timber strapping beneath the *Via Praetoria*

Plate 3.10: (below) Roman road between Ribchester and Burrow-in-Lonsdale This was as photographed in 1973)

structures were still standing. The most significant conclusion of these excavations was that the gateway-timbers had been felled during the second half of A.D. 72. This, of course, put the presence of Cerialis' army beyond doubt, and thus provided the opportunity for the major re-assessment of conquest in the north west which is the subject of this chapter.

The early development of the fort clearly involved some enlargement, which included the construction of an annexe located beneath the areas now covered by the buildings of BBC Radio Cumbria and Carlisle Museum and Art Gallery (Tullie House). The turf-and-timber mode of construction appears to have lasted, possibly with a break of some kind in the early Hadrianic period, until being replaced in stone in the early Antonine period. It is likely that modifications of the structure will have taken place as Roman policy in the north changed (see below).

The high standard of preservation of organic material has facilitated a close study of the area of the southern gateway; this had two 'carriageways' of timber, one of which had been so deeply rutted by cart-wheels that it required replacement. This gateway gave access to a gravelled roadway inside the fort which had been laid onto a corduroy of logs. Flanking this road were drains, lined and capped with timber. Excavations have also revealed well-preserved sections of turf-rampart, also laid on a corduroy of logs, and climbed by a gravelled service-trackway, known as an *ascensus* ('ascent'). Located inside the fort were the *intervallum*-road ('interior service road'), and elements of barracks constructed of wooden uprights supporting sections of wattle-and-daub. This was probably a normal method of construction of fort-buildings, as structures of similar type have been located at many north-western forts, including Ribchester and Lancaster. There were also sheds inside the fort, constructed by the post-and-wattle method, some of which may have been concerned with leather-tanning. This latter feature prompts the suggestion that the site at Carlisle was initially more akin to a depot than simply a fort, raising the possibility of comparison with the site at Corbridge (Red House),[42] at the eastern end of the Stanegate road.

In addition to the southern rampart and gateway and fragments of internal buildings, elements of the western rampart were located in excavations in 1999 just inside the medieval walls. The major excavation-programme of 2000–01 on Castle Green revealed sheds and workshops of various periods, as well as part of the stone phase of the headquarters (*principia*). As this sat directly in line with the road to the south gate, it is a reasonable assumption that the stone *principia* stood on the site of its timber predecessor. It was in the central area of the fort that substantial sections of personal body-armour (*lorica segmentata*) were recovered. Immediately outside the fort, further industrial activity was located in the Castle Street area,[43] though a substantial 'timber platform', observed in the past beneath the Museum, has yet to be explained. Tile-stamps of all of the British legions have been recovered from Carlisle, and one of the Vindolanda-documents refers to the presence there of a *centurio regionarius* – a kind of 'District Commissioner'.[44] The same source makes it clear that Carlisle's Roman name was *Luguvalium*, making it one of the few sites in north-west England of which the Roman name is known for certain.[45]

The recently-refined dating for the origin of Roman Carlisle has implications also for the understanding of the Stanegate road; it is possible that this, too, should be seen as an achievement of Cerialis and Agricola in the early 70s, presumably serving, initially at least, as a line of lateral communication. The chronologies of other sites along the Stanegate, between Carlisle and Corbridge (with the *possible* exception of Nether Denton), are less certain[46] and will be discussed later in the context of consolidation and frontier-development.

Plate 3.11: Roman
road (Fairmile) to the
south of the fort at
Low Borrow Bridge

Plate 3.11: Roman road (Fairmile) to the south of the fort at Low Borrow Bridge

This revision of the establishment-date of the military site at Carlisle has more far-reaching implications for the traditional chronology of conquest: as we have seen, the Flavian poet, Papinius Statius, suggests the penetration of Scotland as early as the governorship of Vettius Bolanus.[47] The evidence of early coin-loss, indeed, offers support for a proposal that, early in the 70s, Roman troops proceeded northwards from Carlisle, crossing the country to Newstead (*Trimontium*), possibly a crucial point of juxtaposition between the Selgovae and Votadini, the latter of whom may already have been clients of Rome. It is understood[48] that a re-assessment of fort-development at Newstead shows that the first-phase fort faced westwards, with its main gate orientated towards Carlisle. From Newstead, a route may have been forged to Cramond, Camelon, Strageath and possibly as far north as the river Tay. So extensive an advance would also create the real possibility that either Bolanus or Cerialis was responsible for the initiation of the Gask Ridge *limes*[49] through Strathearn and Strathallan, the purpose of which was probably to police contacts between the inland tribes and the coastal Venicones who may already have been supplying grain to the Roman army. As we shall see, such an hypothesis has considerable implications for the assessment of subsequent activity in the area.

What, therefore, was the strategy of the emperor, Vespasian, which underpinned these movements? Tacitus appears to herald the meaning for Britain of the opening of the Flavian era, a period of 'great generals and brilliant armies leading to the destruction of enemy-morale'.[50] The work of Bolanus and Cerialis appears to have been principally concerned with, first of all, the handling of the 'Brigantian crisis' precipitated by the overthrow of Cartimandua and secondly achieving a broad stability in the north. Tacitus[51] seems to confine the work of Cerialis' successor, Julius Frontinus, to the defeat of the Silures of south Wales; however, in view of the extent – and probable political difficulties – of the territory covered between A.D. 70 and 74, it does not seem reasonable to suppose that Frontinus was in any way able to relax Roman vigilance with regard to the north. His armies, too, must have been active in an area from the southern Pennines to the Tay, and this presumably included continuation of a fort-building programme; indeed, it has been suggested that Corbridge (Red House) may have been completed in his governorship, and it seems very likely that the construction of the legionary fortress at Chester probably began no later than Frontinus' governorship; this site was clearly related to the permanent occupation of the north, rather than to conquest. Chester, apart from its 'maritime links', was away from the main route into the north and was 'separated' from north Wales by marshland. Thus the conquests both of northern England and of north Wales were probably directed from the base of legion XX *Valeria Victrix* at Wroxeter.

It has recently been suggested, however,[52] that the structural evidence from Chester may offer a clue to the intentions of Vespasian. At sixty acres, the new fortress occupied approximately twenty percent more space than others in Britain; the cause of this appears to have been a group of major buildings in the middle of the fortress, of which the most striking – and enigmatic – is the so-called 'Elliptical Building'. Indeed, one of the puzzles surrounding this structure is the fact that it was not completed – that is, until the third century and then in a different format. Various purposes have been proposed for this building which appears to have been planned with a central courtyard surrounded by twelve 'shrines', perhaps for the Olympian deities. Although a practical purpose – that of a *ludus* or arena – has also been suggested,[53] it seems a reasonable likelihood that its meaning was symbolic of Rome and the Empire.

Such a symbolic role has been associated with Vespasian's 'new beginning', a theme which, in various contexts, echoed through the new emperor's coinage.[54] Did Vespasian, perhaps, have in mind the creation of a second British province, to include all of the north and Ireland, with its nerve-centre at Chester? Of course, events soon overtook such an ambition: the Elliptical Building did not grow beyond foundation-level and Ireland was never annexed. Yet, the discovery of Roman material of Flavian to Hadrianic date at Drumanagh (Co. Dublin) suggests that there were contacts which were more than simply casual; further, the occasion[55] when, during Agricola's fifth campaign (A.D. 81), his biographer depicts him gazing across the sea and speculating about the possibility of taking Ireland, appears to carry an air of 'wistful nostalgia', perhaps recalling a dream whose moment had by that time passed. The

significance of Ireland had perhaps lain in trade, particularly in supplies of grain for the Roman army from its eastern coastal areas.

Frontinus was succeeded by Agricola, evidently late in the summer of A.D. 77;[56] his 'brief' was presumably to advance Vespasian's policy of further expansion. It seems clear from Tacitus' account that little of the military activity of his father-in-law's governorship took place in what is now England; the first campaign was a strike, late in the season of A.D. 77, against the Ordovices of north Wales. Tacitus' rather vague account of the second campaign, with its mention of 'estuaries and woods',[57] points to north-west England as the location. The historian's description of Agricola's isolation of various groups suggests an area that was rather loosely organised politically and socially, which effectively conforms to the impression of Lancashire at this stage as conveyed by archaeological work.[58] It seems likely that Agricola was responsible, probably as a result of the success of the military activity of this campaign, for enhancing communications in the north west. It was evidently he who laid out a road from Chester, through Northwich and Manchester, to run northwards through Ribchester joining the existing route up the Lune Valley at Burrow-in-Lonsdale.

At Northwich, the intermediate point between Chester and Manchester, though significantly *not* on the crossing-point with the 'King Street route', a fort-site was examined in the 1960s[59] on Castle Hill. Elements of a turf-and-timber structure were taken as Agricolan; these were overlain by later structures, probably of second-century date. At any rate, the military site may have been short-lived, giving way to activities that were chiefly of an industrial nature (see below in chapter 6). Excavation and observation over the years have established the layout of an auxiliary fort on Castlefield at Manchester.[60] Recent work on the northern and western defences[61] has revealed elements of the northern gateway, rampart and ditch-system of a fort which evidently had two turf-and-timber phases, the earlier of which is regarded as of Agricolan date and the second as late Flavian/Trajanic. The fort was evidently substantially enlarged around the middle of the second century, perhaps following the withdrawal from the Antonine Wall in Scotland in the late-150s/early-160s.

A number of roads converged on Manchester: one ran across Saddleworth Moor,[62] heading for York; there are military sites along it at Castleshaw and Slack. At the former, there is a fortlet, which has timber buildings and which has been assumed to be Agricolan, and a smaller fortlet inside and partly contiguous with it.[63] The later fortlet, which is taken as Trajanic in date contained a rather strange collection of buildings consisting of a barrack-block, a courtyard-building, a commander's house (with a bath-house), latrines and a granary which was apparently larger than this fortlet alone would have required. Both fortlets, each of which probably had two phases of construction, were contained within turf ramparts, and together saw an occupation of around forty years. Another road heads from Manchester to Ilkley,[64] though doubt persists regarding the relation to it of the dramatically-sited paved surface which runs over Blackstone Edge.[65] Yet another heads south-eastwards towards Melandra (Glossop) and Brough-on-Noe.[66]

North of Manchester, the situation becomes more complex: a road runs northwards via Affetside, where Roman material has been recorded in the past,[67] to Ribchester. The third-century road-list, known as the *Antonine Itinerary*,[68] indicates a route from Ribchester to Manchester which has an intermediate site, named *Coccium*. This has usually been taken to be Wigan,[69] where many Roman finds have been made and where, in recent years, excavations have revealed timber buildings with three phases of occupation, which have been placed between the early-second and early-third centuries. There is nothing to suggest a military origin for these structures nor that they played any part in the original conquest of the north west. If *Coccium* is indeed Wigan – and not another site between Manchester and Ribchester – then we should regard the route given in the *Antonine Itinerary* as of later significance, when consolidation of the original conquest had resulted in a greater complexity of site-distribution.

Ribchester, as we have seen, was early on a key-point on the Ribble-Aire line of communications, and the fort was at least as early as the governorship of Cerialis; a good deal of the fort-area – approximately thirty percent – has been lost to erosion caused by the lateral movement of the Ribble within its valley. What remains provides evidence of fort-phases both of turf-and-timber and of stone construction. The excavated remains probably indicate re-orientation or realignment of the fort at some stage; certainly, the known remains of stone buildings (of which the ends of the granaries are still visible) do not belong to a fort on the same orientation as the turf-and-timber structures located in the churchyard. Possibly, structural changes were related to a change of role and/or a change of garrison; Ribchester seems to have been affected by developing

Plate 3.13: Ribchester: Tombstone of a cavalry-soldier; Ribchester Museum Trust

Plate 3.14: Ribchester: Cavalryman's parade-helmet; Ribchester Museum Trust

frontier-strategies in the late-first and second centuries. It seems likely, for example, that an early garrison of Asturian cavalry (from Spain) was redeployed on Hadrian's Wall early in the second century A.D., whilst later in the same century, Ribchester received a part of the large group of Sarmatian cavalry which, according to the historian, Dio Cassius,[70] was sent to Britain by the emperor, Marcus Aurelius. It is, in any case, likely that the complex troop movements associated both with the British frontiers as well as with commitments in other parts of the empire[71] will have necessitated considerable, and perhaps frequent, changes of garrison and manning-levels at individual forts.

Elements of the defences of the Ribchester forts have been observed in a number of recent excavations;[72] a clay-and-turf rampart rested on a log base (corduroy), and at one point it could be seen that the turves were approximately one foot square and that each pair of layers was interleaved with brushwood. The multi-phased ditches include three different types – a conventional V-shaped ditch with a drainage-channel/'ankle-breaker' at the bottom, a 'Punic' ditch (characterised by a near-vertical outer face), as well as a much shallower type of ditch which can still be seen as a feature in the fields adjacent to the churchyard. It also appeared in the excavations of 1978 that there were ditch-like features at a considerable distance from the fort-rampart; these may have been part of a complex of 'outworks' which have been noted at other sites. Ribchester's role as a cavalry-fort has been demonstrated in two other ways: first, the 'Punic' ditch (referred to above), when excavated, contained very large sections of horse-carcass. Secondly, a hoard of metal-work recovered in the eighteenth century included a very fine cavalryman's decorated parade-helmet, recalling those found at Newstead (in Roxbrughshire).[73]

As well as holding its position on the north-south road, Ribchester also lay on a road which ran along the north bank of the Ribble and to the north of Preston; it made for Kirkham and may from there have turned northwards to the mouth of the Wyre at Fleetwood; local tradition has long held that a site has been lost to coastal erosion at the river-mouth.[74] Many have believed this to have been the site of Ptolemy's elusive *Portus Setantiorum* although, as we have seen (in chapter 1), it now seems more likely that the Setantii and their *Portus* (harbour) were located on the northern side of Morecambe Bay – perhaps in the vicinity of Newby Bridge at the southern end of Windermere (see further below in chapter 4).

We have already noted the possible significance of Kirkham in the context of Rome's early incursions into the north west; excavation (in 1994)[75] on the last available area of the Roman site at Dowbridge (Kirkham) revealed a complex succession of structures, although the discovery in 1800 of a decorated shield-boss[76] had long ago determined a military character for the site. The earliest phase of activity appears to be marked by more than one campaign-camp, which could have belonged

Plate 3.15: Kirkham: *Pilum Murale.* Photograph by courtesy of Oxford Archaeological Unit Ltd.

Plate 3.16: *Pila Muralia* used in groups of three to form the outer defence of campaign-camps

to Cerialis' governorship – or earlier. This was evidently superseded by a watchtower, protected by a circular ditch which was, in its turn, replaced by an auxiliary fort of more than one phase. A clear chronology for all of this has proved difficult to establish, although the watchtower may date to Agricola's governorship, and the inception of the fort-phase to the period of reorganisation which accompanied the Flavian evacuation of Scotland in *c.* A.D. 87. This fort appears to have been maintained in operation until at least the middle of the second century A.D.

South of the Ribble, at its confluence with the river Darwen, lies Walton-le-Dale: this site, too, had over the years proved to be something of an enigma, although excavations in the 1980s and 1990s appear to have put beyond doubt that the chief role of the site was military. On the other hand, it has to be said that the buildings excavated[77] are not those of a conventional fort lay-out. Though of a large scale, they would appear to be more consistent with a manufacture, storage and supply role. The recovery at this site, as we have seen, of early imperial coins leaves alive the possibility that it had seen some kind of military activity in the 50s or 60s relating to Rome's early interventions in the area. If this is so, the subsequent chronology is likely to have seen the site abandoned by the early 70s and the storage buildings constructed late in the first century or early in the second, after an interval of inactivity.

It is likely that the Ribble–Aire corridor was equipped with a signalling system similar to that over Stainmore; a small earthwork on Mellor Hill, above Ribchester, may be a fragment of it. It is also possible that a site of a similar nature awaits discovery near Whalley, to judge from occasional finds of Roman material in the area, and the presence of an altar, evidently to the god, Mars, in Whalley church – unless, that is, this has been transported to its present location from another site.[78]

The new military road ran northwards from Ribchester to Burrow-in-Lonsdale;[79] whilst the road itself has some impressively-preserved stretches – such as that which can be seen from Jeffrey Hill crossing the valley of the river Hodder – there is little surviving of the fort at Burrow. Like many, however, it was protected by a confluence of rivers – in this case, of the Lune with Leck Beck; it lies at a distance from the main road, prompting the suggestion that it may not have been the earliest military site in the area. Limited excavations tell us more about the later stages of the fort's development, although a turf-and-timber phase was located which, although not certainly dated, would not be inconsistent with construction in Agricola's governorship.

However, Burrow will have occupied a critical position in the Lune Valley 'control-system', looking north to Low Borrow Bridge, south to Ribchester and westwards towards Lancaster, up to which point the Lune was certainly navigable. A sign of Burrow's significance may be seen in the apparent 'Jupiter-capital', which is preserved at Burrow Hall. Such a monument may well have stood at the fort's main gate, an impressive reminder of the power of 'Jupiter's city'.

As we have seen, the fort at Lancaster was founded probably in the governorship of Petillius Cerialis, although Castle Hill has revealed a complex structural history in the Roman period;[80] a well-preserved clay-and-turf rampart has been located on the north, north-east and north-west portions of the fort. A gateway, albeit heavily robbed, was located in excavations during 1973, associated with the butt-ends of two ditches and a double palisade of wooden stakes. Two roads appeared to issue from this gate – one following the line of modern Church Street, the other swinging northwards from it and making apparently for the river. This fort had been enlarged at some stage, perhaps at the time of the Trajanic refurbishment implied on a fragmentary inscription found beneath the Priory Church.[81] Artefactual evidence suggests the possibility of a short break in activity in the later years of the first century.[82]

It remains unclear how the river Lune was crossed at Lancaster in this early stage of development – whether by ford or bridge – and whether harbour (and perhaps ship-building) activities commenced in the first century: it should be noted, however, that ships may simply have been beached, thus obviating the need for formal harbour-structures. It is certain that a road ran along the south side of the Lune, its presence dramatically demonstrated by the recovery from the Artle Beck (Caton) of a fine cylindrical milestone of Hadrianic date.[83] Stretches of this road were also recorded in the early-1990s during pipeline-work in the areas of Quernmore, Caton and Brookhouse. This road joined the north-south route possibly at its crossing of the river Wenning.[84] This part of the route, at least as far as Carlisle, had, as we have seen, already been traversed by earlier governors. There has been little recent work on the forts themselves at Low Borrow Bridge and Brougham, although the results of excavations in the vicinities of both forts will be alluded to in a later chapter.

We have seen that the fort at Carlisle is now established as a foundation of Cerialis' governorship, although the site may well have grown in size and complexity to equip it to take on a supporting role in Agricola's advances further north.[85] Like Vindolanda, Carlisle has also produced evidence in the form of writing tablets,[86] two of which mention Agricola by name – one concerning his acquisition of supplies for his northward advance, the other indicating that the governor chose his personal bodyguard (*equites singulares*) from the then-garrison at Carlisle, the *Ala Gallorum Sebosiana*, a unit which had evidently been transferred to Britain from the Rhine in the early 70s.[87] Whilst the details of Agricola's advance through Scotland do not strictly concern us, a brief discussion is relevant to the understanding of changing Roman imperatives in northern Britain.

As we have seen, Vespasian's intention appears to have been the complete conquest of Britain, and probably Ireland also. Vespasian died in the summer of A.D. 79, by which time (according to Tacitus)[88] Agricola had reached the Tay estuary. It seems likely that both Carlisle and Corbridge were equipped to act as bases and winter-quarters for these activities, and that Agricola had probably opened northward-running routes from both, heading respectively for the Clyde and the Forth, supplementing the earlier north-easterly route of Petillius Cerialis.

Plate 3.17: Low Borrow Bridge: Roman fort (arrowed) at the head of the Lune valley

Agricola, therefore, had access both to the sites of the Gask Ridge (which he probably refurbished) and to a line of forts to the west of this, terminating at what was to become a new legionary fortress (presumably for legion XX) at Inchtuthil;[89] this latter line is usually given the title of 'glen-blocking' forts, which policed access to the Gask Ridge and served as a means of controlling the Highland tribes.

The new emperor was Vespasian's elder son, Titus; his perspective appears to have differed – perhaps because of changing imperial circumstances – from that of his father. Agricola's next two campaigns look decidedly like 'holding operations' – fortifying the line of the Forth and Clyde, and bringing under control the territory of the Novantae in the south west.[90] Presumably, the question exercising the new emperor was whether he could, in the face of an increasingly fluid situation on the Danube, continue to embrace his father's grandiose dream in Britain: was it worth what would be required to take Scotland, let alone Ireland, too? There are a number of indications that Titus was coming down on the side of caution.

Signs of this are evident in Tacitus' narrative: as we have seen, Agricola's fortification of the line of the Forth and Clyde was taken by some as representing the imposition of a frontier in *Britannia*. This provoked an acrimonious dispute between different schools of thought. Some, presumably Titus' supporters, approved, whilst others regarded it as a slur on the Roman name and those who advocated it were branded as 'cowards', a view evidently held by Tacitus and, perhaps, by Agricola himself.[91] The other indication lies in Agricola's wistful observations about Ireland[92] during the fifth campaign, Agricola evidently regretting the passing of the earlier, more positive, policy.

Titus himself died in September of A.D. 81, to be succeeded by his younger brother, Domitian. Again, there appears to have been a shift of policy, for in his final two campaigns (of A.D. 82 and 83) Agricola was again operating in the north of Scotland, his advance marked by a line of campaign-camps characterised by the so-called 'double-*clavicula*' type of entrance; Stracathro is typical of these. Although there are few permanent forts north of the Tay, the campaign-camps carry Agricola's progress along the Moray Firth,[93] as far as Inverness – and perhaps beyond.[94]

Whilst this may carry the appearance of a resurrection of full enthusiasm for Vespasian's policy for northern Britain, Domitian's objectives were probably more limited; their extent is made more difficult to understand in view of the construction of the fortress at Inchtuthil which seems to presuppose the permanent presence in Britain of four legions, despite the fact that, by A.D. 83, detachments appear to have been taken from the British legions for service elsewhere.[95] The fact that this major site was abandoned, still-unfinished, in *c.* A.D. 87, seems to suggest that construction-work on it must have largely post-dated Agricola's governorship.

The climax of Tacitus' 'British narrative' is provided by the battle of *Mons Graupius* in A.D. 83 at a location which is still not pinpointed with certainty.[96] The result of it was evidently a crushing victory for Agricola, which was rapidly followed by the governor's replacement; however, after seven campaigning-seasons in Britain, Agricola's tenure can hardly be regarded as unreasonably cut short. Tacitus, however, clearly regarded it as an act of jealous malice on the part of the emperor. Further, it is possible that the historian's view of two governors of Britain – Vettius Bolanus and Petillius Cerialis – may have been coloured by it. Both of these senior senators were high in the esteem of the Flavian emperors and, because of this, may well have been canvassed by the emperor for their views on Agricola's removal and future career.[97] In the case of Cerialis, such an imperial 'consultation' would have been perfectly natural if the Quintus Petillius Rufus, who was consul in the year of Agricola's removal from Britain, is to be identified with Cerialis.

It is unclear whether Agricola's victory at *Mons Graupius* was followed by further conquest,[98] although, as we have seen, construction-work does appear to have continued in Scotland for a few more years. Indeed, it is likely that the victory was viewed by Domitian as an end in itself, which may offer a clue regarding the emperor's objectives. As against the Ordovices of north Wales in A.D. 77, Agricola's victory over the Caledonians at *Mons Graupius* probably represents an act of genocide in the destruction of a generation of fighting-men. As a result, Domitian was left free to pursue the policy of his choice without serious threat of harassment by the enemy.

The emperor decided upon a policy of consolidation: he had, in fact, little choice, with further deterioration on the Danube requiring the removal from Britain in *c.* A.D. 87 of a complete legion (II *Adiutrix*). The vacant fortress at Chester required a garrison; there was little option but to remove XX *Valeria Victrix* from Inchtuthil to fill this gap. Accordingly, in the north, everything was abandoned to the north of the line of the Forth and Clyde, and much south of this line also.[99] The new frontier of *Britannia* was to be the Stanegate road, running from Corbridge to Carlisle; only a few 'outliers' were retained to the north of it.

It was not a complete or ideal solution: the region north of the Stanegate remained a mixture of hostile, neutral and a few friendly tribes, such as the Venicones and Votadini in the east. To Tacitus,[100] it was a negative sell-out, a shaming of Roman tradition: 'Britain', he wrote, 'was completely conquered and immediately thrown away'; Agricola's efforts had been wasted. But Tacitus was not only taking a view far narrower than could be afforded by the emperor of Rome, but he was also failing to do justice to the strength of the consolidation that was initiated on and to the south of the new *limes* ('frontier'). The importance of this work is highlighted from

Plate 3.18:
Carlisle: *Dupondius*
of Vespasian.
Photograph by
courtesy of Oxford
Archaeological
Unit Ltd.

two contrasting standpoints; Carlisle, as we have seen, is credited with the presence of a *centurio regionarius* (a kind of 'District Commissioner'), indicating the importance attached to the continuing task of organisation required in the new frontier-zone;[101] at the same time, a Vindolanda-tablet, with its reference to *Brittunculi* ('nasty little Brits'), points to the scale of what was perceived as needing to be done to Romanise the north west.

Notes

1. The dating of Agricola's governorship is dependent on the dating of his consulship; for this, see Campbell, 1986, 197ff.
2. For new evidence regarding Tacitus' public career, see Birley A. R., 2000.
3. The fullest edition of the *Life of Agricola* is that by R. M. Ogilvie and I. A. Richmond (published in 1967); it must, of course, be kept in mind that archaeological discoveries and interpretations have advanced considerably since then. For a new translation, see Birley A.R., 1999.
4. That is, Marcus Vettius Bolanus (A.D. 69–71), Quintus Petillius Cerialis Caesius Rufus (A.D. 71–74), and Sextus Julius Frontinus (A.D. 74–77). The name of Agricola's successor is not known for certain, though some believe it to have been Sallustius Lucullus, who certainly occupied the governorship at some stage after Agricola (Suetonius, *Life of Domitian* 10; see Birley A. R., 1981, 62–72).
5. Jones, 1968, 6; Shotter, 2001b.
6. Shotter, 1999a and b; 2002a.
7. Shotter, 2002b; Cartimandua's 'fate' is not known, though for a suggestion, see Reed, 1977.
8. *Life of Agricola* 8,1 and 16,5.
9. Shotter, 2001c.
10. Birley A. R., 1973.
11. *Life of Agricola* 17,1.
12. *Life of Agricola* 8,2–3.
13. Shotter, 2002a.
14. *Life of Agricola* 25,1.
15. Shotter, 1998b; 2000b; 2001c.
16. For Chester, see Mason, 2001; for Northwich, Jones, 1972; for Manchester, Jones, 1974 and Bryant, Morris and Walker, 1986; for Castleshaw, Walker, 1989 and Booth, 2001; for Ribchester, Buxton and Howard-Davis, 2000 and Edwards, 2000. Such evidence as there is for Burrow-in-Lonsdale is summarised in Shotter and White, 1995, 36–46.
17. Rogers, 1996; Edwards, 1998. Finds of Roman material have been made at Warburton on the southern side of the river Mersey; since some of this is evidently early in date, it leaves open the possiblility that there may have been an early 'conquest site' in this area.
18. See Jones and Shotter, 1988; Shotter and White, 1990; Shotter, 2001a.
19. Howard-Davis and Buxton, 2000.
20. Welfare and Swan, 1995, 144–145.

21. For Watercrook, see Potter, 1979; Shotter, 1998a; for evidence from Hincaster, see Shotter, 2000c, 208.

22. Excavations at Ravenglass in the 1970s found evidence of a military enclosure earlier than the Hadrianic fort (Potter, 1979; Shotter, 1998a). See Gerrard and Mills (2002) for an account of early *aes*-coins found near Muncaster Castle; the significance of these remains unclear.

23. Evans and Scull, 1990.

24. *Life of Agricola* 20; Tacitus includes the observation in his account of Agricola's second campaign (A.D. 78). It is suggested by A. R. Birley (2000) that Tacitus may have been a military tribune in Britain between A.D. 77 and 79.

25. Ramm, 1978, 28ff.

26. See Graystone, 2002.

27. Lambert *et al.*, 1996, 87ff; Birley E. B., 1947; Hildyard, 1951; (for a recently-reported Claudian copy-*as* from Low Borrow Bridge, see Shotter, 2003b). For Burrow-in-Lonsdale, see Birley, E. B., 1946 and Hildyard, 1954.

28. Summerson, Trueman and Harrison, 1998, 7f; Cool, 2004 (forthcoming).

29. Bishop and Dore, 1988.

30. Birley E. B., 1932.

31. For example, Bowes (*Journ. Rom. St.* 58 (1968), 179f); Brough-under-Stainmore (Birley E. B., 1958; Jones M. J., 1977); Maiden Castle (Richmond, 1951); Kirkby Thore (Gibbons, 1989, 108; Charlesworth, 1964). For the most recent assessment of the Stainmore-sites, see Vyner, 2001.

32. Welfare and Swan, 1995, 57–60 (Rey Cross); 34–36 (Crackenthorpe); 39 (Kirkby Thore); 43–44 (Plumpton Head); also Vyner, 2001.

33. Gilliver, 1993; 1999.

34. Howard-Davis and Buxton, 2000, 60–61.

35. See Higham and Jones, 1975; Woolliscroft and Swain, 1991.

36. It should be noted that the remnants of a camp have been identified at Langwathby (near Brougham; Welfare and Swan, 1995, 41).

37. Austen, 1991.

38. Poulter, 1982.

39. See Welfare and Swan, 1995, 36ff; for Scalesceugh, see Bellhouse, 1971.

40. Excavation-reports are awaited on a number of the military sites, though see Caruana, 1992; overall treatments are, however, available in McCarthy, 1993 and 2002.

41. E.g. Bushe-Fox, 1913.

42. Bishop and Dore, 1988; Hanson, Daniels *et al*, 1979.

43. McCarthy, 1991; It should be noted that the excavations of 1988 in the grounds of Carlisle Cathedral did not reach the early-Roman levels.

44. Bowman and Thomas, 1983 (Doc. no. 22); Birley, Birley and Birley, 1993. For a reference on a tablet from Carlisle itself, see *Britannia* 19 (1988), 496 and Tomlin, 1998.

45. There are numerous discussions of Roman place-names in north-west England, and the interpretative difficulties of the evidence relating to them (Richmond and Crawford, 1949; Rivet, 1970; Goodburn and Bartholomew, 1976; Rivet and Smith, 1979; Strang, 1997 and 1998; Smith, 1997, 372–383; Shotter, 1997, 111ff). It should be noted that Roman names for sites may not have remained the same throughout their lifetime – a suggestion recently made with respect to the use, in the *Notitia Dignitatum*, of the name, *Arbeia*, for South Shields (Graeme Stobbs, *pers. comm*).

46. Birley E. B., 1961, 141ff; Jones M. J., 1975, 169.

47. Statius *Silvae* V.2. 140–149; Pliny *Natural History* (4.103) appears to corroborate such an early penetration of Caledonia; for supporting coin-evidence, see Shotter, 2000a.

48. Jones R. F. J., *pers. comm.*

49. See Woolliscroft (2002) for a discussion of evidence relating to the inception and development of the Gask Ridge *limes*.

50. *Life of Agricola* 17, 1.

51. *Life of Agricola* 17, 2.

52. Mason, 2000; 2001.

53. The late Professor Barri Jones, *pers. comm.*

54. Levick, 1999, 65ff; *The Roman Imperial Coinage* II (Vespasian), pp.66ff; see also Shotter, 2004 (forthcoming).

55. *Life of Agricola* 24; see also Robinson, 1999.

56. For the dating, see particularly Campbell, 1986.

57. *Life of Agricola* 20, 2–3.

58. Cowell and Philpott, 2000, 175ff.

59. Jones G. D. B., 1972; Jones M. J., 1975, 170f. For more recent work, see *Britannia* 15 (1984), 288.

60. Bruton, 1909; *Journ. Rom. St.* 56 (1966), 200.

61. Jones G. D. B., 1974, 23f; Bryant, Morris and Walker, 1986; Shotter, 1995a.

62. Booth, 2001, 14ff.

63. For the most recent work and a full discussion, see Walker, 1989; earlier work is described in Bruton, 1908 and 1911; Start, 1985; Booth, 2001. Discussion of the site at Slack may be found in Dodd and Woodward, 1921, 1–92 and Hunter, Manby and Spaul, 1967.

64. For Ilkley, see Hartley, 1987.

65. This road is discussed by Richmond (1925).

66. Jones M. J., 1975, 166f (Melandra); Jones and Wild, 1970 and Dearne, 1993 (Brough-on-Noe).

67. Coin-finds from the area are discussed in Shotter, 1990, 168f.

68. Rivet, 1970.

69. *Britannia* 15 (1984), 286; Jones and Price, 1985; Tindall, 1985; Waddelove E., 2001.

70. Dio Cassius, *History of Rome* 72. 16, 2.

71. For example, see Speidel, 1987.

72. See Buxton and Howard-Davis, 2000; Edwards and Webster, 1985–88.

73. For the hoard, see Edwards, 1992; the Ribchester-helmet is in the British Museum, whilst those from Newstead are in the Royal Museum of Scotland (Edinburgh). For Newstead, see Curle, 1911, 164ff.

74. Jones G. D. B., 1980; for the road, see Lightbown, 1996.

75. Howard-Davis and Buxton, 2000.

76. See Watkin, 1883, 207 for an illustration. The shield-boss is in the British Museum.

77. Full publication of the excavations at Walton-le-Dale in the 1980s and 1990s is in preparation; a brief description of buildings located in the 1980s may be seen in *Britannia* 13 (1982), 352.

78. Jones G. D. B., 1970, 3.

79. Birley E B., 1946; Hildyard, 1954; Shotter and White, 1995, 36–46.

80. See Jones and Shotter, 1988; Shotter and White, 1990; Shotter, 2001a.

81. *RIB* 604.

82. Shotter, 1979.

83. *RIB* 2272.

84. Birley E. B., 1946, 145; Graystone, 2002, 41ff.

85. Caruana, 1992.

86. Tomlin, 1998; see especially *Tab. Luguval.* 44 (Tomlin, 1998, 74f).

87. *ILS* 2533.

88. *Life of Agricola* 22, 1; See Strang, 1997 and 1998; Smith, 1987; Maxwell, 1989; Breeze, 1996.

89. Pitts and St. Joseph, 1985.

90. Cf. Reed, 1971.

91. *Life of Agricola* 23 and 25, 3–4.

92. *Life of Agricola* 24.

93. Jones and Keillar, 2002, 1ff.

94. See Henderson, 1985.

95. See *ILS* 1025 and 9200.

96. Maxwell, 1990.

97. It should be noted, in addition, that Agricola's immediate predecessor in Britain, Sextus Julius Frontinus, was associated with Domitian in his German campaigns of the early 80s.

98. See the views of S. Wolfson (in 'Tacitus, Thule and Caledonia': http://myweb.tiscali.co.uk/fartherlands/ shetland.htm).

99. Hobley, 1989; Jones G. D. B., 1990.

100. *Histories* I. 2, 1; see Shotter, 2004 (forthcoming).

101. Bowman and Thomas, 1983 (Doc. no. 22); Birley, Birley and Birley, 1993, 37.

CHAPTER FOUR

The Consolidation of Occuption

We have seen in the preceding chapter that the recall of Agricola from Britain in A.D. 83 and the subsequent withdrawal of legion II *Adiutrix* four years later incurred a withering censure from Cornelius Tacitus. We need now to set these changes into two contexts – the situations which brought them about and the manner in which they were handled in Britain. In this way, we shall be in a better position to judge the extent to which Tacitus' criticisms might have been justified.

First, however, some observations are required on the nature and quality of the sources available to us for a study of the Roman north from the mid-80s to the early-120s, when Hadrian's Wall was put in place. It was a period characterised by momentous events – the complete withdrawal from Scotland and the establishment of the first east-west frontier in Britain along the Stanegate road between Corbridge and Carlisle; not only this, but it contained the events leading up to the building of Hadrian's Wall.

We have no continuous narrative of the period from classical times: Tacitus' *Histories*, which covered the period A.D. 69–96, is lost apart from the account of A.D. 69 and part of 70; further, the *Roman History* of Dio Cassius survives only in the form of extracts made by various Byzantine Epitomators. Beyond these, we have only occasional references in works such as Suetonius' *Lives of the Caesars* and the later *Scriptores Historiae Augustae* ('Writers of the Augustan History'), a work that is full of interpretative problems,[1] together with occasional references in poets, such as the satirist, Juvenal. Some useful information is contained in the writing tablets from Vindolanda (*Tabulae Vindolandenses*)[2] and in surviving inscriptions. Other than these, we rely on archaeological evidence which is itself often capable of more than a single interpretation.

As we have seen, the majority of the surviving classical sources are highly critical of the emperor Domitian; most of the writers concerned, however, were from the higher ranks of Roman society – the senatorial and equestrian orders – and it was their members who appear to have suffered most from an emperor who was both autocratic and suspicious. Other groups – especially the army and the ordinary people – entertained

Figure 4.1: Late-Flavian/Trajanic sites in north-west England

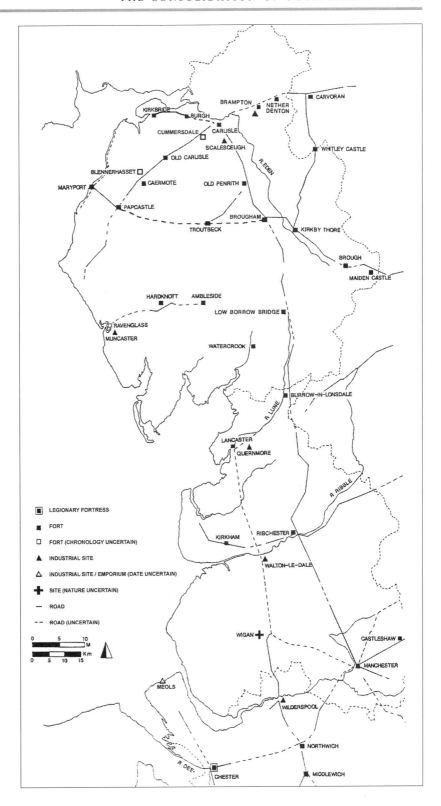

Plate 4.1:
Vindolanda: The
Stanegate road to the
west of the fort

a generally more favourable view.[3] For his part, Tacitus suggests that Domitian's motives for changing policy in Britain were, at the least, weak and capricious and, at worst, malevolent; we should keep in mind, however, the very real difficulties encountered during his reign.[4]

First, the emperor had little option but to respond to a threat on the Danube that was not new, but developing; the security of Italy was under a far greater threat from that source than ever it was from Britain; the withdrawal of a legion from Britain, therefore, was inevitable. Secondly, central European instability was again highlighted by campaigning on the Rhine in the mid-80s; this was necessary and positive in its results, and not the fiasco that Tacitus would have us believe.[5]

The emperor was also under pressure from nearer to home, as is seen from the attempted rebellion amongst the Rhine-garrison in A.D. 89, instigated by one, Antonius Saturninus. The potential seriousness of this would have made an impact on an emperor who will have been familiar with similar events on the Rhine in A.D. 68–69. Further, these events will have also been recalled by the execution of Sallustius Lucullus, allegedly for naming a new piece of weaponry after himself rather than after the emperor;[6] it is more than likely that Lucullus, who may have been governor of Britain between A.D. 85 and 89, was associated with Saturninus. That relations between Domitian and the senate worsened still further seems clear from Tacitus' references to the latter years of the reign and from the likelihood that another serious (but ultimately unsuccessful) conspiracy was mounted in A.D. 93, the year of Agricola's death.[7] Finally, the emperor's assassination in A.D. 96 is less likely to have been a 'bedroom plot', as is often suggested, than a conspiracy mounted by senators determined to replace the 'last of the Flavians' by the aged Marcus Cocceius Nerva, regarded perhaps as an innocuous, but safe, 'pair of hands'.

These events, then, formed part of the backdrop against which developments in northern Britain have to be viewed and in the light of which Tacitus' condemnation must be judged.[8] As we have seen, the question of a frontier *within* Britain had been raised before:[9] during Agricola's governorship the possibility of using the line of the Forth and Clyde had been raised. It may have been related to this that, presumably in his fourth campaign (of A.D. 80), Agricola had built forts at Barochan Hill and Mollins, and perhaps at Mumrills and Balmuildy also, to sit alongside the existing fort at Camelon.

At first sight, it may have appeared that Domitian, when he succeeded Titus in A.D. 81, was attempting to resuscitate the 'grand design' of their father by re-introducing a forward-policy in Scotland in his first summer in office (A.D. 82). His objective, however, may, as we have seen, have been of a more limited character – to bring the Caledonians to a battle which effectively would result in 'male-genocide', a repetition perhaps of the treatment already meted out by Agricola in A.D. 77 to the Ordovices of north Wales; indeed, it may have been Agricola's experience of securing such an outcome in mountainous terrain that had persuaded Domitian to retain in office the governor originally appointed by his father, albeit in circumstances that looked (and were) very different from those currently prevailing. Domitian needed a decisive outcome in Scotland in order to leave his options open for whatever the longer-term conditions might require. That those options remained open after Agricola's departure is clear from the fact that consolidation in northern Scotland evidently continued for another three years; indeed, the fact that the new fortress at Inchtuthil (for legion XX *Valeria-Victrix*) was eventually abandoned, still incomplete, in A.D. 87 suggests that its construction may not even have been commenced until after Agricola's departure.[10]

We have already seen that the construction of the 'Elliptical Building' in the fortress at Chester, perhaps the symbol of Vespasian's policy, was

stopped before the building had progressed beyond foundation-level.[11] Now, in approximately A.D. 87, the fortress at Inchtuthil was abandoned, with all installations on and to the north of the Forth-Clyde line, together also with a number to the south of it;[12] only a few sites – Newstead, for example – were kept up as 'outliers' to a frontier-system being developed on the line of the Tyne and Solway. The retention of a few sites, such as Newstead, may have been intended to facilitate continued support for Rome's 'regional allies', such as the grain-growing Votadini.

There is no indication that the Roman withdrawal from Scotland was undertaken under pressure from local tribesmen; such evidence as there is – for example, the burial of nails at Inchtuthil – suggests that it was part of an orderly, presumably pre-planned, strategy. The line chosen for the focus of the frontier-zone was that provided by the Stanegate road. The early history of this road is none-too-clear, although it has been established that the two terminal sites – at Corbridge and Carlisle – belong to the early to mid-70s. It is possible that other forts, such as Nether Denton, may also belong to an early phase of construction. Despite the fact that dating-evidence remains sparse, there is an argument, based upon the structural sequence at Burgh-by-Sands (I),[13] that the watchtower, which pre-dated that two-phase fort, should be dated to the governorship of Agricola or, perhaps more likely, to that of

Plate 4.2: Vindolanda: Late fc and *vicus*, with the Stanegate road running from left to right at the bottom of the picture. Photograph by G.D.B. Jones

his unknown successor. This watchtower revealed only a single constructional phase, whereas its 'neighbour' to the west, at Farnhill, had two before its incorporation into a palisade-structure which may have constituted a secondary phase of construction on the frontier itself. A further two-phase watchtower has been identified at Easton (Finglandrigg), and it is possible that a four-post structure, discovered in 1973 beneath the western gate of the stone-built fort at Bowness-on-Solway, and interpreted at the time[14] as the timber predecessor of this gate, may in fact have been a further watchtower. It remains unclear how (or if) watchtowers at Gamelsby Ridge and Crooklands (between Kirkbride and Beckfoot) and the complex of structures (camp or fort?) at Cummersdale may relate to these.[15] It is not inconceivable, however, that all of these structures represented measures to provide protection for the Solway Plain and its agricultural land both from the Novantae (from across the Solway) and from the Brigantian hill-people to the south.[16]

A two-phase sequence has been proposed for the development of the Stanegate-frontier itself:[17] the first phase appears to have consisted of the road itself between Corbridge and Carlisle, now augmented by a series of large forts of approximately eight acres, and capable of housing double auxiliary garrisons – a necessary expedient, perhaps, in view of the large influx of troops from Scotland. Evidence from Vindolanda[18] suggests that the first phase of the fort there – a large one – should be dated to *c.* A.D. 85; it should, however, be noted that the evidence of aerial photography suggests the possibility of an earlier fort (or forts) on a different part of the site in the vicinity of the Stanegate.[19] The dating and sequence at

ate 4.3: Burgh-by-
nds: Air
notograph of late-
st century fort-
rtline (arrowed).
notograph by
.D.B. Jones

Vindolanda, however, appear to corroborate the suggestion that the evacuation of sites to the north was, indeed, pre-planned, and that frontier-forts were being constructed from the mid-80s in anticipation of the withdrawal. Similar large-sized forts were evidently established at Newbrough, Carvoran, Nether Denton and Brampton.[20]

At some stage – and it could have been soon after the inception of the system – the Stanegate was extended westwards: a two-phase fort, where the second represented a major reduction of the first – was constructed at Burgh-by-Sands (I), requiring the demolition of the watchtower (already mentioned). The excavators believed, on the evidence of the fill of the watchtower's ditch, that it had not been in use for long when the change-of-plan occurred.

An eastward extension from Corbridge – to forts at Whickham (Washing Well)[21] and South Shields, on the Tyne-estuary – seems certain, although the nature of these forts is less clear both in terms of size and chronology; this extension might have coincided with a decision to modify the original plan.

The chief evidence for the modification consists of the substantial reduction in size of the forts and the construction of intermediate sites between them – fortlets and watchtowers: a number of these are known, but by no means can they yet be seen as a coherent system. Evidence from the extension to the west of Carlisle suggests that there, at least, the road was enhanced by a running-ditch and palisade, as seen at Finglandrigg. The watchtower at Farnhill appears to have been integrated into this 'enhanced system'. Dating for this modification is hazardous, although, at Vindolanda, major reconstruction work appears to have taken place both in the mid-90s and very early in the second century.

Plate 4.4: Burgh-by-Sands: Four-post watchtower beneath the first-century for

The modifications, taken as a whole, bring the Stanegate-systems much more closely into line with contemporary frontier-construction on the Rhine. If it could be shown that the forts and the intermediate and running structures were coherent and integrated *throughout* the frontier-zone, then it would certainly be reasonable to regard the Stanegate-system as a true precursor of Hadrian's Wall, constituting a zone in which movement back and forth across it for a variety of purposes could be monitored.

The writing-tablets[22] provide us with a variety of information regarding the nature and organisation of life in the frontier-zone: we see, for instance, the flexibility with which troops were employed. Tablets inform us, for example, of the sending of eighteen men from Carlisle to Vindolanda to take part in the construction of a bath-house – presumably that which has recently been uncovered immediately outside the south gate of the fort at Vindolanda;[23] again, on another occasion, 200 men were sent from Vindolanda to *Coria* – evidently Corbridge.[24] We see the wife of the commanding officer (Flavius Cerialis) inviting her friend to join her for a birthday-party,[25] and read of soldiers writing to request new socks and underpants[26] and to complain about the ignoring by superiors of their rights.[27]

Perhaps the most significant tablets are those which deal with the relationship between the troops of the frontier and local people. Although, as we have seen, one tablet seems to evince a rather low opinion of the *Brittunculi* ('wretched little Brits'), others point to a developing economic relationship in which local farmers were evidently supplying the forts with a variety of commodities and presumably receiving Roman goods and/or money in return. This echoes the most

Plate 4.6:
Vindolanda: The
early-second centur
bath-house.
Photograph: The
Vindolanda Trust

Plate 4.7:
Vindolanda: Toilet-
block of the late-
first/early-second
century fort.
Photograph by
courtesy of The
Vindolanda Trust

recent discoveries in the area of the earlier Gask Ridge *limes* in Scotland,[28] where native sites have yielded evidence pointing to trading-contacts between the Roman army and the subject-population. Such developments encourage us to view these, and other Roman frontiers, not as 'thin red lines' but as zones in which a Romanising influence developed.

The creation of the Stanegate-*limes*, then, was a response to a crisis – but one that was conceived positively and for which preparations had been made. Contrary to what Tacitus seems to imply about the post-Agricolan period, positive measures were taken over an area wider than

the frontier-zone alone: as far as can be seen, the earlier conquest of the north west had not been all-embracing. Areas of considerable size had not been included: in particular, territory to the west of the 'conquest-route' (the valleys of the Lune and the Eden) had received little attention, a point that has been progressively appreciated through studies of coin-loss and of the samian pottery recovered from a large number of sites which were at one time assumed, without question, to have been of Agricolan origin, but which are now classed as 'post-Agricolan'.[29]

The chief sites that penetrate and surround the Lake District, in addition to those earlier sites on the Lune and the Eden, are Cummersdale, Old Carlisle, Papcastle, Caermote, Old Penrith, Troutbeck, Ambleside, Hardknott, Ravenglass and Watercrook. As well as these there are the coastal forts of Beckfoot, Maryport, Burrow Walls and Moresby which will be discussed more fully in the next chapter. It is worth adding, too, particularly in view of the discovery in recent decades of previously unrecognised forts, that we probably as yet do not have the 'full tally' of Roman forts in the area and that others still await discovery.

Few of the sites given in the previous paragraph have seen archaeological work of any great extent; in the north, a road ran from Carlisle in a south-westerly direction through Old Carlisle (Red Dial), Caermote and Papcastle to the coast at Maryport. It remains unclear whether the newly-discovered site at Cummersdale bears any relation to

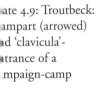

this; excavation of this large, evidently two-phased, site has so far failed to produce any positive evidence of its development, its role or its chronology – or even whether it was, in fact, a fort at all. Old Carlisle, on the other hand,[30] has revealed much of its layout through aerial reconnaissance; this fort, which evidently had an extensive extramural settlement, has seen virtually no excavation, although casually-recovered artefactual material would suggest that it should not be dated any earlier than the latest years of the first century.[31] At Caermote,[32] two turf-and-timber forts have been identified, one inside the other. The larger of the two is the earlier, and a Trajanic date for this and a Hadrianic date for the smaller fort would not be inconsistent with the dating-evidence. An earlier foundation in the Flavian period seems unlikely, though this has been argued on grounds of gateway-style.

Papcastle[33] has seen a certain amount of excavation, although the most substantial (and most recent) work has been concentrated in the extramural settlement. This provided evidence of a temple, possibly dedicated to Apollo (see below in chapter 6), and possible military connections with eastern Europe. Earlier work[34] revealed evidence of timber structures for which a late Flavian origin cannot be ruled out. General observation suggests a fort and settlement which are probably more substantial than most others in Cumbria; this may, in its turn, point to special 'command-responsibilities' in the Lake District for a fort whose position in the 'policing-system' for the region appears pivotal.

On the eastern flank of the Lake District, excavations in an area of the extramural settlement at Old Penrith have indicated a date not earlier than late in the Flavian period,[35] although we should remember that, on analogy with other sites, chronological coincidence between occupation in the fort and extramural settlement should not be assumed without question; virtually no excavation has as yet taken place on the site of the fort itself. The fort at Brougham has produced no secure dating-evidence, although its proximity to Clifton Dykes suggests the likelihood of early-Flavian occupation somewhere in the vicinity; burials in the cemetery, however, are dated mainly to the second and third centuries A.D.[36] At Low Borrow Bridge, there is some suggestion that an early (possibly Cerialian) fort was later enlarged. This secondary structure has been recognised in the form of a pebbly-clay rampart which may have been associated with a stone wall. The dating-sequence, however, remains hazardous, although a second-century date for the 'larger' fort seems possible.[37] Between Penrith and Keswick, adjacent to the known (but undated) camps at Troutbeck, lies a fort-site which was recognised in the 1970s. Although not firmly dated, this fort, which had a rampart of clay blocks, is probably not earlier than the Trajanic period. At a later date, it was evidently reduced in size.[38] The site would 'fit' into the 'policing-network' in the Lake District, and its existence perhaps strengthens the

Plate 4.10: Waterhead (Ambleside): Roman fort (arrowed) at the head of Windermere. Photograph by Messrs. Sanderson and Dixon

case for an as-yet unrecognised site beneath or in the vicinity of Keswick.

Relatively large-scale excavations were carried out at Ambleside (Waterhead) early in the twentieth century, revealing a slightly irregular quadrilateral fort defended by clay ramparts.[39] Outside there were two and, in places, three ditches. The central range of buildings was uncovered, although these related to a later stone-built phase of the fort. The evidence of pottery suggested that the original construction of the fort should be assigned to the later years of the Flavian period,[40] whilst the stone-buildings were probably first erected under Hadrian. It is, however, worth noting that during site-clearance in 1982 approximately half-a-mile to the north of the fort, features were observed which would not be inconsistent with a defensive system. The associated pottery, however, was largely of second-century date. It is possible, therefore, that these ditches represent part of a system of 'outworks' to the Hadrianic fort.

The position of the Ambleside fort at the head of Windermere emphasises its peculiar advantage in that men and supplies could be brought to the fort by ship independently of the road-system. This, together with the large size of the granaries of the stone-built fort, suggests that the fort and its associated civilian settlement constituted a kind of emporium and supply-centre for forts in the Lake District. Such a proposition also serves to highlight the poor state of our knowledge of Roman activities in southern Cumbria and of sites which may have been linked to Ambleside by the lake. It may be, for example, that at both ends of Windermere jetty-structures await discovery;[41] it also makes it reasonable to suggest that *Clanoventa* ('Market by the Shore') would provide a more suitable name for Ambleside than *Galava*.

Plate 4.11: Waterhead (Ambleside): Granaries of the Roman fort

Presumably as a vital part of the communications and policing system for the Lake District, a road[42] was built leading from Ambleside to the coast at Ravenglass. Although it seems that the latter site is of Hadrianic date, the intermediate fort at Hardknott is regarded as having a Trajanic foundation.[43] This almost-square fort is superbly sited with excellent visibility down Eskdale to the sea; it is stone-built, although it is assumed that a rampart-bank was originally provided, as this would have supplied the only access to the internal-towers; the fort had two ditches where necessary, although on parts of the site natural features obviated the need to cut ditches. Excavation of interior features revealed two phases of

Plate 4.12: Hardknott: Air photograph of the Roman fort

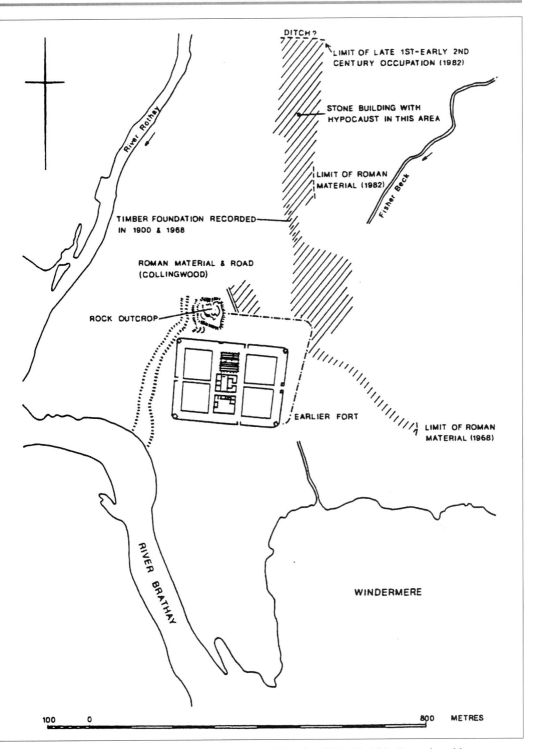

Figure 4.2: The Roman site at Waterhead (Ambleside): Reproduced by courtesy of Oxford Archaeological Unit Ltd.

barrack-block – of timber and stone. Much of the interior would, however, have been difficult, if not impossible, to build upon because of the shallow depth of soil. An oddity of the surviving buildings is the 'commander's house' (*praetorium*), which has either been left unfinished or built on a smaller scale to accommodate a presence on the part of the *praefectus* which was occasional only. It is thought that the granaries, although 'double', were covered by a single pitched roof.

Ravenglass[44] will be discussed more fully in its 'coastal context' in the next chapter, but for the present purpose it is sufficient to say that the most recent excavations have suggested that a fort of mid-Hadrianic date was preceded by an earlier fort (or fortlet) on a different alignment. The dating – and even the locations – of other coastal forts is hazardous. Maryport,[45] of which a stone wall and rampart have been discovered and of which a recent geophysical survey[46] has revealed more (both in the fort

Plate 4.13:
Hardknott: The fort-headquarters
(*principia*)

Plate 4.14:
Hardknott: The fort's
external bath-house

itself and in the extramural settlement), appears on the evidence of coin-loss and pottery to have been a foundation of the late-Flavian or, more likely, Trajanic period. However, given the evident complexity of arrangements in Solway (discussed above), it may be that an earlier fort awaits discovery nearby – or even beneath the known fort.

Of Moresby, Burrow Walls and Beckfoot, little is known apart from a Hadrianic building-inscription from Moresby.[47] This has prompted the suggestion that on the coast some of the forts may have been later additions[48] – as, of course, was the case with the forts of Hadrian's Wall itself. On the other hand, the fortifications being put in place on the Solway from Flavian times may suggest that Beckfoot, at least, could have been established in the later-first century.[49] Further sites may remain to be discovered on the coast of Cumbria; clusters of Roman material between Barrow and Ravenglass and between Ravenglass and Moresby – (for example, in the area of Beckermet) may point in this direction.[50] On similar grounds, there is reason to suspect the existence of sites on the southern flank of the Lake District – in the areas of Barrow and Cartmel,[51] although coastal change may now have substantially removed these.

One fort, however, which does survive in southern Lakeland is Watercrook (Kendal); this site, regarded for many years as an Agricolan foundation, was shown conclusively in excavations of the 1970s[52] to have been established in the later years of the Flavian period. Although the recent excavations were largely confined to areas of the extramural settlement, they showed that the first phase of rampart, constructed of turf and timber, should not be placed earlier than the late Flavian years. On the east angle, the outer defences consisted of three ditches: between

Plate 4.15:
Hardknott: The
parade-ground

Plate 4.16:
Watercrook: Air
photograph of the
Roman fort, situated
in a deep loop of the
river Kent

the first and second were a palisade and a bank constructed of stones excavated from the ditches. The fort, which is nearly square, was protected on three sides by a bow of the river Kent, prompting the suggestion that it, rather than Hardknott, may have been MEDIBOGDO of the *Ravenna Cosmography* – the name meaning 'fort in the middle of a bow', which closely describes Watercrook's disposition. It is quite likely, to judge from alluvial deposits,[53] that the site suffered from periodic flooding of the river, which may explain why the Roman site was not succeeded precisely by the development of Kendal.

The picture across Stainmore[54] in the period of consolidation is unclear. At Greta Bridge, occupation from late Flavian times is assumed on the basis of finds, whilst at Bowes the elaborate Flavian rampart was modified, though at a date not certainly proved. The fort at Brough (as noted above) has produced no clear evidence of its structural sequence, although its long-term importance is attested by the large collection of lead sealings of various army-units found there. Kirkby Thore certainly had a second phase of turf-and-clay rampart, although its date is uncertain.

Further south, other Pennine routes received attention: Castleshaw, as we have seen, was reduced in size – the early Flavian fort of three acres being replaced by one of 0.6 acres built inside its predecessor. Whilst the second fort was undoubtedly of the second century, its exact date of construction is unclear.[55] These changes of size, noted here and elsewhere in the north west, must surely point to considerable flexibility in garrison-arrangements over the years, as we have seen demonstrated in the writing-tablets of Vindolanda.

This network of policing newly-acquired territory was substantial: to it, we must add similar work further to the south. Most of the known forts in Lancashire were established at some point in the Flavian period, and will, therefore, have been in need of refurbishment by the turn of the first and second centuries.[56] On present evidence, in structural terms, the most complex was the multi-period military site at Kirkham:[57] campaign-camps and a watchtower in early Flavian times were evidently followed in the later Flavian years by a turf-and-timber auxiliary fort which was later rebuilt in stone – perhaps in the Hadrianic period. This complexity of development may have been due to the proximity of the site to the coast and its use as a point of entry for men and materials.

At Ribchester,[58] it is likely that the fort, established in all probability during the governorship of Petillius Cerialis, underwent frequent, small-scale, modifications (on the analogy of Carlisle), until a major change, probably early in the second century, saw its conversion into stone conjoined, perhaps, with re-orientation through 90 degrees. The re-orientation of forts – Lancaster evidently saw a similar adjustment – presumably reflected changing imperatives as frontier-policies changed in the later-first and early-second centuries. We may be certain, especially if the river Ribble was, indeed, tidal up to this point, that the fort and extramural settlement at Ribchester remained a significant part of the infrastructure – a point emphasised by the discovery of a timber-

late 4.17: Watercrook: Remains of a double-
·alisade, situated between the fort's second and
hird external ditches

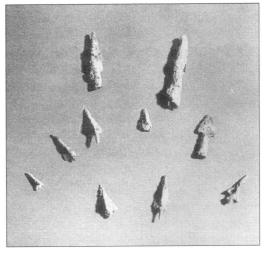

Plate 4.18: Watercrook: Iron-weaponry recovered from the fort's inner ditch. Photograph by Joe Thompson

workshop and considerable amounts of industrial waste between the north gate and the fort's ditch-system. There may have been some connection within the developing infrastructure in the hinterland of the frontier between the fort at Ribchester and industrial activities higher up the Ribble-valley.[59] The evidence of Roman coin-loss at Ribchester, however, suggests that the fort may, temporarily at least, have been wholly or partly demilitarised in the Hadrianic period.

Excavations at Lancaster[60] have suggested that this Cerialian fort was enlarged at some stage during the later Flavian period and almost certainly, like Ribchester, re-orientated through 90 degrees. Thus its main axis now

Plate 4.19: Lancaster Fragment of a building-inscription of the Trajanic period. Lancaster City Museums

pointed northwards towards the Lake District, an area in which in the later-first century, as we have seen, new forts were being established in the hinterland of the frontier. This re-orientation was perhaps also linked to the construction of a timber bridge across the river Lune. As at Ribchester, the tidal nature of the river at Lancaster gave the fort and extramural settlement great potential value as an emporium. A surviving fragment of a commemorative inscription[61] indicates that this enlarged fort was rebuilt in stone under Trajan; this period perhaps, with the developing importance of the use of the river, also saw the construction of a second road out of the fort's east gate[62] which appeared to cross the fort-ditches before swinging northwards towards the river.

In the south of the region the legionary fortress at Chester, which had been a base for part, at least, of legion II *Adiutrix* since the 70s, in *c.* A.D. 87 saw its replacement by XX *Valeria-Victrix* which was moved from bases at Wroxeter and Inchtuthil. Fragments of a Trajanic building-inscription[63] indicate that, like the forts further north, the fortress was rebuilt in stone. We may be certain that, in view of the scale of such a project, it will have prompted its own infrastructural developments in the hinterland at sites such as Holt, Heronbridge, Wilderspool, and probably Wigan, too.[64] The Flavian fort at Manchester was rebuilt in stone and, as at other forts, there appear to have been substantial developments of a commercial and industrial nature in the adjacent extramural settlement.[65] Although little is known in detail of fort-development at Northwich,[66] Middlewich[67] and, probably, Nantwich,[68] all of these probably remained in military use into the second century, perhaps in a role connected with the salt-industry. This industry will obviously have assumed an increasing importance as the army settled into permanent occupation – particularly in connection with the large-scale

ate 4.20: Lancaster:
mber-lined well of
e early-second
ntury A.D.

preservation of foodstuffs and preparation of leather required by the
army for tents, footwear and other equipment.

Although some infrastructural sites,[69] such as Holt (for Chester) and
similar, but smaller, such sites at Quernmore (for Lancaster), Muncaster
(for Ravenglass) and Scalesceugh (for Carlisle) were probably operated
largely by military personnel, others at Heronbridge, Wilderspool/
Stockton Heath, Wigan and Walton-le-Dale appear to have provided
opportunities and access to markets for local tradesmen. In this sense, the
'market-place', as Dio Cassius said of Germany,[70] proved a great
encouragement to the process of Romanisation. It is important to bear in

ate 4.21: Whitley
astle: Air
notograph of the
eavily-defended
oman fort

mind that these developments were not confined to the later years of occupation, but appear from examination of the sites themselves to have been in 'full swing' before the close of the first century A.D.

In all, therefore, taking together developments in the thirty years or so between A.D. 90 and 120 on the frontier itself and in its hinterland, we find little or no sign of the negative, even negligent, attitude implied by Tacitus. Perhaps Tacitus' bitter criticism reflects how far he felt that reality fell short of the 'spin' put upon events by Domitian as demonstrated by an inscription on the great monument at Richborough;[71] commissioned by Vespasian to commemorate Claudius' invasion of A.D. 43, this in its completion was a stark reminder, to Tacitus' mind, of the way in which events in Britain in the later Flavian period had fallen short of earlier Flavian aspirations.

However, for obvious reasons Tacitus had had a vested interest in these aspirations; once it was clear that overall imperatives were not such as to permit the achievement of Vespasian's objectives, the consequent re-assessment was evidently managed in such a way as to ensure both the security and the developing prosperity of *Britannia* within the frontier from Tyne to Solway. What is less clear, though pertinent, is the question of whether (or how far) the unnecessary military adventures of Trajan's later years compromised the stability of what had been achieved under his predecessors.

Notes

1. Syme, 1968.
2. Bowman and Thomas, 1983; Birley, Birley and Birley, 1993; Birley A.R., 2002.
3. Shotter, 1983a.
4. Southern, 1997; Jones B.W., 1992.
5. Tacitus *Germania* 37, 6, though compare Frontinus *Strategemata* I. 1, 8. For a modern assessment, see Schönberger, 1969, 155–167. Domitian took the title, *Germanicus*, for this – as the coinage shows. The fact that Tacitus reached the senior rank of *praetor* in A.D. 88 (*Annals* XI. 11, 1–4) indicates that he must surely have known the seriousness of problems in Europe.
6. Suetonius *Life of Domitian* 10.
7. Tacitus *Life of Agricola* 45; also Rogers, 1960.
8. Tacitus *Histories* I. 2, 1; see Shotter, 2004 (forthcoming); for Nerva, see Grainger, 2002.
9. Tacitus *Life of Agricola* 23 and 25, 3–4.
10. Pitts and St. Joseph, 1985.
11. Mason, 2000; 2001, 89.
12. This hypothesis has been advanced largely on the basis of the evidence of coin-loss (Hobley, 1989).
13. Jones, 1994/95.
14. Potter, 1975 (esp. pp. 33f and 56f); in retrospect, the late Timothy Potter (*pers. comm.*) accepted this as a possible alternative interpretation.

15. *Britannia* 27 (1996), 405; 28 (1997), 415; 29 (1998), 382 and 30 (1999), 334.

16. It is clear that more work is yet needed to elucidate the relationship(s) between these structures in Solway. They may, perhaps, be seen as enhancing measures put in place by Petillius Cerialis (above in chapter 3).

17. Jones, 1990; Hodgson, 2000.

18. Birley R., 1994, 21.

19. Robin Birley, *pers. comm.* (2002).

20. For Nether Denton, see *Britannia* 8 (1977), 373f.

21. *Journ. Rom. St.* 63 (1973), 215; *Arch. Ael.*[4] 49 (1971), 120.

22. See above in note 2 for references; also Bowman, 1994.

23. Birley A.R., 2002, 30f.

24. Birley A.R., 2002, 61.

25. Birley A.R., 2002, 136ff.

26. Birley A.R., 2002, 22.

27. Birley A.R., 2002, 100.

28. *Britannia*, 34 (2003), 302; Dr. David Woolliscroft, *pers. comm.*

29. Shotter, 2001b.

30. Birley E.B., 1951; for a plan of the fort and extramural settlement, see Higham and Jones, 1975, 18.

31. For the coins, see Shotter, 2000c, 35ff.

32. Bellhouse, 1960a; Jones M.J., 1975, 135; *Journ. Rom. St.* 63 (1973), 215.

33. For a summary, see *Britannia* 16 (1985), 276; a full report of the excavations of 1984–85 is pending; more recent field-work has suggested that the site may have been considerably more complex than once thought.

34. Birley E.B., 1963; Charlesworth, 1965.

35. Austen, 1991.

36. *Journ. Rom. St.* 57 (1967), 177 and 58 (1968), 179; Cool, 2004 (forthcoming).

37. Jones M.J., 1975, 164; Lambert *et al.*, 1996, 87ff.

38. Jones M.J., 1975, 180; Allan, 1994.

39. For a general account and references to earlier excavations, see Shotter, 1998, 339–351.

40. Hartley, 1966, 12; for work to the north of the fort, see Leech, 1993; for more recent work, see *Britannia* 21 (1990), 320 and Mann and Dunwell, 1995.

41. Shotter, 1995; the name, *Galava*, would be more appropriate to a site in the Lune valley.

42. See Richmond, 1949.

43. Hartley, 1966, 12; *Journ. Rom. St.* 55 (1965), 203; Jones, M.J., 1975, 154f; Shotter, 1998, 343ff; Bidwell, Snape and Croom, 1999.

44. Potter, 1979, 48f.

45. Jarrett, 1976; Wilson, 1997.

46. *Britannia* 32 (2001), 337–9; For the results of geophysical surveys of other northern sites, see *Britannia* 32 (2001), 322ff.

47. *RIB* 801, which is dated to later than A.D. 128.

48. Potter, 1979, 359.

49. The late Professor Barri Jones, *pers. comm.*

50. Shotter, 1980, 163.

51. Shotter, 1995.

52. For the excavations of 1974–75 and a discussion of results, see Potter, 1979; for the possible name of the fort, see Shotter, 1998, 348f.

53. Potter, 1977.

54. Greta Bridge (Jones M.J., 1975, 154); Bowes (Jones M.J., 1975, 130f); Brough-under-Stainmore (Richmond, 1936; Jones M.J., 1977); Kirkby Thore (Jones M.J., 1975, 158; Gibbons, 1989).

55. Walker, 1989; Booth, 2001, 28ff.

56. The current condition of the 1970s-reconstruction of parts of the Lunt (Coventry), particularly the rampart-sections, provides a good idea of what might have happened to a turf-and-timber fort over a period of 20–25 years; other such experimental reconstructions have indicated shorter periods of decay.

57. Howard-Davis and Buxton, 2000.

58. Buxton and Howard-Davis, 2000.

59. See, for example, Dearne and Lord, 1998.

60. Jones and Shotter, 1988; Shotter and White, 1990.

61. *RIB* 604.

62. Jones and Shotter, 1988, 52ff.

63. *RIB* 464; Carrington, 1994; Mason, 2001, 127ff.

64. Holt (Grimes, 1930); Heronbridge (Mason, 2002); Wilderspool (Grealey, 1976; Hinchliffe and Williams, 1992; Strickland, 1995); Wigan (Jones and Price, 1985; Tindall, 1985).

65. Jones, 1974; Bryant, Morris and Walker, 1986.

66. Jones, 1972.

67. Strickland, 2001.

68. *Britannia*, forthcoming; *Archaeology North-West* (forthcoming).

69. For a fuller discussion of such 'infrastructural sites', see below in chapter 6.

70. Dio Cassius *History of Rome* 56. 18, 2–3; for indications of the presence of local tradesmen, see Hartley K.F. and Webster, 1973, 92–95.

71. For the Monument, see Strong, 1968, 40–73; Shotter, 2004 (forthcoming).

CHAPTER FIVE

The Northern Frontier

Our knowledge of events in Britain during the reign of Trajan (A.D. 98–117) is regrettably slight;[1] much of the reign was taken up with warfare which was conducted at a considerable distance from Britain – across the Danube and in the east. Whether this had any effect in Britain – in terms, for example, of further troop-reductions – is not clear. It does appear, however, as we saw in the previous chapter, that consolidation proceeded in the north west, with the construction of new forts (as at Hardknott)[2] and the rebuilding of older ones (as at Chester and Lancaster).[3]

Yet, the *Life of Hadrian*, in *Scriptores Historiae Augustae*, indicates what appears to have been a disturbing situation that greeted Hadrian on his accession in A.D. 117: 'the Britons could no longer be held under Roman control'.[4] Whilst the reference gives no indication of location, there are clues in the archaeological record which would tend to place it at the western end of the frontier-zone, perhaps principally involving the Novantae (of Dumfries and Galloway). It appears that Trajan's governor, Quintus Pompeius Falco, successfully dealt with the outbreak, as a coin proclaiming victory was issued in A.D. 119.[5] A western location, whilst not proved, is strongly suggested by the fragment of the tombstone of a centurion, found at Vindolanda,[6] which states that he died 'in the war' and is dated to A.D. 118. It has also been suggested that the fine masonry incorporated into the structure of the western gate at the fort of Birdoswald may originally have been part of another structure – possibly a victory-trophy related to the war of A.D. 117–119.[7]

The strongest indication of the location – and seriousness – of the recent troubles is perhaps given by the building of Hadrian's Wall itself. There has long been a mystery surrounding the fact that the western end of the Wall – from the Irthing-crossing to Bowness-on-Solway – was built of turf, rather than of stone. Most explanations offered have tended to regard the 'Turf Wall' as the weaker part of the structure,[8] and it has been ascribed to a shortage of better materials – a completion of the wall-building, but in inferior materials.

The preconceptions which underlie such an interpretation may, however, be flawed, and we may, therefore, make progress by examining the 'positive features' of the 'Turf Wall'. First, we cannot readily accept

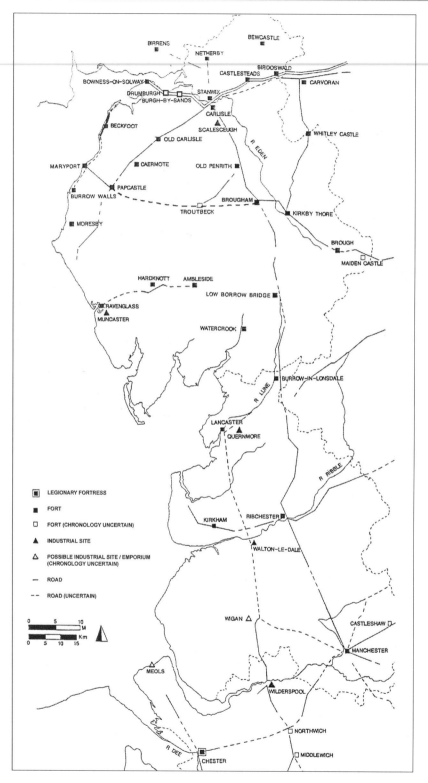

Figure 5.1: Sites in
north-west England
occupied at the
death of Hadrian
(A.D. 138)

Plate 5.2: Hadrian's Wall: The Turf Wall Appletree

the notion that stone-construction was the norm, and turf regarded as a weaker alternative, particularly since not only the Wall in this sector, but also the milecastles (but not the turrets) were built from turf and timber.[9] In the wake of the disturbances in Britain which greeted Hadrian's accession, it would have been natural to impose in the frontier-zone a line with regular gateways to facilitate the monitoring of movement in either direction. Assuming that Hadrian, in the aftermath of victory, sent instructions to his local military commanders, their natural response to such an order would have been to carry out the instructions using turf and timber, the normal building-materials.

Whether this proved to be a satisfactory solution is not clear, although the fact that Hadrian himself came to Britain in A.D. 122, bringing a new governor (his friend, Aulus Platorius Nepos) and a new legion (VI *Victrix* from the Rhine, replacing IX *Hispana* at York),[10] suggests that, whilst the principle, as demonstrated in the Turf Wall, was satisfactory as far as it went, it was not the total answer to problems in Britain. We have no evidence of further hostilities between A.D. 119 and 121, and the reference on the career-inscription[11] of Marcus Maenius Agrippa (the sometime-commander (tribune) of the *Cohors I Hispanorum* at Maryport) to an *expeditio Britannica* is not now seen as applying to so early a point in Hadrian's reign.[12]

In the absence of references to fresh warfare, it is perhaps best to suggest that Hadrian, recognising a continuing urgency in the British frontier-situation, came with a completely new initiative in mind. We should also remember that his work on the Wall was not the only project in which he became involved whilst in Britain. For example, it is likely that, at this point, he initiated a scheme to 'soften' the military grip at least on the eastern portion of the Brigantes by giving them the status of a partly-autonomous *civitas* with a centre at Aldborough (*Isurium Brigantum*).[13] This may have been part of a review of the *civitates*, as Hadrian also appears to have helped the leaders of the *civitas Cornoviorum* in the development of the former legionary fortress at Wroxeter as their centre (*Viroconium Cornoviorum*).[14] It may be, too, that Hadrian celebrated the completion of a project to drain the East Anglian Fens with the construction of a brand new town at Stonea (in Cambridgeshire, and on the 'island' that may have been the site of Boudica's centre).[15] This town, although eventually something of a

Plate 5.3: Maryport: Dedication to *Jupiter Optimus Maximus* made by Hadrian's friend, the fort commander, Marcus Maenius Agrippa. Photograph by the Senhouse Roman Museum

Plate 5.4: (Left) Hadrian's Wall (Cawfield Crags): The Stone Wall, Cawfields Milecastle the *Vallum*. Photograph by G.D.B. Jones

Plate 5.5: Hadrian's
Wall (Wallsend fort):
reconstructed wall-
section, remains of
Hadrian's Wall, triple
post-emplacements

failure, was distinguished by having a 'tower-block' at its centre instead of
the more normal type of Romano-British *forum*.[16] Such a departure is
redolent of the innovative hand of the emperor-architect.[17]

It was, however, Hadrian's Wall which is seen as the centrepiece of the
emperor's 'British initiative'.[18] It is possible that he based himself at
Vindolanda; fragments of an extensive timber building have in recent
years been located beneath the later extramural settlement.[19] The plan
now was to put in place a wall which ran from the Tyne (initially from
Newcastle, but soon extended to Wallsend) to join the already existing
turf wall at Willowford (at the Irthing crossing). It seems probable that,
despite the celebratory inscription from Jarrow,[20] a number of separate
'construction-starts' were made, and it is believed by some that the first of
these was at the crossing of Dere Street.

The plan now was to build in stone: the Wall was approximately nine
feet wide and perhaps twelve to fifteen feet in height, and crowned by a
parapet-walk which must have been a platform more for observation
than for fighting. The construction-process of the Wall itself involved
four stages – the digging-out and laying of a foundation, the building of
a northern and a southern 'skin', and the in-filling with a rubble-and-
mortar core of the void between these; the core and the 'skins' were not
structurally bonded. The legions and other groups within and without
the army will have been split into small parties to execute the work, as is

shown by the survival of small commemorative 'centurial' stones which were incorporated into the fabric at intervals.

To the north of the Wall was a deep 'V'-shaped ditch; recent excavations at Byker (Newcastle) have shown[21] that, between the ditch and the Wall in that sector at least, were three staggered, but closely-set, rows of pits running parallel to each other and to the Wall and ditch. It is suggested that these may have comprised 'man-traps' (*lilia*: pits containing sharpened stakes and covered in bracken – as also to the north of the Antonine Wall at Rough Castle); alternatively, they may have provided a 'framework' for packed brambles, and thus may have constituted the equivalent of a linear emplacement of 'barbed wire'. The Wall itself had fortlets ('milecastles') at a distance of one Roman mile (1620 yards) from each other, with two equally-spaced elevated turrets (towers for observation and/or signalling) between each pair of

Plate 5.6: Willowford: 'Narrow Wall on a 'Broad' foundation

Plate 5.7: Vindolanda: Reconstructions of Stone and Turf Walls

ate 5.8:
ousesteads: Air
notograph of the
rt

milecastles. Depending on size, the milecastles could have housed between one and two dozen men in barracks which were situated on each side of a roadway which ran from south to north through the milecastle. In effect, these milecastles provided eighty fortified gateways through the Wall. Initially, the main concentrations of troops were held in the still-maintained forts of the Stanegate to the south. The relationship between these two lines was that, whilst the Stanegate road itself ran through the valleys of the rivers Tyne, Irthing and Eden, the Wall occupied the northern crests of those valleys. It has been suggested that the Wall may have been originally painted white or cream, but the deposits on some of the stones, interpreted initially as the residue from such a process, are now regarded by many as probably constituting the residue from the brush-pointing of the mortared joints between the stones.

A change of plan was made in *c.* A.D. 124–125, with the decision to build forts on the Wall to accommodate auxiliary units of cavalry and infantry; the forts on the Stanegate were, as a consequence, mostly closed down. It is unclear what had prompted this move, unless it was simply to improve ease of deployment. However, taking into account the fact that the *vallum*, to the south, was routed so as to avoid the forts and their defences, it may be that, together, the resiting of the forts and the construction of the *vallum* were intended to heighten security for the troops by placing them within a cordon which was marked off on its southern side by the *vallum*. Some of the forts[22] overlie the foundations of the Wall and some of its intermediate structures which were already in place before the decision was made to add the forts. Evidently contemporaneous with the building of the forts was another change – to narrow the gauge of the Wall to approximately six feet. In some locations

Plate 5.9: Birdoswald
Air photograph of
the fort (1976)

Plate 5.10:
Birdoswald fort:
Masonry at the west
gate

– for example, at Willowford, it is now possible to see the 'new' Narrow Wall sitting on the northern edge of the Broad foundation which was already in place when the decision was made. It remains unclear why the Wall was made narrower, unless it was simply to cut down the volume of material required and, perhaps, to accelerate the construction-process.

The placing of the forts in relation to the Wall differs: some lie across the Wall and are joined by the Wall at their east and west gates, whilst others used the Wall as their own northern ramparts. It was once suggested that this difference marked a distinction between cavalry forts, which thereby had three gates exposed north of the Wall, and those for infantry which had one gate only exposed. However, nowadays, it is believed that those that lie (or lay) across the Wall had been abandoned before the fort-building had been completed. As a confirmation of this, it might be pointed out that none of the forts on the Antonine Wall in Scotland protrudes across that Wall.[23] The last fort to be built on Hadrian's Wall was at Carrawburgh – in the early-130s; that this was an 'afterthought' to close the long gap between Chesters and Housesteads seems likely in view of the fact that this last fort was built across the already-completed *vallum*.

The *vallum* is probably, in interpretative terms, the most controversial feature of the whole wall-complex. It consists of a steep-sided, flat-bottomed ditch, some ten feet deep, with linear mounds running parallel with it to both the north and the south; the whole feature was 120 feet across – intentionally, as the mounds did not consist of 'carelessly-thrown' earth, but were placed deliberately and held together by revetments provided by banks of turves.

Controversy has always surrounded the question of the purpose of the *vallum*: its importance is clear, for no part of the *limes* lacks it; it was even constructed in terrain that defeated those who were digging out the northern ditch. That it remained from an earlier phase of frontier cannot be entertained because of the fact that it avoids all of the forts (except Carrawburgh); that it performed the purpose of demarcating the southern side of a military zone seems possible, although this does not explain its flat-bottomed character. It is possible that it was used for covert lateral communication, although there must have been many occasions when it carried a depth of water, and there has never been any report of the 'duck-boards' that one would have thought necessary to facilitate movement along the ditch-bottom.

The structure was in place by the 130s: the remaining structural phase was the replacement and, in some places, re-alignment of the turf Wall in

ate 5.11: Bewcastle: e fort-rampart

stone. The dating of this has been much disputed, though recent excavations at the fort at Birdoswald have suggested that it was, in fact, completed within the period of Hadrian's reign – that is, by A.D. 138.[24]

It is less clear what kind of reaction the building of Hadrian's Wall evoked amongst the local population, for it will certainly have disrupted life for some, particularly when we take into account not just the land required for the frontier installations themselves, but also, in the short-term at least, for the camps for those involved in the construction of the Wall.[25] Given the fact that deforestation will have led to major agricultural development in the area, it is likely that many small farmers were removed from their land; indeed, one such site was revealed many years ago at Milking Gap.[26] It is also the case that the Wall cut crudely through the territory of the western Brigantes (or Carvetii), and that the 'outpost-forts' of Birrens, Netherby and Bewcastle[27] effectively enclosed that portion of the tribal territory that had been left adrift to the north of the Wall. It would be surprising if these factors did not cause some upset amongst the northern tribes, and it remains a possibility that the *expeditio Britannica*, mentioned in the career-inscription of Maenius Agrippa, had some connection with such events.

What, then, were Hadrian's intentions in building the Wall? Clearly, one purpose must have been to provide a base for patrolling the region to the north which, in terms of political geography, contained some tribes hostile to Rome (for example, the Novantae and perhaps the Selgovae) and some who had a claim to Roman protection (for example, the grain-growing Votadini). It is clear that Hadrian's purpose elsewhere in the empire was to strengthen the territory which he wished to designate as Roman, and to provide a means to oversee and control those outside it. In that sense, the Wall 'carried a message' that Hadrian had made a decision on what should constitute the province of *Britannia*, but was indicating that, although formally and institutionally outside the area of *direct* control, the Romans retained an interest in what went on 'beyond the frontier'. His strengthening of the infrastructure elsewhere in the province lends some weight to this.

Plate 5.12: Maryport Air photograph of the fort

ate 5.13: Beckfoot:
r photograph of
e fort, showing
ternal streets and
ternal ditches and
lisade trenches.
otograph by
D.B. Jones

Secondly, there was the sense of achievement: this is reflected in the brief entry in the *Life of Hadrian*[28]: 'He built a wall eighty miles long, *the first to do so* (my italics), to separate the barbarians from the Romans'. Early in his reign, in particular, Hadrian needed some good publicity, and Britain was an ideal theatre in which to achieve it. His success is reflected perhaps in a later series of coins which commemorate the province and its armies.[29]

But Hadrian's interests went beyond the purely military: for example, whilst it is patently obvious that a wall penetrated by eighty gates at

ate 5.14: Biglands
ouse: Air
hotograph of
ilefortlet 1,
owing 'ditch-
rdon' (arrowed)

regular intervals was not meant to shut the northern tribes away it clearly was intended that movement across the Wall in either direction could take place only under strict supervision: *personae non gratae* could be weeded out. If we go further, and enquire as to who might wish to cross, the most likely group would be those involved in trade; indeed, commerce would probably be the most effective means of introducing a degree of Romanisation north of the frontier; surveys of Roman coins found in southern Scotland do, indeed, suggest that business 'across the frontier' was brisk.[30] Such business would also attract taxation; the Wall and its milecastles must have provided a successful means of identifying and collecting such revenues; the presence of *beneficiarii consulares* would suggest that this was, indeed, done.[31]

Finally, Hadrian was an emperor who understood well the 'political power' of buildings: his effort to portray himself as 'the New Augustus'[32] will have received added emphasis, for example, from his decision to rebuild the Pantheon in Rome and to retain on the porch the inscription commemorating Augustus' friend, Agrippa. Building the Wall in Britain *in stone* provided for people in the region a symbol of Roman power and organisation, especially when the Wall was constructed on the top of such dramatic natural locations as the Great Whin Sill. However, just as the Wall was a symbol of Rome's power, so, too, was it of the emperor who caused it to be built – Hadrianus Augustus; it was his monument as much as Rome's and as much as the famous Column in Rome[33] belonged to his very different predecessor and adoptive father, Marcus Ulpius Traianus.

Since the 1880s, and the pioneering work of Joseph Robinson, a bank official from Maryport,[34] we have become even more aware that the frontier-fortifications of the Hadrianic period did not terminate, as apparently did the Wall itself, just to the west of the village of Bowness-on-Solway. Indeed, a complex of structures continued along the coast to

Plate 5.15: Swarthy Hill: Milefortlet 21

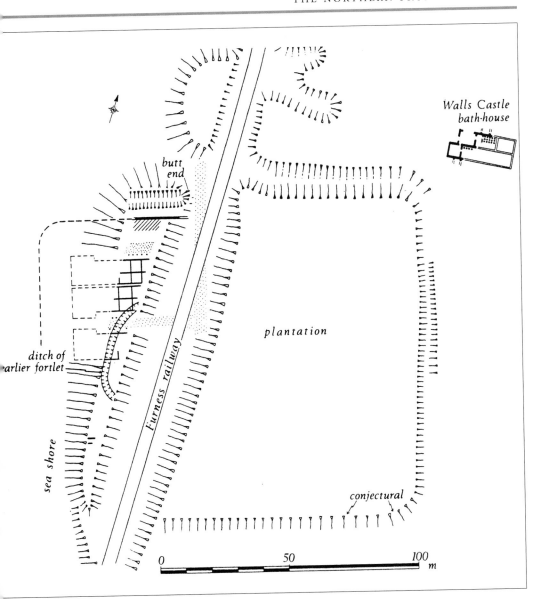

Walls Castle
bath-house

butt
end

ditch of
earlier fortlet

Furness railway

sea shore

plantation

conjectural

0   50   100
                     m

Figure 5.2: The
Roman fort and
bath-house at
Ravenglass:
Reproduced by
courtesy of
Cumberland and
Westmorland
Antiquarian and
Archaeological
Society

a terminal point the location of which has itself caused much discussion. As we have seen in the previous chapter, some of these fortifications pre-date the Hadrianic period and form part of the arrangements which were put in place in the late-Flavian/Trajanic periods as part of the extended 'Stanegate-scheme'; some, indeed, may have been even earlier than that.

The fortifications which date to the Hadrianic period have gradually been revealed by ground-based field-survey, aerial reconnaissance and some excavation. However, although they date from the Hadrianic period, the fact that the first milefortlet (at Biglands) is more than a mile from Bowness-on-Solway may suggest that the Wall and the coastal sites may not have been planned in conjunction. Beside the questions of the nature and dating of these fortifications, the chief questions surround their extent and purpose(s) – questions which have been made more complex because of coastal changes which have led to the erosion of some sites and the fact that others may now be some distance from the present coastline.

It is now accepted[35] that, although a system of enumeration is used which assumes a continuous set of fortifications running westwards from Bowness-on-Solway, in fact the system is in two parts separated by the large inlet, referred to by Ptolemy of Alexandria as *Moricambe*,[36] which formed a natural harbour at the confluence of the rivers Waver and Wampool. Thus, the two parts are now considered to consist of a section from Bowness-on-Solway to Cardurnock, recommencing with a southern section from Skinburness to Risehow (south of Maryport). In numerical terms, this 'translates' into Milefortlets 1 (Biglands)[37] to 5 (Cardurnock)[38], and 9 (Skinburness) to 26 (Risehow). In general terms the inter-relationship of sites strongly resembles that of Hadrian's Wall itself, with auxiliary forts, milefortlets and towers (two of which are located between each pair of milefortlets).

Dating-evidence is very restricted in amount from the great majority of the sites; it is generally assumed that, although some of the forts (for

Plate 5.16: Campfie\ Air photograph of Tower 2B. Photograph by G.D.B. Jones

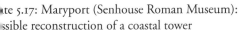

Plate 5.17: Maryport (Senhouse Roman Museum): Possible reconstruction of a coastal tower

Plate 5.18: Silloth: Palisade. Photograph by G.D.B. Jones

example, Beckfoot and Maryport)[39] may have been earlier than the Hadrianic period, the smaller installations are possibly in the first instance contemporaneous with the building of Hadrian's Wall. First, the forts themselves: although the fort at Beckfoot, which is clearly visible from the air in favourable conditions, is generally accepted as Hadrianic, there may well have been an earlier fort in the vicinity relating to pre-Hadrianic fortifications on the Solway. The fort at Maryport, which can be seen as a pronounced platform behind the Senhouse Roman Museum, appears, on the evidence of coin-loss,[40] to have been pre-Hadrianic; again, there may be an earlier fort awaiting discovery in the vicinity. Further south, forts at Burrow Walls (Workington) and Moresby are less well-known, although the latter has produced a Hadrianic building-inscription.[41] To the south of St. Bees Head, there may have been a fort in the Beckermet-area,[42] whilst the coastal fort at Ravenglass also appears to have been of Hadrianic date,[43] although the discovery of an earlier fortification beneath the fort, but on a different alignment from it, again leaves open the question of when the earliest site was constructed here. Beyond Ravenglass, speculation over the years has suggested the existence of forts around the coast of southern Cumbria,[44] but no firm evidence has come to hand, although it might be said that the volume of Roman material reported from the Barrow-area has served to keep the speculation alive.

Some work has been carried out on some of the smaller installations: whilst the fortlet at Cardurnock (MF 5) appears to have been in use in the second century and again in the fourth, occupation at Biglands (MF 1) and Swarthy Hill (MF 21)[45] seems to be restricted to the second century A.D. Biglands was evidently rather poorly constructed: a turf rampart was pierced by a six-post gateway on its north side (and *presumably* on its south side as well), and was protected by a single ditch with a timber palisade between the ditch and the rampart.

Inside the Biglands milefortlet, there were two buildings, rather roughly-constructed of turf and timber, on either side of the street which ran from south to north through the fortlet. These buildings, which were presumably barracks, were not even properly aligned on to the street. At Swarthy Hill (Milefortlet 21), the rampart was considerably less substantial than at Biglands, with an inner and outer face of stacked turves in-filled with earth and sand. The characters of milefortlets differ in other ways: it would appear that, with the exceptions of Cardurnock (Milefortlet 5) and Skinburness (Milefortlet 9),[46] which are larger than average, the areas of the milefortlets are approximately 300–350 square metres in each case – that is, capable of holding a small patrol-group. The larger ones, which housed larger than normal garrisons (perhaps a *centuria*) are probably to be explained in relation to their occupying terminal positions in the sections to which they belonged.

It was thought that the Biglands milefortlet had seen three phases of occupation, all within the second century A.D., although it would be hazardous to guess too precisely at the dates of these three phases. It can, however, be said that, at Biglands, Phases I and II, which were separated by a period of deliberate demolition, bore a close resemblance to each other. Phase III, on the other hand, was rather smaller, the inland gateway appeared to have been closed and the rampart pierced by a single gateway giving on to the coast; this entrance was structurally markedly less impressive than the earlier gateways. Similar deterioration and size-reductions have been observed elsewhere than at Biglands.

It seems reasonable to propose that the first phase should be seen as Hadrianic (that is, *c.* A.D. 124–138/9), coming to an end when Antoninus Pius decided upon a re-occupation of territory up to the Forth–Clyde line. Whilst the structural sequences of the Antonine Wall continue to arouse debate,[47] it may be suggested that the abandonment of the Antonine Wall in *c.* A.D. 160 led to the re-occupation not only of Hadrian's Wall itself, but also of some of the coastal fortifications, though perhaps limited to those north of *Moricambe*. Beyond that, a dating-

Plate 5.19:
Birdoswald:
centurial stone ('The
Century of Julius
Primus, of the 8th
Cohort, built this')

scheme for the coastal sites becomes extremely difficult, though it may be said that there is currently no evidence to connect occupation of any of the coastal sites with the campaigns of the emperor, Septimius Severus, in A.D. 209–211 (see further below). Further, milefortlets south of *Moricambe* appear to have only one construction phase; the available dating-evidence suggests that the milefortlets in this sector did not remain in use after *c.* A.D. 140.

Few of the towers have seen much excavation, though that at Campfield (T2B) had had a complex life with at least three phases of construction (two in timber and one in stone).[48] Further, a few of the towers have shown signs of activity in the third (and possibly fourth) century. Aerial reconnaissance has led also to the identification of linear features in places, though by no means, on present evidence at least, cohering into a 'system'. East of Biglands, for example, crop-marks have suggested that the coastal fortifications there may have been contained within a cordon consisting of two linear ditches, whilst in the Cardurnock peninsular, two phases of a palisade and a single ditch, followed by a Tower,[49] have been revealed. Further south, palisades have been excavated in the Silloth-area, recalling a reference in the *Life of Hadrian*[50] to that emperor separating barbarians from Romans: 'During this period, and frequently at other times, in a great many places where barbarians are separated off not by

Plate 5.20: Chesters
Fort: Barrack-block

Plate 5.21: Antonine Wall: Man-traps (*Lilia*) at Rough Castle

Plate 5.22: Vindolanda: Commander's house (*Praetorium*) of the Severan fort

rivers but by frontier-barriers, he set them apart by great stakes driven deep into the ground, and fastened together in the manner of a palisade'. Whilst this description related specifically to Germany, its application was clearly wider than that.

Whilst the dating of the coastal sites continues to be resistant to certainty, we can see some progress on the matters of extent and purpose. First, their extent: it now seems clear that an integrated system of fortifications does not continue south of Risehow, although, of course, some Roman military structures do; we have already noticed the forts at Burrow Walls and Moresby, and there is some evidence of smaller structures (as at Harrington Parks),[51] although conceivably some smaller structures may emerge to have been Romano-British rather than the work of the Roman army. It has been suggested[52] that there may have been tighter fortification of the coast in the area of Ravenglass: not only was a smaller military site on a different alignment located beneath the known auxiliary fort, but a concentration of artefactual evidence a mile to the south (at Eskmeals) may suggest a coastal stretch which merited closer supervision. It may not be fortuitous that, between Maryport and Ravenglass, natural cliffs offer better protection to the coastal hinterland.

Secondly, what purpose(s) did these coastal fortifications serve? The traditional response to this question has been that the coastal sites prevented the outflanking of Hadrian's Wall, presumably by armed bands from Dumfries and Galloway (the Novantae), crossing the Solway Firth. This may well still contain a part of the answer, although it should be kept in mind that such bands were probably engaged not so much on purely military enterprises aimed at the Roman army, as perhaps on 'economic raiding' and cattle-rustling activities against the farmers of Solway. It is clear that this area was of especial significance because of the density of farms which it evidently supported,[53] farms which may well have had a part to play in the provisioning of the garrisons on Hadrian's Wall. On a more general note, destroying the prosperity of such farmers may have been intended to make them less accommodating in their attitude to the Roman authorities. As we have seen, over the years, the Novantae were 'regional enemies', and it is possible that the *expeditio Britannica*, led by Maenius Agrippa from Maryport had some connection with such problems. Hadrian's frontier-philosophy was based upon supervising the activities of enemies from *outside* enemy-territory. It is also worth remembering that to

ate 5.23: South
ields: Granaries

the south of the Solway Plain, this agricultural land was provided with protection (presumably from hill-farmers to the south) by the road which ran south-westwards from Carlisle, through Red Dial (Old Carlisle), to Papcastle and Maryport. It is thought that Papcastle, because of its size and location, may have been the 'control-fort' for north-west Cumbria.[54]

There is also another possible motive for the construction of the coastal fortifications: if one of the purposes of Hadrian's Wall was to act as an extended 'customs-barrier', then the outflanking of it would have done damage to the empire's revenues. The task of evading payment of revenues by coastal shipping will have been made rather more arduous and time-consuming by extending the coastal fortifications to Maryport.

Plate 5.24: South Shields: Reconstructed fort gateway. Reproduced by courtesy of Tyne and Wear Museums

The building of Hadrian's Wall and the coastal fortifications represented a very substantial investment in terms of money, men and sheer effort: so why, within months of his accession in A.D. 138, did Hadrian's successor, Antoninus Pius, decide to discard Hadrian's frontier and advance Roman-held territory to a new frontier between the Forth and the Clyde? Although a full examination of the complex problems which surround our understanding of the new frontier [55] would be out of place in the present volume, some discussion is required of issues which bear upon the Hadrianic frontier and Roman activities in northern England.

Plate 5.25: South Shields: Reconstructed barrack-block. Reproduced by courtesy of Tyne and Wear Museums

As with Hadrian's Wall, surviving comments by classical authors are minimal: the *Life of Antoninus*[56] (in the *Scriptores Historiae Augustae*) talks of Antoninus 'driving back the barbarians', whilst the Greek writer, Pausanias, alludes to problems with the Brigantes,[57] but then appears to confuse the British Brigantes with a tribe of the same name in Switzerland. It is to be assumed that, whatever the Brigantes had done, the reference is likely to have been specifically concerned with that part of the tribe that lay to the north of the Hadrianic frontier. Signs of building-work have been detected at both Corbridge and Carlisle, presumably as a preparation for embarking northwards on the former Flavian routes.

As far as can be seen, Hadrian's Wall was largely, or even wholly, abandoned, and the *vallum*-ditch was in-filled to form causeways and its mounds breached at forty-five yard intervals. Studies of the samian pottery from both walls[58] have indicated that the two walls were *not* held in conjunction. Antoninus' purpose may not have been simple and straightforward: as Hadrian's 'unexpected' successor, he may have needed to make his mark, much as Claudius had had to do almost exactly a century earlier with the invasion of Britain. It would appear most likely that control of the tribes between the Walls was a principal issue: Rome's friends in the east, the Votadini, may have required extra protection, perhaps from interference mounted by their neighbours, the Selgovae, possibly acting in concert with the Brigantes and the Novantae. There are certainly signs of new fortifications in the west of the region – for example, at Carzield and Barburgh Mill.[59] In this case, Antoninus' purpose may have been an indication of his dissatisfaction with the Hadrianic policy of patrolling Rome's enemies from outside, preferring instead to include them in the province and to patrol them as part of the regular policing. Such a view would account for the decision, also taken at this time, to demilitarise the coastal fortifications of Cumbria as 'surplus to requirements'.

A further purpose may have had to do with the natural resources of the area: gold, silver and lead were all evidently available[60] in the area around Leadhills; new supplies of silver would obviously have been welcomed in a situation where the quality of the silver coinage was deteriorating rapidly[61] and, with an acceleration of the provision of public buildings in stone, especially in the towns of Roman Britain, lead itself will have been a vital commodity for tying adjacent stone-blocks together.

Although many doubts continue to surround the history of the Antonine Wall itself, it is now thought that an original plan to follow the Hadrianic pattern of a small number of large forts (six, in this case) with a regular system of intervening smaller sites, was abandoned in favour of a more flexible scheme with a larger number of forts of variable sizes, and thus garrisons of variable size and type. Although some problems arose in the north to occasion the issuing of the 'dejected Britannia' coin of A.D. 154–155,[62] it does not now appear to have led to a short break (followed by a resumption) of occupation on the Antonine Wall. Rather, it seems that, after a single phase of occupation, the forts of the Antonine Wall were gradually evacuated over a period between the late-150s and early-160s,[63] in favour of a refurbishment and a resumed occupation of Hadrian's Wall. It is unclear what had led to this – whether it was some instability in northern Britain that called for a concentrating of available

Plate 5.27: Vindolanda: 'Round Huts' of the Severan period. Reproduced by courtesy of The Vindolanda Trust

troops or (perhaps more likely) the developing problems on the Rhine, the Danube and in the East, which characterised the reign of Marcus Aurelius and will probably have occasioned some troop-withdrawals from Britain.

The remainder of the second century is unsatisfactorily recorded for us: Britain certainly received in *c.* A.D. 175 an injection of 5,500 Sarmatian cavalrymen from the Danube,[64] of which one unit (presumably of 500 men) has been identified at Ribchester. In A.D. 181, Commodus' governor, Marcus Ulpius Marcellus, a stern disciplinarian and a hard man, is recorded by Dio as achieving success which was also recorded on the coinage.[65] It appears that the real problems were now seated well to the north – amongst Agricola's old enemies, the Caledonians – and that Rome's policy was initially one of 'carrot-and-stick', or military threat followed by an attempt to buy peace with subsidies. Indeed, Dio[66] marks the breakdown of such policies by his admission that the Caledonians had 'broken their promises'. There are certainly inscriptions which point to hostilities between Roman troops and local tribesmen,[67] including a band of the otherwise-unknown Corionototae.

Although the long-held idea that northern Britain was hit in the last years of the second century by a widespread 'military cataclysm' is no longer favoured, the distribution of building-inscriptions on Hadrian's Wall and its hinterland[68] permits the likelihood of intermittent local raiding and, as a result, protracted uncertainty. Continuing building-work in the frontier-area and its hinterland[69] under governors of the turn of the second and third centuries (Virius Lupus, Valerius Pudens and Alfenus Senecio, A.D. 197–208) points to developing pressure from the north, and this despite efforts by the Roman authorities to relieve the situation by diplomatic initiatives.[70]

The climax came with the decision of Septimius Severus, an emperor who always appreciated the importance of the loyal support of the army, to make a further attempt at a military solution.[71] Thus, in A.D. 209, the emperor himself, his wife (Julia Domna), two sons (Caracalla and Geta), together with the imperial entourage, established themselves with legion VI *Victrix* at York, taking the opportunity to split Britain into two provinces (*Superior* in the south, and *Inferior* in the north). York, now upgraded to the status of a *colonia* (the fourth in Britain), was designated as the 'capital' of the new northern – and inevitably more military – province. The cult of the tutelary deity, *Dea Brigantia*, was encouraged in the north, with its centre based upon the fortress and *colonia* at York. It may also have been Severus who initiated plans to create a new *civitas* in the north west for the Carvetii (probably originally a 'sub-group' of the Brigantes), with its centre at Carlisle (see below in chapter 6).

Severus' campaigns were organised somewhat differently from their predecessors of the Flavian and Antonine periods; little use appears, for example, to have been made of the western route, through Carlisle, into southern Scotland. Instead, the eastern land-base at Corbridge was utilised, together with a far greater reliance on sea-borne transportation up the east coast. The earlier fort at South Shields[72] was enlarged and its buildings completely remodelled as granaries, perhaps to supply the military expeditions and, in the longer term, to receive grain from the Votadini for the army in northern Britain. The emphasis on a sea-borne approach on this occasion is demonstrated by the renewed significance of sites such as Inveresk and Cramond,[73] and by the construction of a vexillation-fortress at Carpow on the Tay.

The chief trouble appears to have lain to the north of the Forth/Clyde isthmus, in the shape of the Maeatae, the third-century northern neighbours of Agricola's Caledonians. There was little, if any, campaigning in southern Scotland, nor was the Antonine Wall reactivated, unless some individual sites along it were reused on a temporary basis. Campaign-camps take Severus' armies up towards the Moray Firth in what looks much like a reiteration of Agricola's final campaign – though on a grand scale, and with the objective of taking the heart out of the Maeatae.[74] Evidently contemporary with these activities are the mysterious stone-built (but short-lived) round-houses,[75] which have been uncovered at Vindolanda; it has been conjectured that the fort at Vindolanda may temporarily have been converted for use as a prisoner-of-war camp, or perhaps as accommodation for those evacuated from the war-zone in the interests of their own safety.

Severus died at York in A.D. 211 before the completion of his work; his elder son, Caracalla, did produce a 'diplomatic solution' which, though sneered at by ancient writers,[76] appears to have secured almost a century of peace in the north. The diplomatic solution probably consisted, as had Severus' earlier attempts, of the payment of subsidies in return for the giving by local tribes of 'undertakings'.

The garrison-pattern in the north west during the third century is difficult to establish without much more excavation; in any case, the ceramic and numismatic evidence provide far less clear indications than they do for earlier periods. We may well expect that the internal upheavals which separated the death of Commodus in A.D. 192 and Severus' full establishment of himself in 197, together with Severus' own emphasis on the army as the principal source of his power, will have led to the reorganisation of some existing garrisons. In addition to this, a reduced threat to the northern frontier and the new civilian role for the *civitas Carvetiorum* will have allowed for a greater flexibility of manning.[77] Watercrook, for example, appears to have lost its garrison early in the third century, and to have remained unmanned until the late-260s or early-270s. Hardknott may present a similar picture. Rebuilding, evidenced at a number of sites, again points to a flexibility, which was perhaps aimed at toughening the heart of the new northern province. The construction of the 'Elliptical Building' at Chester,[78] a century-and-a-half after its original inception, and the introduction of the officially-sponsored cult of *Dea Brigantia*[79] suggest that powerful symbolism played a substantial part in this intensified move to Romanise the north.

It is ironical, therefore, that, just as the northern enemy seemed to have been brought under control – temporarily, at least – and Romanisation was beginning to bear fruit in the north, the uncontrolled power of the army led to a series of dangerous self-inflicted wounds – rivalry for power taken to the point of civil war, economic collapse and the loss of frontier-integrity; these were the problems contributing to the great third-century crisis, out of which (as we shall see in chapter 7) a radically-different Roman Empire and, with it, a changed *Britannia* were born.[80]

Notes

1. For a recent account of Trajan's reign, see Bennett, 1997; for Trajan's Column, see Richmond, 1982; Coarelli, 1999.

2. See Bidwell, Snape and Croom, 1999.

3. E.g. *RIB* 464 (Chester: *Britannia* 9 (1978), 429f) and RIB 604 (Lancaster).

4. *Scriptores Historiae Augustae, Life of Hadrian* 5. 2; for the *Historia Augusta*, see Syme, 1968.

5. *RIC* II (Hadrian), 577.

6. Birley A.R., 1998; cf. Fronto 2. 22, referring to troops killed in Britain in Hadrian's reign. A.R. Birley (2002, 74) suggests that principal amongst the 'troublemakers' may have been the Anavionenses, who were angry at the recruitment of some of their fellow-tribesmen into the Roman army.

7. Wilmott, 2001, 89; the context and date of this masonry must remain uncertain.

8. For the complexities of construction, see Breeze and Dobson, 2000, 25ff; Wilmott, 2001, 39ff.

9. The forts in the western sector were also built initially of turf-and-timber, although these were, of course, subsequent to the original construction of the Wall itself.

10. It is not clear precisely when *legio* IX *Hispana* was transferred to Europe, nor whether the provincial garrison may, as a result, have been temporarily reduced to two legions in the early years of Hadrian's reign. It is thought that its replacement (*legio* VI *Victrix*) came to Britain at the time of Hadrian's visit in A.D. 122.

11. *ILS* 2735; Birley A.R., 1981, 292 (See also the career-inscription of T. Pontius Sabinus (*ILS* 2726)).

12. Frere, 2000, 23ff.

13. See Hartley and Fitts, 1988, 41ff.

14. Although the major buildings at Wroxeter must have been started in the 90s, the forum-inscription (*RIB* 288) commemorates Hadrian, perhaps because of a benefaction to speed up the building-work.

15. Jackson and Potter, 1996, 42ff and 671ff.

16. See, for example, Marsden, 1987; Shotter, 2000d, 32ff.

17. Birley A.R., 1997; Boatwright, 1987.

18. The bibliography of Hadrian's Wall is extensive, though the best and most accessible account remains the fourth edition (2000) of Breeze and Dobson. Also available are Breeze, 1982; Johnson, 1988; Shotter, 1996; De la Bédoyère, 1999; Jones and Woolliscroft, 2001.

19. *Britannia* 33 (2002), 297f.

20. *RIB* 1051; this may have been attached to a celebratory monument.

21. Bidwell, 1999, 95ff; *Britannia* 33 (2002), 293f.

22. For example, at Housesteads: *Journ. Rom. St.* 36 (1946), 134ff.

23. Robertson, 1990, 20.

24. Bidwell, 1999, 149.

25. E.g. Welfare and Swan, 1995, 5ff.

26. Kilbride-Jones, 1938; Gillam, 1958.

27. See Woolliscroft, 1988; Austen, 1991; Caruana, 2000.

28. *Scriptores Historiae Augustae, Life of Hadrian* 11, 2.

29. *RIC* II (Hadrian), nos. 845–846; 882; 912–913.

30. See, for example, the regular surveys by the late Professor Anne Robertson of Roman coins found in Scotland, published in *Proceedings of the Society of Antiquaries of Scotland*; her last survey was in *PSAS* 113 (1983). The surveys are continued by Dr. Donal Bateson.

31. *RIB* 602 (Lancaster: *Contrebis* 26 (2001–02), 5); Breeze and Dobson, 2000, 156.

32. Shotter, 2003a, 321ff.

33. Coarelli, 1999.

34. Bellhouse, 1992.

35. Bellhouse, 1989.

36. Bellhouse, 1962.

37. Potter, 1977.

38. Simpson and Hodgson, 1947.

39. Jarrett, 1976; Caruana, 1997, 40ff.

40. Shotter, 1993; 1997b, 132ff.

41. *RIB* 801.

42. Shotter, 1990, 188 and 234ff; Daniels, 1978, 283f.

43. Potter, 1979, 1ff.

44. Shotter, 1995b.

45. Turnbull, 1998.

46. Bellhouse, 1954b.

47. Hodgson, 1995; Swan, 1999.

48. Jones, 1993, 34ff; Woolliscroft, 1994.

49. Jones, 1982, 285ff.

50. *Scriptores Historiae Augustae, Life of Hadrian* 12, 6.

51. Daniels, 1978, 279.

52. Potter, 1979, 48.

53. Higham and Jones, 1985, 68ff.

54. Dr. A.C.H. Olivier, *pers comm.*

55. Hanson and Maxwell, 1983; Swan, 1999.

56. *Scriptores Historiae Augustae, Life of Antoninus Pius* 5, 4.

57. Pausanias, *Description of Greece* 8. 43, 3.

58. Hartley, 1972.

59. Breeze, 1974.

60. Innes, *Origines Parochiales Scotiae*, Bannatyne Club, 1851–1855, I. 171. (I am grateful to my colleague, Dr. Sandy Grant, for this reference).

61. See G.C. Boon, Counterfeiting in Roman Britain, *Scientific American*, Vol. 231 (No. 6), 120–130.

62. *RIC* III (Antoninus), 930; Speidel, 1987; an event commemorated on the coinage of A.D. 154 can hardly have occurred later than A.D. 152 or 153.

63. On the strength of this date, see Hartley, 1972; Shotter, 1976; Swan, 1999; Abdy, 2002.

64. Dio Cassius *History of Rome* 72, 16; Edwards, 2000, 49.

65. Dio Cassius *History of Rome* 73, 8; *RIC* III (Commodus), 440 of A.D. 183–4; *Scriptores Historiae Augustae, Life of Commodus* 8,4.

66. Dio Cassius *History of Rome* 75, 5.

67. *RIB* 946, 1142, 2034.

68. Potter, 1979, 362.

69. Hartley, 1980.

70. Dio Cassius *History of Rome* 75, 5.

71. Dio Cassius *History of Rome* 77, 12–15.

72. Dore and Gillam, 1979; *Britannia* 32 (2001), 322–326; it has been suggested, on the strength of the discovery at South Shields of a lead sealing depicting Severus and his sons and of major architectual changes at the southern end of the fort, that Severus and his family may have been resident for a time at South Shields.

73. Rae and Rae, 1974.

74. Described as a policy of 'genocide' in *British Archaeology* No. 6 (July, 1995).

75. Blake, 2001, 7–11.

76. Herodian 3. 15, 6.

77. Breeze, 1988.

78. Mason, 2001, 173ff.

79. Hartley and Fitts, 1988, 86; Joliffe, 1941.

80. A number of recent excavations have produced evidence of newly-recognised features of Hadrian's Wall (both general and applicable to individual sites). As these are not yet in the public domain, it would not be proper to include them at this stage.

CHAPTER SIX

The *Pax Romana* in the North West

Romanisation

Traditionally in Rome,[1] military glory was regarded by members of Rome's senatorial aristocracy as an ambition of great merit in itself. Under the emperors, the importance of military glory persisted, because, as Virgil's *Aeneid* showed,[2] part of Rome's purpose was to 'war down the proud'. There were, however, new preoccupations: again, Virgil's 'prescription' for Rome included offering the 'olive branch' to those who submitted. The reason for this stemmed largely from the growing realisation in the late Republic and early Principate that the purpose of empire went beyond the ransacking of conquered provinces and beyond, too, the mere acquisition of military glory. The empire was a 'buffer' which stood between Rome and Italy on the one hand and Rome's real and long-term enemies who lay beyond the empire's frontiers. Such traumatic events as the loss of three legions under the Augustan general, Quinctilius Varus, in A.D. 9 beyond the Rhine forced Romans to think seriously and hard about the protection that their empire could provide.[3]

It simply, therefore, served no purpose for Rome to act in the manner caricatured by the Caledonian chieftain, Calgacus, when (in an oration 'provided' for him by Tacitus[4]) he said of Romanisation: 'They create a desolation and they call it peace'. Military power secured initial conquest, and it also provided the 'policing' of a province which not only guarded security in the interests of Rome, but also protected law and order which was of obvious concern to the Romano-British in their everyday lives. Nor was it Rome's concern to force an identical face on to every province; Romanisation[5] was a two-way process of cultural assimilation which recognised that 'Romano-British' consisted of two parts. We very rapidly see, therefore, that Romano-British was distinct from Gallo-Roman, and certainly from Graeco-Roman. The third-century historian, Dio Cassius,[6] vividly describes the way in which this process occurred on the Rhine in the Augustan period when he says that the native population 'became different without knowing it'. A peaceful process was, from the Roman point of view, essential, as it was neither economically nor politically feasible to maintain an army large enough to cope with constantly recalcitrant provincial communities.

Tacitus[7] makes it clear that the British were in general ready to embrace the culture of their conquerors, provided that they were not subjected to abuse; the number of British tribal leaders (eleven) who submitted to Claudius seems to confirm this,[8] and it was part of the provincial governor's job, by encouragement, to develop this willingness.[9] The dangers inherent in failing to tackle this task positively and sensitively were, in Britain, made patently obvious by the uprising of the Iceni and Trinovantes under Boudica in A.D. 60. It is worth noting, however, that, in Britain in particular and, indeed, in the empire generally, genuine *provincial* uprisings were relatively rare occurrences.

How, then, should we perceive Romanisation in Britain? It was at one time assumed that, in the wake of the military conquest of Britain, there followed immigration by farmers and others from Europe who were anxious to capitalise on the 'rich pickings' to be had in the new province. Such a view was generated partly by the evident luxury of life-style demonstrated by some of the villas. It is now appreciated that the 'villa-system' was a natural development out of the pre-Roman organisation, that many villas were (and remained) extremely straightforward in style and scope, and that the luxurious villas, which were in any case small in number, represented a level of wealth achieved by relatively few and, usually, only after a considerable period of time. Further, the observation of the Greek 'geographer', Strabo (writing in the early-first century A.D.), that Iron-Age Britain produced an exportable surplus of grain[10] shows that, whilst the architecture of the Iron-Age farm may not have been particularly impressive, the methods employed by the farmers themselves clearly were. It is not unreasonable to see these successful Iron-Age farmers as forming the ruling cliques of their tribes, and thus those who represented economically and socially the class upon which a system of Romanised local government in the new province could be based.

We now recognise that forestry-clearance was at the time of the Roman invasion much further advanced than was once thought and that the application of words such as 'sparse' and 'backward' to Iron-Age populations was wholly inappropriate. Nor should we assume that such advances were restricted to the south; our view of the wealth and power of rulers, such as Cartimandua and Venutius, indicates that they, too, were part of such sophisticated developments.

In both south and north, farming and other trades were stimulated by the presence of Roman troops who constituted a 'market' which required satisfying, as well as providing physical focal points around which such economic and social intercourse developed. In the south, an economic network was thus established which provided the basis for the physical and political organisation of the lowlands, once the army moved on from the later-60s and early-70s. Much of the north remained in essence a 'military district', but even here the army's presence was on the whole stimulative, rather than coercive.

The Cotswolds, in fact, offer in microcosm a 'model' of what developments Romanisation might bring: in the early days of conquest, the area was policed through a legionary fortress at Gloucester and an auxiliary fort at Cirencester; together, these guarded against any militant tribalism which might have been based upon hillfort sites, such as Bagendon. Many, however, in the tribal territory of the Dobunni were probably ready to embrace the new opportunities; early villa-building suggests the enthusiasm, and it also assumes the wealth or the ability and readiness to borrow to finance it. Romanisation, therefore, probably anticipated the thinning out of military garrisons in that area.

Before long, however, military imperatives were less concerned with this area, and Romanisation accelerated. By the end of the first century A.D., as legion II *Augusta* moved on to a new permanent base at Caerleon, the fortress and its settlement (*canabae*) at Gloucester were made into a *colonia*, a type of town which was high in the Roman urban hierarchy, but by definition largely self-sufficient. Although a *colonia* was intended to act as a 'flagship' for Romanisation in its area, Gloucester, it seems, remained somewhat on the margins of this. The real impact on the social, political and economic landscape was made by Cirencester (*Corinium Dobunnorum*): after its unit of auxiliary cavalry moved on (in the early 70s), the civilian settlement which had established itself outside the fort was sufficiently strong as a town to 'stand on its own feet'. It had replaced Bagendon as the focus of local attention, and had developed to the point of being the natural administrative, economic and cultural centre of this part of Britain; it is in no way surprising, therefore, that it was chosen to act as the *civitas*-centre of the Romanised Dobunni. Many of those who prospered and who, on the basis of that prosperity, could be entrusted with the 'burden' (*munus*) of local government will have been the descendants of those who, in the 40s, had used Bagendon and other such sites as their bases for resistance to the new military occupation.

Whilst such a picture as had been painted of the early development of Romanisation in southern, lowland, Britain is now broadly accepted, there is still in some quarters stronger resistance to the idea that parts, at least, of northern Britain may have displayed some similarities in their development; emphasis continues to be placed upon such concepts as sparseness of population, cultural and economic backwardness – marginality, in fact. No-one would deny that such descriptions remain appropriate in parts of the north,[11] but it is now clear that the north should not be treated as homogeneous. Thanks to more excavation of military and non-military sites, of substantial programmes of aerial

reconnaissance[12] and of the unique type of evidence provided by written
'documents' found at sites such as Vindolanda and Carlisle[13], we are now
in a much stronger position than we were to assess the social and
economic impact of the military presence in the north, and of the
relationship that developed between Roman and native in the highland
zone.[14] We can begin to see what levels of wealth may have been achieved
by native farmers and, on the analogy of what happened further south,
what kinds of responsibilities may have been opened up by the
acquisition of wealth.

The Roman Army

Obviously, crucial to this discussion is the question of changing military
imperatives in the area.[15] The 'Roman army' is a term redolent with
misconceptions both in fact and impression: it conjures up the notion of
a ruthless foreign force, dedicated to the reduction to quiescence, even
serfdom, of the native population amongst whom it worked. As we have
seen, Rome could not afford to view her army's purpose in such crude
terms.

For economic and political reasons, the Roman army was not allowed
to grow endlessly: in fact, over the first two centuries A.D., the average
number of troops under arms was approximately 350,000 *over the empire
as a whole*. Of these, perhaps ten percent were committed to Britain as its
permanent garrison – legions and auxiliary troops in approximately equal
numbers. We have seen, however, that emergencies elsewhere led to
occasional reductions in that number; further, there must have been
many more such troop-transfers than are reported in surviving
documentation.

Three legions were posted permanently to Britain – VI *Victrix* at York
(replacing, in the early 120s, IX *Hispana*), II *Augusta* at Caerleon and XX
Valeria-Victrix at Chester – though these could be used more flexibly,
with detachments (*vexillationes*) serving away from their main bases, as
plainly happened, for example, during the building of the Hadrianic and
Antonine frontiers in the second century A.D. The legions[16] consisted of
5,500 men each, and were made up largely of infantry, with just a small
number of cavalry and administrative and 'technical' personnel[17] besides.
All legionary soldiers were, by definition, full Roman citizens, although
this did not, of course, mean that they were necessarily Roman, or even
Italian. The conscious spreading of Roman citizenship[18] through the
provinces of the empire meant that large numbers of men from all over
the empire were eligible for legionary service, which represented a well-
paid job. Thus, in terms of the men who made them up, the legions were
diverse units, with an intense unit-pride focused on their standards
('eagles'); they brought with them to the provinces in which they served a

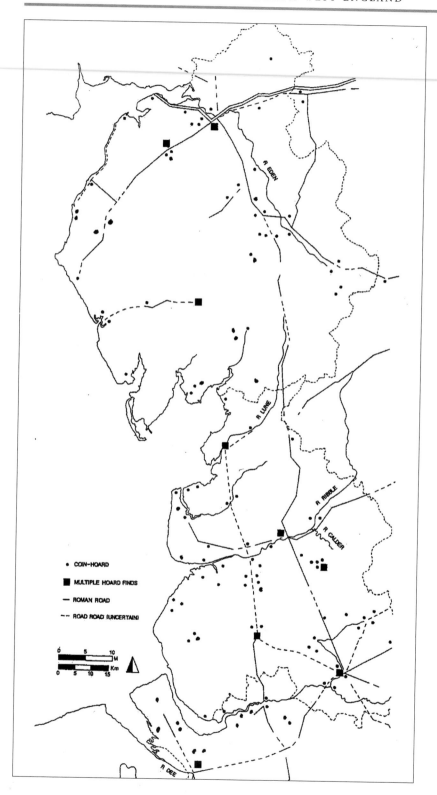

Figure 6.1: Findspot
of Romano-British
coin-hoards in nortl
west England

great variety of background and custom. It is likely that in time, at least, some Britons found their way into the legions, possibly even serving in Britain itself.

Serving alongside the legions were units of auxiliary troops (*auxilia*);[19] these were organised in groups smaller than the legions – basically 500- or 1000- strong[20] – and could be made up of cavalry (*alae*), infantry units with some cavalry (*cohortes equitatae*) or units consisting solely of infantry (*cohortes peditatae*). These, too, could be sub-divided, as must have happened on the Antonine Wall, where small fortlets were undoubtedly manned by detachments from larger neighbours. Further, documents from Vindolanda indicate the detaching of bodies of men, large and small, for service elsewhere.[21]

Auxiliaries were recruited from amongst those members of the empire's subject-population who were not Roman citizens; the unit-names indicate the place of original recruitment – for example, First Cohort of Spaniards. How far the territorial integrity of unit-recruitment was maintained is not clear, though it seems likely that they must have been kept up to strength by local recruitment.[22] The non-citizen auxiliaries were made Roman citizens on demobilisation after twenty-five years, although the privilege could also be earned on the battlefield. The forts of the auxiliary units constituted the 'policing-network' in north-west England, and will have been a dominant feature of the Romanised landscape – both physically and in other ways; these forts, both collectively and individually, will by their needs and facilities have served to give shape to the local economies of which they provided the chief focal points.

The auxiliary units had originally been intended to bring variety to the Roman army, though the general success of Romanisation across the empire meant that they became increasingly similar to the legions. Hadrian introduced a new element of variety into the army by beginning to recruit units of infantry and cavalry of various sizes, to which we give the generic title of 'Irregulars'. These are distinguished from other types of unit by such titles as *pedites* (infantry-soldiers), *equites* (cavalrymen), *numeri* (detachments) and *cunei* (formations). Little is known of the organisation of these, though some appear to have had 'specialised skills', such as the *Numerus Barcariorum* ('Detachment of Bargemen'), who served at Lancaster, and others that are recorded in the *Notitia Dignitatum*.[23] They appear to have been housed in existing auxiliary forts, perhaps alongside auxiliary units; one such unit in the north west was made up of Sarmatian cavalry (from north of the Danube) who were stationed at Ribchester and may have been part of a large consignment of such soldiers brought from the Danube following the wars of the reign of Marcus Aurelius.[24] In all, such a diverse army will have added a distinctly cosmopolitan note to the population make-up of Roman Britain, particularly if, as seems likely, many of them chose to settle locally on demobilisation from the army.

All of these troops owed allegiance to the emperor and, through him, to Rome; a group of altars, recording the annual oaths of allegiance to Jupiter, was found at Maryport where they had been ceremonially buried or 'stored' at the years' ends.[25] These altars, amongst other things, help to provide information on the garrison-sequence at Maryport, and some were dedicated by a fort-commander, Marcus Maenius Agrippa, who was a friend of the emperor, Hadrian, and who, as we have seen, was involved in an *expeditio Britannica* launched by that emperor.[26] It is upon such altars and other inscriptions and dedications, upon stamped bricks and roofing-tiles and occasional references in documents,[27] such as the writing-tablets from Vindolanda or discharge certificates (Diplomas) of soldiers, that we are dependent for our knowledge of the disposition and movement of the Roman army in the north west. Occasionally, too, finds of metal-work which are characteristic of particular units or of particular areas of the empire may offer clues to the nature and identity of units which may have been in garrison (permanently or temporarily) at individual forts.[28] Conceivably, finds of characteristic metal-work could in the future lead to the location of other deployments of Marcus Aurelius' Sarmatians.

Plate 6.1: Lancaster: Altar to Mars dedicated by a unit of Bargemen (*Numerus Barcariorum*). Reproduced by courtesy of Lancaster City Museums

Following their period of service, soldiers were discharged with land and other bounties: legionaries might receive theirs within the context of a town (*colonia*), as happened to veterans of legion XIV *Gemina Martia Victrix* at Colchester (*Camulodunum*) shortly after the initial invasion of Britain in the 40s. Auxiliaries and irregular troops probably received theirs in the form of small-holdings close to where they had served. Thus, Julius Januarius, a retired cavalry NCO (*decurio*), appears to have farmed land at Bolton-le-Sands, presumably after seeing service at Lancaster.[29] On a larger scale, as we have seen, Sarmatian veterans appear to have constituted a significant settlement around the fort at Ribchester; such a status could account for apparent defences (in the form of a turf-bank and ditch) which were located at one point and which are not normally found in association with extramural settlements.[30]

In the organisation of landownership and tenure in north-west England, some – perhaps, the best – land may have been appropriated by the authorities for the purpose of veteran-settlement. That it was for the forts themselves is made clear by the frequency with which what may have been pre-Roman ploughed land has been noted beneath the Roman levels. Inevitably, therefore, the occupation will have brought with it some disruption of existing practices. However, the peace which appears generally to have settled over the region indicates that reasonable solutions to such problems must have been sought and found. Obviously, too, such settlement will have brought constant diversification into the social and economic faces of the north west, leading to an enhancement of opportunities for wealth-generation.

Nor should we forget the presence of the fleet (*Classis Britannica*) and of units with naval capabilities.[31] As we have seen, a 'Unit of Bargemen' was at one time stationed at Lancaster, and Ravenglass was garrisoned by a cohort with naval connections (*Cohors I Aelia Classica*); we have noted, too, that the conquest of the north may have gained vital diversity from the temporary presence (A.D. 71–87) of a legion that had been recently recruited from the Ravenna fleet (II *Adiutrix*).[32] Whilst naval units did have an offensive role, a larger part of the fleet's work was probably concerned with the transportation of men and materials – as may, for example, have happened on Windermere.

It is thus crucial that we avoid taking a blinkered view of the Roman army as a blunt instrument of oppression; yet, whilst we can see, in principle, the inadequacy of such a view, our ability to look at the army's role in detail is severely hampered by the nature of surviving evidence, which is patchy in terms both of chronology and location. Major

ate 6.2: Old
arlisle (Red Dial):
ir photograph of
e fort and *vicus*.
notograph by
.D.B. Jones

documents such as the *Antonine Itinerary*, the *Notitia Dignitatum* and the *Ravenna Cosmography*, not to mention Ptolemy's *Geographia*,[33] provide us with information on political arrangements, road-routes, place-names and troop-dispositions. However, the fact that we lack even basic chronologies for many sites – periods of occupation and demilitarisation – means that we cannot make full use even of the information which we have in such sources. At best, we may be able to piece together a number of alternative interpretations, although occasionally (as with the Roman frontier in the mid-second century)[34] we may be able to use such artefactual evidence as pottery and coins to achieve some degree of clarity. We should, however, remember that the regular discovery of new major sites and stretches of road emphasises[35] just how fragile and incomplete the state of our understanding remains.

The paucity and, often, obscurity of our evidence, therefore, make it hard to study in detail the political, social, economic and cultural impact of the Roman army in the north west; the generally-accepted picture remains heavily dependent upon information derived from the excavation of small areas of a relatively small proportion of available sites. Further, such evidence is often difficult, if not impossible, to relate to accounts given in classical written sources, which may be truncated, stereotyped – or even wrong. Whilst a picture of broad outline is established, we are left pondering such questions as the significance, even the existence, of Juvenal's chieftain, Arviragus.[36] Is he meant to be symbolic of a continuing truculence amongst Brigantian leaders at the turn of the first and second centuries? What are we to believe when one source, Pausanias, has evidently confused the Brigantes of Britain with a European tribe of the same name? Does the undated tombstone of Flavius Romanus from Ambleside[37] point to a Brigantian rebellion, or

Plate 6.3: Lancaster: Inscription of the mid-third century A.D., recording the rebuilding of the bath-house and *basilica* which had 'collapsed through old age'. Reproduced by courtesy of Lancaster City Museums

perhaps to a different kind of event? How are we to interpret inscriptions that refer to buildings which had collapsed through old age? Are we to take them literally, or assume that a more sinister explanation is being deliberately obfuscated?[38] The superficiality of some of our understanding is simply highlighted by such dilemmas.

Town-life

Traditionally, we think of the north as 'the military zone' of Roman Britain; the ever-present Roman forts provide a reminder of continuing military imperatives in the area. Yet considerable portions of Brigantian territory progressed to some form of local self-administration as a *civitas*. The meaning[39] of such a progression in the military zone remains unclear: was it, perhaps, a level of self-administration exercised in conjunction with local army commanders? It has to be said that it is difficult to see how it could have worked otherwise, if only because of the ubiquity of the Roman forts.

It is believed that a *civitas* of the Brigantes was established in the second century, possibly by Hadrian, and located to the east of the

Plate 6.4: Carlisle: female personification of Carlisle, wearing the 'ated crown'. Reproduced by courtesy of Tullie House Museum and Art Gallery, Carlisle

Pennines with its centre at Aldborough. The territory's agricultural land, particularly in the Vale of York, suggests that prosperity was attainable by some local leaders to enable them to undertake the burdens of *civitas*-status, a status which their loyalty to Rome had secured for them. *How* they exercised their role is less clear, as is their relationship with the legionary commander at York. Further, did some of those who lived in the *colonia* at York also hold office at Aldborough? The identities, therefore, of the 'Brigantian grandees', and the extent of their role remain less than clear. It seems possible that the decision, evidently by Septimius Severus, to promote the cult of *Dea Brigantia* in the early-third century could have been a response to a lack of coherence and drive in the *civitas Brigantum*.

Inscriptions from Old Penrith[40] and Brougham[41] indicate that in the third century – possibly early in the century – the Carvetii, who are usually taken as originally a 'subgroup' of the Brigantes, were 'promoted' to *civitas*-status.[42] It is assumed that the administrative centre of the *civitas* was located at Carlisle; excavations and casual discoveries over the years have pointed to the extent of the town, and have also indicated that there were substantial structures,[43] including a large courtyard-house on Keays Lane, with a hypocaust.[44] It is possible that changes in layout which have been detected reflect a changing status.[45] Carlisle seems, in fact, to have exercised a pivotal regional role from an early date, as it is mentioned in Vindolanda-documents as the seat of a *centurio regionarius*.[46] It is further worth noting that, in early frontier-developments, Carlisle appears to have remained 'independent', as it seems possible that the Stanegate road bypassed Carlisle through Cummersdale,[47] just as Hadrian's Wall did through Stanwix.

The extent of the territory included within the *civitas* is similarly difficult to determine; as we have seen, our most direct evidence consists of inscriptions found in the north of the region. These certainly point to the inclusion of the Solway Plain and part, at least, of the Eden valley; all of this is noted as agricultural land of good quality. Did the *territorium* extend further eastwards up the Eden valley, perhaps enjoying a boundary with the *civitas* of the Brigantes? In the south, it has been suggested[48] that the milestone at Middleton-in-Lonsdale, which marks a distance of fifty-three miles, presumably from Carlisle, may represent the southern boundary of the *territorium* of the *civitas*; or did it, perhaps, follow the Lune to its mouth? In addition, there are doubts about the northern extent: as we have seen, tribal territory, normally regarded as Brigantian, had been isolated to the north of Hadrian's Wall: was any (or all) of this included, in the third century, in the *territorium* of the Carvetii?

Besides this, there may have been other 'sub-groups' in the north west similar to the Carvetii; it has been suggested[49] that other *civitates* could have been established in the region. One group, which has the support of documentary evidence, is the tribe of the Setantii, whose *Portus* ('Harbour'/'Haven') is mentioned by Ptolemy. Various suggestions have been made with regard to its location; as we have seen (in chapter 1), some strength attaches to a position in Lancashire,[50] north of the river Mersey, and many have been convinced that the *Portus* is a site 'lost' off the mouth of the river Wyre. An alternative proposal, which does not necessarily exclude what has been said, is that the Portus Setantiorum was located in southern Cumbria, perhaps at the southern end of Windermere:[51] we have noted already (in chapter 1) that hillforts in the area may point to a local centre of economic power in the late-Iron Age.

It is, at any rate, clear from the granting of *civitas*-status to the Carvetii and thereby 'ceding' some administrative responsibility to the tribe, that there were men of sufficient loyalty, wealth and potential for continued wealth-generation to have had some responsibility for local administration devolved to them. Such a development highlights

economic success on the part of farmers and tradesmen which derived
from supplying the needs of the Roman army: such a group probably
brought together men of local origin with others from distant parts of the
empire drawn by the gains to be made in such trade. The 'Carvetian
leaders' should not, therefore, be thought of as an exclusively indigenous
group of men. It is also clear that the achievement of such economic
success was no easy matter: one writing-tablet found at Carlisle indicates
that the Roman army could 'drive a hard bargain' in terms of the effort
demanded of those who worked for it.[52]

In the early days of occupation, the north-west's landscape was
dominated by the physical signs of conquest and policing – the forts
themselves and the roads that linked them. Nor will these have been
placed exclusively on 'virgin territory'; evidence has accumulated which
shows that agricultural land was taken for such projects, thus presumably
creating disruption and loss of livelihood for some local people: here, we
may see some justification for the 'desolation' alleged by Calgacus –
temporary though this may have been.

If we can draw analogies from other places, the land between the forts
will have become the *territoria* of those forts, and thus the responsibility
of the fort-commanders. The manner of its treatment will obviously have
depended upon a number of factors. For example, areas containing
resources of precious metals will probably have been regarded as imperial
estates, and operated directly by the army or, perhaps, by 'trusted' groups
treated as lessees – as evidently happened in the case of the lead mines of
Derbyshire. Such an explanation as this may apply to communities living
west of the river Ribble in the Settle-area of north Yorkshire.[53] The
heavily-defended fort at Whitley Castle (near Alston) perhaps oversaw

ate 6.5:
indolanda: The
itcher's shop

local operations in the lead/silver industry. Some land will have been taken over by army-units for their own purposes: for example, some forts, such as Carlisle and Ribchester,[54] took land adjacent to the forts for the construction of annexes in which manufacturing of various types was carried out. Land was also taken for the construction of 'outworks' and parade-grounds (as at Hardknott). Especially in the vicinity of cavalry-forts, extensive areas of grassland must have been kept for the corralling and grazing of animals, as well as for taking as hay for winter-bedding. A demand will also have been made for agricultural land – presumably of good quality – for distribution to demobilised soldiers.

Thus, the presence of units of the Roman army had an inevitable and direct effect on landscape-management; the demand for timber for building and burning may also have led to a return of some forestation in an area in which deforestation had evidently seen a significant advance in late-prehistory. The 'other side of the coin' was that the Roman army, because of its requirements and because of the infrastructure which it created, offered clear advantages for those prepared to take them.

The north west illustrates this well: the roads themselves, which penetrated some very difficult terrain, held advantages for civilians as well as for soldiers. The military arterial routes, such as that from Chester to Carlisle, became central features of a growing network of roads which served to link local farmers and tradesmen into the Romanised economy; finds of Roman material – particularly of coins and coin-hoards[55] – demonstrate this by their geographical distribution. As we shall see, many farmers were left as landowners or tenants to pursue their traditional trades – but now with large new markets to satisfy. However, those most directly affected by the army's presence were the merchants and tradesmen who followed in its wake, and settled in the small towns which grew as extramural settlements outside the forts. Such developments usually occurred in 'ribbon fashion' along one or more of a fort's access roads (as is visible at Vindolanda), or may, as at Old Carlisle (Red Dial), have focused on a nearby main road.

There was evidently no standard size, shape or mode of development attaching to such extramural settlements, though caution needs to be exercised over such matters because of the small amount of excavation that has, as yet, taken place at such sites. Most forts in the north west appear to have had extramural settlements; only Hardknott appears not to have done, its small bath-house servicing a military community alone. The reason for this was presumably either the inhospitable environment in this part of the Lake District, or perhaps the evidently very disjointed nature of occupation at the fort[56] which will not have offered extramural settlers much security of livelihood. It is worth noting, however, that the equally inhospitable Maiden Castle-on-Stainmore shows evidence of building-terraces created on the slope running south from the fort; on these, there are signs of small rectangular stone buildings. Presumably, proximity to a major road, as well as a fort, made all the difference in terms of business-prospects. Clearly, the size of the settlement would depend on the size and importance of the adjacent fort: a legionary fortress, such as Chester, with its 5,500 soldiers, would support much more extensive settlement than an auxiliary fort intended for only 500 troops.

The hinterlands of legionary fortresses appear to have assumed a similarity around the empire: indeed, a similar pattern has been observed at Chester, Caerleon and, on the Rhine-frontier, at Bonna (Bonn). Immediately adjacent to the fortresses, and on land which was the property of the Roman state, were the *canabae* which were similar in legal status and role to the much smaller extramural settlements around auxiliary forts. At a short distance (about two miles) from the fortresses, however, were further settlements which were presumably out of immediate military jurisdiction. In the north west, such a 'separate' settlement is known to have existed at Heronbridge, to the south of the fortress at Chester; a similar arrangement appears to have existed in the relationship between the legionary fortress at Caerleon and a more 'distant' settlement at Great Bulmore.[57]

Thus, a fort such as Papcastle,[58] which was large and which probably exercised a key role in the management of security in the interface between the northern Lake District and the high-quality agricultural land of the Solway Plain, seems to have supported an extensive extramural settlement; so, too, Ambleside, presumably because of a regional supply-role deriving from its position at the northern end of Windermere.[59] Aerial photography suggests that such settlements were not planned homogeneously (as happened in the larger towns of southern Britain), but developed according to the stimulus to do so. They appear to have lacked most of the 'prestige-buildings' which usually featured in larger towns, although the aerial photograph of Old Carlisle suggests the possible presence of an hotel (*mansio*) at that site; the absence of such major buildings is explained by the fact that those who lived in these extramural settlements do not appear to have enjoyed any element of control over their own affairs, but deferred to the fort commander. Informal 'associations', however, did occur, as is shown by a dedication to the god, Vulcan, made by the *vikani* (townspeople) of Vindolanda.[60] Such religious gatherings may be best compared to modern 'trades-unions', as they brought together people who, in this case, had a shared interest in the 'smith-god'; it is possible that some local administrative potential might have resided in such religious 'guilds'.[61]

Some extramural settlements appear to have been relatively densely settled (as at Piercebridge in County Durham), whereas others, often referred to as 'dispersed settlements', seem to have had small nuclei giving way to occasional small settlements or farms on the roads leading away from them (as appears to have happened at Brougham).[62] As we have seen, it is generally assumed that such settlements as these were not walled – unless special circumstances obtained, as may have been the case at Ribchester. Indeed, it remains unclear if even Carlisle had walls in the Roman period.

Extramural settlements appear to have begun development shortly after the establishment of the forts;[63] as at Watercrook, buildings were initially of timber, but were in most cases converted to stone later. Typical of these buildings were long, narrow, structures with their gable-ends facing on to a street; such an arrangement may be seen at Vindolanda, where there is structural evidence indicating that some of these were converted from earlier barrack-blocks. These buildings had internal divisions which may, typically, have provided for a shop (or workshop) on the street-frontage, with living-accomodation behind and perhaps a 'yard' at the rear where the resident family (or families) engaged in producing goods which could be offered for sale in the shop. Recent excavation at Lancaster (Church Street), for example, revealed such a building with a metal-worker's workshop on the street-frontage.[64]

Inhabitants (and/or users) of such buildings may have been traders or craftsmen attracted over long distances by the market which the fort represented,[65] though most of those who lived and worked in the extramural settlements were probably more local in origin; many young women, for example, may have been attracted by 'unofficial liaisons' formed with serving soldiers which could be formalised into marriage after a soldier's demobilisation. This will obviously have meant that many

Plate 6.6:
Manchester: Iron
reduction hearth

of such people were literally 'camp-followers', who moved around as units of the army moved. Amongst the reforms introduced by Septimius Severus to strengthen his relationship with the army was one which permitted soldiers to marry whilst still on active service. The discovery of wooden toys in excavations at Vindolanda provides a clear reminder of the presence of children, too.[66]

Although we still have little direct evidence of the make-up of populations in these settlements, it seems certain that they were diverse in nature and origin, though linked by their common ability to provide something which soldiers and fellow-settlers needed. Population-sizes, and thus potential markets, are hard to judge, but it would not seem unreasonable to suggest that an auxiliary fort and its extramural settlement might amount to as many as three thousand people; thus, that market was substantial and varied in its tastes and needs.

Clearly, there will have been opportunities for a wide assemblage of craftsmen; over the years, extramural settlements have produced evidence of industrial activity in the form of furnaces, weaving equipment, kilns, tanning pits, as well as waste-products from many processes[67] – not to mention activities connected with the provision of food and drink. Metal-working will obviously have occupied a major place in the industrial life of the settlements in order to facilitate repairs to items of military and civilian property, and to produce a wide range of tools, utensils, fittings and decorative objects. Much of this was probably organised on an individual basis, though the settlement which lay to the north of the fort at Manchester[68] had a considerable area devoted to furnaces, housed apparently in sheds and 'lean-to' structures, which might justify its description as an 'industrial estate'. It is not surprising, as we have seen, to find that Vulcan, the 'patron-deity' of metal-workers, was the object of a dedication recovered from the extramural settlement at Vindolanda.[69]

In the early days of the extramural settlements at least, the military and civilian communities will have depended upon locally-based potters to supplement the supply of vessels which could be acquired from other sources, such as travelling salesmen. In some cases, the need for a range of terracotta products – tiles and bricks, as well as pots – was such that military units themselves might, presumably in a location adjacent to a good supply of suitable raw materials, establish industrial complexes – as happened, for example, at Holt, Quernmore, Muncaster, Scalesceugh and Brampton.[70] Supply-arrangements, however, did not remain static: it has been shown, for example, that whilst the Quernmore-kilns evidently supplied Lancaster until some time in the second century, products from entirely different sources appear in later Roman deposits.[71]

Fine wares, such as the high-status red-glazed samian pottery, were imported from Europe, and presumably sold by travelling salesmen to local shops for selling-on to individuals. In the course of time, the supply of such products as samian ware, colour-coated ware (from the Nene Valley), as well as the black and grey cooking-pots, appears to have been organised on a much larger scale, with the army placing contracts with favoured manufacturers, most of whom were located in the south of the province. In the north west, large industrial complexes, sufficiently well-organised to handle substantial contracts developed at such centres as Heronbridge, Stockton Heath and Wilderspool (see below). Besides such 'practical items', it should also be remembered that metal-workers and potters will have had thriving businesses also in the field of religious and dedicatory objects, which will have been in great demand from populations who were nothing, if not superstitious.

There will have been plenty of work, too, for joiners in the extramural settlements, particularly when many buildings required timber in their construction and when much repair- and restoration-work of wooden structures and vehicles will have been necessary. Joiners' tools have often been found, and they, of course, will have constituted an important product for the metal-worker. Nor should we forget that the timber used by the joiner as his raw material and by other tradesmen for the firing of furnaces presupposes the availability of local supplies which could have been maintained only by a programme of woodland-management.[72]

Plate 6.7: Bowness-on-Solway: Group of British and imported pottery vessels of the mid-second century

Plate 6.8: Watercrook: Enamelled 'duck' brooch

Plate 6.9: Watercrook: Head of a bone hairpin

The supply of raw materials serves to emphasise the importance of the relationship between the forts and extramural settlements on the one hand with the adjacent and more distant countryside on the other. The supply of iron ore (from Cheshire and south-west Cumbria), of copper (from north Wales and the Lake District), lead and sometimes silver also (from Alderley Edge and the Pennines) were organised by road, as well as by coastal shipping and inland waterways to the tradesmen who needed them. All of this provides a vivid demonstration of the interlocking of vital mutual interests on the parts of soldiers and civilians, of town and country, of producers and suppliers. The market-economy, of which the Roman army itself was the apex, clearly drew in a large part of the north west and its people.

Of course, the most 'populous' form of employment in the area will have been in agriculture and, as the Vindolanda writing-tablets indicate, in facilitating the supply of food and drink to the forts and to individual traders in the extramural settlements. It goes without saying that local farmers will have geared their activities not only to supply their own families and satisfy the taxman, but also to produce a surplus to be sold. Writing-tablets, for example,[73] show the amounts given by soldiers for quantities of items such as boot-nails, eggs, salt, bacon and beer: it is a 'sobering thought' that a *denarius* (a day's pay for a legionary soldier) would purchase nearly 180 pints of local beer. Agricultural products must have taken account of the tastes of the market; studies of butchered bones, for example, indicate that optimum ages for slaughter were both recognised and observed.[74] One site at Vindolanda has been identified as a likely butcher's shop because of its counter and the provision of an internal drain linked to the main sewer outside in the street.[75]

We may imagine farmers bringing their animals into a town 'on the hoof', selling them to a butcher. The butcher might cook the meat for sale as 'take-away' meals, or he might arrange its preservation with salt. It is easy to see the value that would have been attached to the virtually unlimited supplies of salt to be obtained in the Northwich, Middlewich and Nantwich areas of Cheshire, all of which have provided ample evidence of salt-working.[76] The curing of meat will have been of major importance in the military zone. There were, of course, 'by-products' to the meat: fleeces and hides, for clothes and shoes, will have provided businesses in the extramural settlements, although it is worth noting that hides might be taken as an alternative form of taxation,[77] to be used for the manufacture of military tents. Hooves and horns may well have been reduced for glue.

Thus, the evidence, whilst admittedly available only in a fragmentary form, points to a vibrant trading-situation in the extramural settlements and to the close relationship that must have developed between the traders in the settlements and the wider tribal community. There were, of course, many other services available: we may, for example, with some confidence postulate a 'leisure-industry' in the form of bars, restaurants and brothels. The bath-houses represented, under official auspices, the closest equivalent that the Roman world had to our 'leisure-centres', and often provided both for soldiers and civilians not simply bathing facilities, but also a range of other activities for relaxation and, perhaps, for keeping fit. Because of its crowded nature, the bath-house was not just a major social centre, but could provide a suitably anonymous 'cover' for criminal activities, also. Again, the constant heating of water required in the bath-houses emphasises the need for substantial supplies of timber in the areas adjacent to the extramural settlements – and, of course, ample water-supplies, too. Recent excavations in Carlisle (Castle Green) have provided striking evidence of the technology of water-supply within the fort, in the form of pipes of terracotta and wood, as well as 'junction-boxes'.

Our knowledge of the extramural settlements, inadequate though it is, provides evidence of other structures and services. Some may have contained a 'hotel' (*mansio*), a large building consisting of small rooms arranged around an open courtyard, with its own bath-house and stables. Such buildings provided a basic level of accommodation for *official* travellers, particularly the couriers of the imperial post. It is quite possible that evidence of a small bath-house, forming part of a large courtyard building recognised to the north of the fort at Lancaster indicates the presence of a *mansio*[78] – unless it was part of a residence assigned to an important official, such as the tax-officer known as a *beneficiarius consularis*[79] who is recorded as present at Lancaster. In such a case, a residence overlooking the river would seem to have been particularly appropriate.

A final aspect of community-life to be considered is entertainment: traditionally, gambling was popular and was undoubtedly carried on widely in bars and on pavements. Evidence of board-games, possibly of the 'war-game' type, has been found in the north west in the form of 'boards' made of stone and divided into squares. A large collection of counters of bone and pottery was recovered from a barrack-area at Ravenglass.[80] There may well also have been cock-fighting and dog-fighting organised in the extramural settlements.

Plate 6.10: Lancaster: Monumental entrance from the courtyard house to the baths

Plate 6.11: (Below) Chester: The amphitheatre

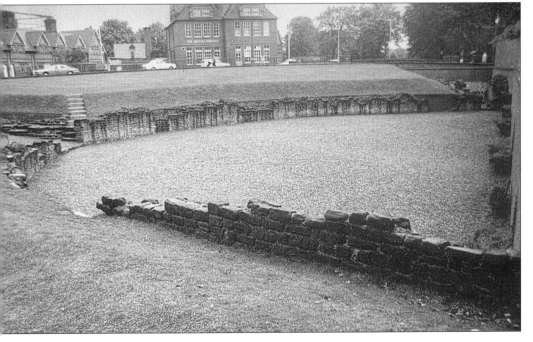

The stone-built amphitheatre at Chester, however, provides evidence of a grander scale of entertainment and ceremonial;[81] such a site has an obvious relevance in the context of the substantial military and civilian population to be expected of a legionary fortress. Some indication of the nature of the entertainment provided may be gained from the scattered evidence in Britain of gladiatorial contests; but we should not overlook the significance of such objects as the pottery face-mask found at Wilderspool[82] and the decorated parade-helmets from sites such as Newstead and Ribchester.[83] An amphitheatre such as that at Chester may well also have been used by the legionaries for weapons-training: recent work at Chester suggests that the visible amphitheatre, which does not appear to have been used until the third century, was preceded not (as once thought) by a timber amphitheatre, but by a substantial bath-building, fed by an aqueduct which led through what is now Grosvenor Park. Smaller arenas may have been located in the vicinity of other forts and extramural settlements in the north west.[84]

A further indication is given by possible evidence of military musicians – both those still on active service and others, perhaps retired but living in the extramural settlements: the 'Apollo-stone' from Ribchester,[85] depicting the god with a lyre – that is, in the *citharoedus*-mode – indicates that the god had a temple in the settlement, which perhaps acted as a 'guild-centre' for military musicians. The recent discovery at Papcastle[86] of a bronze statuette of the satyr, Marsyas, who had the temerity to challenge Apollo to a music-contest and, unsurprisingly, lost, perhaps similarly points to a temple of Apollo, where the god's overseeing of music and musicians was of particular importance.

In sum, therefore, we may see in extramural settlements town-like developments which grew as need dictated, which were generally unwalled and which probably 'tailed-off' into a kind of 'rural suburbia'. No doubt, Latin was only one of many languages which would have been heard in the streets. The *raisons d'être* of such towns were commerce and the servicing of the military community; in achieving this, we may be certain that life in such a settlement was vibrant and noisy, with a mêlée

Plate 6.12: Ribchester: Apollo Citharoedus. Reproduced by courtesy of Ribchester Museum Trust

ate 6.13:
pcastle: Bronze
tuette of Marsyas.
produced by
urtesy of Oxford
chaeological
nit Ltd.

of industrial, commercial and domestic sounds. The air will have often been full of smoke and the intermingled smells of cooking and of industrial processes, such as tanning. These were, in spirit, real towns and we may be sure that, whilst some may have found life intimidating, it will never have been either quiet or dull. It will not have been the 'desolation' predicted by Calgacus, but a life-style that bore many reminders of what the past had been like, but overlain with the excitement of what present and future had to offer.

Religion

It has been observed that religion was the 'cement' that bound Roman and British into 'Romano-British'; traditionally, the gods of the Olympian pantheon had underpinned the Roman state, and were regarded as having built and guaranteed its success. It should be noted, however, that in the Roman world, religion had two distinct faces – the gods of the Olympian pantheon who were primarily concerned with Rome's continuing success, and the so-called 'mystery-religions' in which the gods concerned 'spoke a message' that was personal to the devotees/initiates. In most cases, gods in these two groups were *not* mutually exclusive.[87]

The evidence of surviving inscriptions indicates that a variety of religious practices were catered for in the extramural settlements, though not necessarily all contemporaneously. By nature, Romans and the Romanised Celtic peoples of the west were superstitious, looking to divine help and protection in a wide variety of activities. Because of this, religion – particularly the state-religion of Rome – had always proved to be a powerful weapon in the hands of politicians who, in their priestly roles, advised people on the action required to keep the gods happy.

Initially, it seemed that religion would be the cause of hostility and divisiveness between Romans and Britons, as the Romans sought in western Europe to remove the influence of the Druids.[88] In truth, the Druids were one aspect of Celtic religious practices, and the militant amongst their number were always likely to constitute an implacable foe to Rome: both the Druids and the priests of the Roman gods exercised control by inspiring in the people a fear of what would happen if priestly advice was not taken. Thus, Druids and Rome were essentially 'rivals' for the same ground – the ability to win political control through the medium of religion; the removal of the Druids from the British scene was, thus, a major priority for Rome in the conquest. Not only this, but events early in the conquest made it abundantly clear that the Druids were natural figureheads for any crusade that was based upon tribal nationalism.

Without the influence of militant Druids, the relationship between Roman and Celtic religions was far simpler: both communities were polytheistic and both saw their gods as presiding over particular activities. These were often easily brought together in the so-called *interpretatio Romana*, in which a Roman god and an 'equivalent' Celtic deity were effectively 'fused' into one – for example, *Apollo Maponus* at Ribchester, *Mars Ocelus* at Carlisle, and *Mars Cocidius* at Lancaster. It enabled Rome to cause little disturbance to existing practices, except perhaps to organise them in a more formal way. For example, at Carrawburgh (on Hadrian's Wall), where in the pre-Roman period a natural spring was evidently regarded as a manifestation of the goddess, Coventina, the spring was enclosed in a concrete basin and housed in a square 'Romano-Celtic' temple, of a type that has been recently excavated (and consolidated) at Vindolanda. Dedications to Coventina also show how she came to be perceived in anthropomorphic form, and the large number of coins and other objects found at the site show how it became an object of pilgrimage and veneration – presumably to secure the continuity and quality of the water-supply.[89]

Certain religious observances were required officially: although the great majority of Roman emperors did not view themselves as gods, their extraordinary position in society was paralleled by the 'imperial cult', in which an obligatory demonstration of political loyalty was channelled through the observance of emperors' 'divine spirit' (*genius* or *numen*). Numerous surviving altars and dedications record such statements of loyalty on the part of units of the Roman army, and of other groups and individuals; the finest collection of these in the north west is that from Maryport.[90] As head of the Roman pantheon, Jupiter, the Greatest and Best (*Iuppiter Optimus Maximus*, often abbreviated to *IOM*), was the object of especial attention as symbolic of Rome herself. Individuals might purchase small statuettes, in bronze or terracotta, of emperors or of the 'state-deities' to place on their own household-altars as indications of their loyalty or as recognition of an especial source of protection. In a purely practical sense, the manufacture of such objects was directed towards a market which would never dry up.

Particular groups and individuals would see individual deities as having a particular relevance to their own activities: the army, for example, looked to Mars or Hercules as sources of strength, and

Plate 6.14: Carlisle: Dedication to the Romano-Celtic deity, Mars Ocelus, conjoined with the Imperial Cult: the emperor's name has been subsequently erased. Reproduced by courtesy of Tullie House Museum and Art Gallery, Carlisle

ate 6.15:
ndolanda: Small
›mano-Celtic
mple. Reproduced
˙ courtesy of The
indolanda Trust
ate 6.16: (Below)
aryport: Horned
:ity. Reproduced by
›urtesy of the
:nhouse Roman
`useum

sometimes brought these to Britain in forms familiar to them in their own countries of origin. Thus, a unit of Germans at Housesteads put up a dedication to *Mars Thincsus*,[91] whilst others might equate Mars with a deity native to Britain, such as *Mars Cocidius* (at Lancaster). We have already seen how these gods might be invoked as protectors of groups linked by similarity of trade or skill.

There are also examples of local deities, who were Romanised, but not equated with a specific Roman god; Coventina (at Carrawburgh) has already been mentioned, but we may add Ialonus (probably the deity which presided over the river Lune), who was invoked by a retired soldier at Lancaster, presumably to ensure a prosperous harvest. Similar to this

was the creation of local tutelary deities for towns or tribes: thus the cult of *Brigantia* was encouraged by Septimius Severus, and a fine representation of the goddess as '*Minerva Victrix*' has come from Birrens.[92] Similarly, a small stone bust from Carlisle, wearing a 'gated crown', was presumably the tutelary deity of the principal town of the Carvetii.

What these 'official' cults lacked was any real sense of the spiritual; Cicero had observed that their principal concern was with success in the material world; those who wanted answers to deeper questions regarding the 'purpose of life' could, if they were literate, turn to the works of the philosophers. For others, spirituality or personal salvation were sought through a wide variety of essentially non-Roman mystery cults, most of which originated in the eastern Mediterranean, but which sprang up all over the empire mostly as a result of the mobility of traders and military personnel. Many such cults are represented in Roman Britain, but few appear to have enjoyed a wide appeal; the most celebrated were Mithraism, Isis-worship (from Egypt) and, of course, Christianity.

Participation in these cults was restricted to initiates who, in contrast to the ceremonies of the state's gods, sought the gods' presence and intercession in the secrecy of the *interior* of temple-buildings. Because of the secrecy, our knowledge of the ceremonial is patchy, restricted to what can be 'reconstructed' from the archaeological evidence. Most sites of this nature show only intermittent use, both because 'congregations' were mobile and, as in the case of the hierarchical cult of Mithras, the involvement of a senior figure, such as a fort-commander, was required to lend the necessary authority and resources. In some cases, an element of 'fashion' or 'political correctness' was involved, as when the visit to York of Septimius Severus, his family and entourage prompted the construction there of a temple to the Egyptian deity, Serapis.[93]

Plate 6.17: Bewcastle Silver plaque showing the Celtic deity, Cocidius

Few temples relating to 'mystery-cults' survive in the north west; indeed, many may have been targets in the fourth century for Christian vandalism. The approximate sites of some, however, are attested by surviving inscriptions or cult-objects. Mithraism has,[94] perhaps, left the most tangible evidence: the Persian god of light, goodness and truth attracted interest principally from amongst soldiers and businessmen. The best-preserved *Mithraeum* in Britain is the small rectangular building to be seen off the south-west corner of the fort at Carrawburgh (on Hadrian's Wall). This had four separate periods of use between the mid-second and early-fourth centuries, when it was finally destroyed violently, presumably at the hands of Christians who regarded the Mithraic liturgy as a kind of 'devilish' mockery of their own, and who, in the wake of Constantine I's Edict of Toleration (A.D. 312), enjoyed the impunity that facilitated the adoption of a high profile.

The temple at Carrawburgh shared its general design with others: it had a central nave, which would have been dominated by a brightly-painted relief of Mithras slaying the primeval bull and allowing its blood

Plate 6.18: Kirkham: Altar to three 'Mother Goddesses'; it is now the font at St. John's Church, Lund

and semen to flow to earth, where it evaded the forces of evil (represented by an ant, a serpent and a scorpion) to become the source of life and fruitfulness for mankind. This nave was flanked by raised 'aisles' on which were placed the benches upon which initiates reclined during the ritual meal. At the entrance to the nave were two figures – Cautes ('The Rising Sun') and Cautopates ('The Setting Sun') who, together with Mithras ('The Sun at its Zenith'), made up the 'Mithraic Trinity'. As in Christianity, the Mithraic Trinity also represented 'Three persons in one God'.

Separated from this inner sanctum was an ante-chamber where would-be initiates were probably tested in various ways before admission. The temple was cavernous, lacking natural light and representing the rock from which Mithras was born (as represented in a fine sculpture from Housesteads) and the cave in which he lived. The atmosphere inside was 'heady', due to the burning of pine-cones (as incense) and the very restricted artificial lighting. At Carrawburgh, the latter feature is vividly demonstrated by an altar depicting Mithras with a radiate sun-crown, in which the 'rays' are pierced through to facilitate light shining through from a lamp placed in a recess at the back of the altar.

Although no other Mithraic shrines have been located in north-west England, various sites have produced portable evidence of the cult's presence – Chester, Manchester, Maryport and, perhaps, Lancaster also,

Plate 6.19: Carrawburgh: The Temple of Mithras

where one item in a hoard of sculpture recovered in the late-eighteenth century has some Mithraic features.

The evidence for Christianity in the north west is even less promising: Christians were driven 'underground' by their refusal to engage with the imperial cult, becoming one of the few cults not tolerated by Rome. This illegal status meant that, although active persecution was not regular or particularly frequent, Christians were unable openly to perform their ritual or even communicate publicly with one another. Even after A.D. 312, the administrative classes were evidently slow to renounce traditional paganism. Thus, prior to this date there were no obvious churches, and surviving evidence consists of artefacts which are not always easy to interpret. Indeed, even after 312, there is little evidence of fourth-century church-buildings, and even the identification as a church of the small apsidal building within the commander's house at Vindolanda, whilst reasonable in view of other evidence from the fort, cannot be regarded as completely secure. Nonetheless, it is likely that there were early churches in the north west; it has been suggested that unusual church-dedications may offer clues to the locations of early Christian communities; as an example, a dedication to St. Elphin – Romano-British name, Alphinus – at Warrington may be of significance. Beyond this, any pre-Conquest Christian evidence may conceal the existence of Romano-British Christian centres. Thus, the church-sites at Heysham Head, Urswick and

Plate 6.20: Carrawburgh: The Temple of Mithras: altar-group; that on the left is hollowed out at the back to accommodate a lamp which will have shone through the rays of Mithras' sun-crown

Plate 6.21: Carlisle: Tombstone of Flavius Antigonus Papias, a Greek. The formula, *plus minus* ('more or less'), applied to the age of the deceased, is taken as of Christian significance. Reproduced by courtesy of Tullie House Museum and Art Gallery, Carlisle

Plate 6.22: Vindolanda: Possible Christian Church in the courtyard of the fourth-century *praetorium*. Reproduced by courtesy of The Vindolanda Trust

Aldingham may be of interest, as also the site of Furness Abbey, which has over the years produced a considerable amount of Roman material.[95]

Artefactual 'evidence' of Christianity is generally more difficult to assess, and most of it is not without controversy: for example, excavations in the extramural settlement at Manchester[96] in the late 1970s yielded, evidently from a mid-second century context, a fragment of an amphora-wall, on which was inscribed part of a 'word-square', in which the rearranged letters give the words, PATER NOSTER (twice) with two 'spare' As and Os. The words, PATER NOSTER, of course mean 'Our Father', whilst the letters, A and O, are a Latin rendering of the Greek

'alpha' and 'omega' ('the beginning' and 'the end'). Whilst it is easy to see Christian significance in such formulations, there is by no means unanimity amongst scholars that they should be interpreted in that way. It should be said, however, that, if the Manchester-example is of Christian origin, then it provides one of the earliest pieces of evidence of the Faith in Britain.

Three tombstones from the north west carry possible indications of Christian burials; two – one each from Carlisle and Brougham – employ a formula which indicates that the deceased person lived for so many years 'more or less' (*plus minus*).[97] The sense is that the *precise* length of time spent on earth was of less importance than the eternal life to come. Interestingly, the Carlisle-tombstone (of a Greek, named Flavius Antigonus Papias) opens with the traditional invocation of the pagan gods of the underworld (*Dis Manibus* or, as in this case, *DM*); it is presumably an indication of the conservative nature of tradition, which manifests itself in a wide variety of early Christian contexts. The third tombstone – from Maryport – survives as a fragment[98] which contains the familiar Christian cryptogram, the ligatured Greek letters *chi-rho*, which are the opening of *Christos* ('the Anointed One').

For the rest, personal objects, such as lamps and finger-rings, may point to Christian ownership, although in many such cases the meanings or doubtful provenances may cast doubt on the significance to be attached. However, a recent discovery, which is potentially of considerable importance, consists of lead salt-pans from Shavington (near Crewe);[99] two of these bear the name of one, Flavius Viventius, and one of them describes him as [EPI]SCOPVS (or 'bishop'). These suggest a possible organisational involvement for the late Romano-British Church in this vital industry, anticipating the kind of role which is more familiar in the context of the medieval monastic Church, but which may also recall the 'bargaining-power' of salt, going back into the pre-Roman Iron Age.[100]

Nowadays, of course, we associate the ceremonial surrounding death with the practice of religion; although, as we have seen, tombstones did

Plate 6.23: Shavington: Two sections of a lead salt-pan, bearing the words VIVENTI [EPI] SCOPI ('Of Viventius, the Bishop'). Photograph by The Salt Museum Northwich

ate 6.24: Lancaster:
gures possibly
rming a
ausoleum-group'.
eproduced by
urtesy of Lancaster
ity Museums

invoke the intercession of gods – in this case, those of the Underworld – death and burial were not associated with the temples of the state's gods. Although few of the north west's Romano-British cemeteries are well-known, we do see clearly the effect of Roman law which forbade the placing of any burials, apart from those of infants, within settlement-areas. Instead, the roads that led out from settlements were the focal-points of the burials of the remains of the dead. Lancaster, for example, has produced evidence of cremations at the southern end of Penny Street, and it has also been suggested[101] that a large earthwork, some two miles south of Lancaster, may have been a substantial roadside mausoleum, possibly associated with a large collection of statuary found hoarded nearby in the eighteenth century. It should, however, be noted that many graves will have been unmarked and thus at risk of being overbuilt, as settlement-expansion occurred.

However, the most significant cemetery-evidence from the north west has come from excavation of part of the cemetery associated with the fort and extramural settlement at Low Borrow Bridge (Tebay) and situated at about three-quarters of a mile to the south of the fort and adjacent to the road (now called Fairmile) leading to Burrow-in-Lonsdale.[102] As a result of 'differential drying' in the river-gravels, individual sub-rectangular and sub-circular burial-plots could be made out, presumably belonging to those who had paid into burial-clubs to secure their plots. The fact that many of these plots 'cut' one another suggests that visibly they were hard to distinguish after a while and were not in the main furnished with clear

Plate 6.25: Low Borrow Bridge: Cemetery, showing the outlines of grave plots. Photograph by Oxford Archaeological Unit Ltd.

grave-markers. In fact, only one inscribed grave-slab was recovered from the excavations. This cemetery contained graves of different types: some sixty cremations were recovered, one of which contained a single coin – presumably the 'fare' to be paid to the ferryman for the deceased's journey across the river Styx. There were also a few inhumations, a number of which were in the 'crouched' or 'womb' position – a reminder of the persistence in this Romano-British community even to the second and third centuries A.D. of pre-Roman traditions.

Plate 6.26: (Below) Low Borrow Bridge: Cremation-burial from the cemetery. Photograph by Oxford Archaeological Unit Ltd.

The Rural Hinterland

As we have seen, a great deal of the land of north-west England was deforested and farmed before the coming of Rome. It is a reminder that the bulk of Brigantian and Carvetian tribesmen were already living settled lives, making a living or, at least, subsisting through their own care of the land. Aerial photography[103] indicates that, in principle, this changed little during the Roman occupation, though the steady programme of demobilisation of Roman soldiers on to the land undoubtedly led to diversification amongst the rural population, as well as in the nature of agricultural produce to accommodate changing tastes.

However, we should bear in mind that agriculture was not the only rural occupation.

There must have been many at the margins of society who continued to feed themselves and their families through 'hunting and gathering' in the woodlands, whose extent was probably deliberately strengthened to accommodate the increased need of timber for building and burning. Such people may well have been able to sell to the more organised parts of the community both the hunted meat, as well as by-products (for example, antlers which might find a use as picks). We should probably not, however, regard such people as Romanised in any meaningful sense.

A rather larger, and more organised, minority is represented by people whose interests lay in the recovery of raw materials, and either selling these on or engaging in industrial manufacture themselves. A hint of such business was given in the examination of iron-slags from the excavations at Manchester (Deansgate) in 1972; this showed Cheshire as a major source of ore,[104] but we may wonder whether iron-ore came to major centres, conveyed by road or water, from other sources in the north west, such as south-west Cumbria. The extraction of copper from north Wales and lead from the northern Pennines and from such locations as Alderley Edge will have been of great importance for building, for personal items and, especially, in the case of lead, for the manufacture of tanks for the salt-industry.

How this was organised in the north west is not known for certain, though evidence from other parts of Britain has suggested that ore-extraction may have been a responsibility of the procurator's department or let out to individual companies, as clearly happened in Derbyshire. That the Roman army was involved to some extent is not in doubt – both as an organiser of extraction and of use. We may, in this connection, cite the manufacture of bricks, tiles and pots in locations such as Holt,

Plate 6.27: Caton: Hadrianic milestone. Photograph by courtesy of Lancaster City Museums

Plate 6.28: Blackstone Edge: Paved Roman road

Plate 6.29: Wilderspool: Part of the industrial site, showing circular hut-structure (arrowed)

Plate 6.30: Walton-le Dale: Timber-slots for shed-like buildings

Scalesceugh, Brampton, Muncaster and Quernmore, which must have been close to sources of suitable clay. It is likely, on the example of Holt, that manufacturing work was here in the hands of military personnel. The army may also have been responsible for sites such as Walton-le-Dale, where large, rectilinear, shed-like structures carry the military imprint on a site that may have been concerned with storage and distribution.[105]

The proximity to Chester of the works-depot at Holt needs no stressing, but we should remember that this area of north-west Cheshire contains other manufacturing and trading sites, such as Heronbridge and Wilderspool. Obviously, Chester will have been a major market for such sites, but we should not forget the proximity of what appears to have been a multi-period trading and distribution site at Meols,[106] on the Wirral.

One of the most substantial industrial sites in the north west, however, is that at Wilderspool, the full extent of which is still not known.[107] Excavations in the 1970s revealed a site divided by property-boundaries and criss-crossed by multi-phased aqueducts. A great variety of industrial processes has been identified at Wilderspool, including the manufacture of bricks, tiles and pots, objects of bronze, iron and lead, as well as glass-making and stone-masonry. Pottery products from the site have been identified as far north as the Antonine Wall, and there seems to have been a military connection, perhaps principally with legion XX. The most-clearly identifiable building, however, was a round-house; this prompts the suggestion that, whilst the site may have had military supervision, perhaps to ensure quality-control of products for its markets, the workforce may well have been British, which would explain the 'illiterate' manufacturers' marks – so-called 'trade marks' – on some *mortaria* from the site. This leaves open the question of whether British workers were on the site by coercion or whether, in an area which may have been socially and economically marginal, we should view Wilderspool as a facility intended to benefit British manufacturers. A prevailing 'mystery' surrounding this and other industrial sites in the north west is that, whilst some activity continues on some of them well into the fourth century,[108] the 'heyday' of them all appears to have passed by the close of the second. There is also evidence from Wigan which would appear to be consistent with a site of an industrial nature.[109]

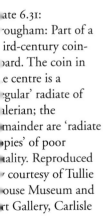

Plate 6.31: Brougham: Part of a third-century coin-hoard. The coin in the centre is a 'regular' radiate of Valerian; the remainder are 'radiate copies' of poor quality. Reproduced by courtesy of Tullie House Museum and Art Gallery, Carlisle

Another area of industrial activity that has been located away from principal sites is that recognised in and around the limestone-caves of west Yorkshire.[110] The presence of considerable numbers of coins and other significant objects in the assemblages collected in and adjacent to the caves argues strongly against these representing the activities of marginal groups: it has, therefore, been suggested that there may have been some economic and social connection between these sites and larger communities located on lower ground at centres, such as the villa at Kirk Sink (Gargrave),[111] or perhaps directly with elements of the Roman army.

We can, however, assume that the bulk of the native population of the north west remained as they had long been – arable farmers and pastoralists. However, the lack of excavation of rural sites in north-west England leaves much doubt as to the nature of the relationship between farmers and the populations of forts and extramural settlements. There are, in fact, many questions about the nature of the rural economy to which the answers, in the present state of our knowledge, can be no more than provisional.

Outwardly, the most obvious difference between the rural economy of north-west England and other parts of Britain is the absence from the former of structures classified as villas.[112] The villa-estate of the lowland zone represented architectural Romanisation in the countryside, which is manifested in various levels of resource; these existed alongside other rural sites whose general nature and appearance were much closer to those found in the north west. The villa-estate assumes a level of wealth, either owned or borrowed, but did not necessarily have a monopoly of

Plate 6.32: Ewe Close: Romano-British rural settlement. Photograph by courtesy of Cambridge University Collection of Air Photographs

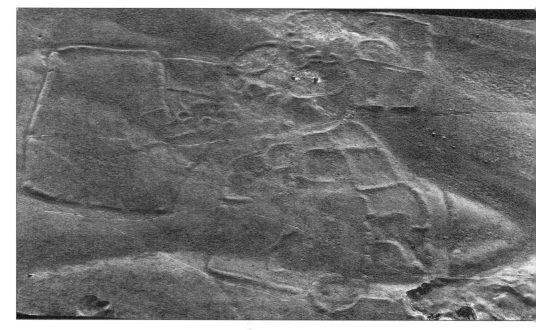

land.[113] It is clearly too crude an assumption to argue that because the north west generally lacks villa-estates, its farmers also lacked land and finance: the establishment of the *civitas* of the Carvetii in northern Cumbria, by definition, assumes a strong level of resources on the part of its leaders. It is difficult to imagine that, for the most part, the source of that wealth was other than agriculture. In any case, as we have seen, some upland Romano-British sites may have been integrated into larger agricultural concerns on lower ground.

The north west has so far yielded two sites which conform to the description of a villa as measured by the criteria established in the lowland zone – Eaton-by-Tarporley (near Chester) and Kirk Sink (near Skipton).[114] The identities of the owners of these villas are not known: they could have come from further south, or they might have been of local origin, though we should not lose sight of the fact that neither site is far from a legionary fortress. There are probably more such sites awaiting discovery, especially, for example, in Cheshire and western Yorkshire. Nevertheless, the vast majority of known rural sites in the north west are not of this type; rather, they are made up of circular or rectangular structures in complexes of varying size and constructed either of stone or of timber. Clearly, such complexes consisted of both domestic sites and fields or yards. Present knowledge of the distribution of such sites suggests that some were small farms whilst others may well have been centres of estates of considerable size.

Such study as has taken place indicates that we cannot employ simple criteria such as chronological development or level of Romanisation to

Plate 6.33:
Holt Park: Romano-British rural settlement

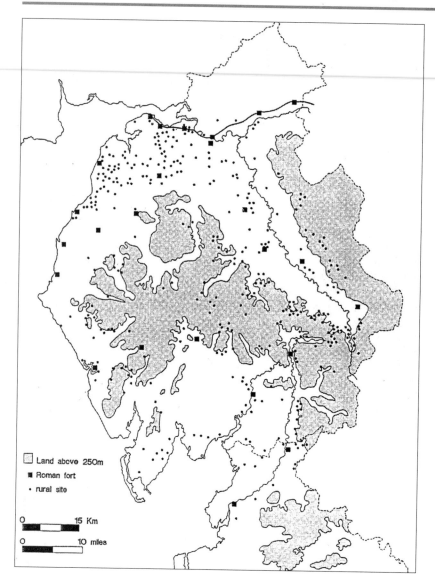

Figure 6.2: Romano-British rural sites in Cumbria and north Lancashire (after R. C. Turner)

Land above 250m

■ Roman fort

• rural site

0   15 Km

0   10 miles

explain the differences in shape and building materials. Indeed, artefactual evidence indicates no obvious distinctions in date or ownership-type; the difference in building materials appears to represent the use of timber on sites located in the valleys with stone used chiefly on sites at higher altitudes, as, for example, at Maiden Castle-on-Stainmore. This probably simply reflects the fact that, due to human agency or environmental process, deforestation had proceeded further at higher altitudes, making timber a scarce (and valued) material – too valuable to use for building. It is clear, too, that some at least of the rural sites of all types enjoyed long histories, stretching back beyond the Romano-British period (as at Ewe Close in the Upper Lune Valley or Urswick 'Stone

Walls') and continuing much later (as at Gauber High Pasture in Upper Ribblesdale).[115] Experience with such sites, however, has indicated that, without excavation, their chronologies can be very misleading.

There can be no doubt that the presence of the Roman army with its dependent extramural settlements will have had considerable effects upon local rural populations: they will have provided opportunities for those involved in agriculture – tastes in food and drink to be accommodated, as well as openings into the 'textile-market', and the provision of hides for tents and for transforming into a variety of leather-goods, not to mention the rearing of working-animals and the provision of fodder for them.

A further major effect will have been in the area of land-distribution, though the details of this must remain largely a matter of conjecture, since we have few inscriptions from rural sites to enable us to identify owners, and since building-types, as we have seen, do not provide an indicator. Clearly, some land must have been appropriated by the authorities for the settlement of discharged soldiers, and it may be assumed that this was likely to have been land of better quality, such as was situated in the valley-floors and in coastal locations – for example, in the area of Penrith. Although the evidence remains inconclusive,[116] it was long ago conjectured[117] that land on the Fylde may have been used for veteran settlement, and it would seem very likely that the veterans of Ribchester, as well as enjoying a stake in the extramural settlement, had allotments of land in the Ribble valley. One piece of evidence from the Lancaster-area, which may offer a pointer, is the altar[118] set up near Bolton-le-Sands by Julius Januarius who described himself as a retired *decurio* – the equivalent of a centurion in a cavalry-unit – presumably from the fort at Lancaster. Preferential treatment in the quantity and quality of land allocated may have been afforded in descending order, to veterans from the legions, from auxiliary cavalry-units and from auxiliary infantry-units. It has been suggested that land designated for such use might show signs of centuriation,[119] the traditional Roman form of land-distribution, although at present no certain evidence of this practice has been generally accepted. Further, it has to be said that finds-assemblages from rural sites do not immediately suggest owners of even fair means – as one might expect of retired members of the Roman army.

Despite such imperatives, however, it is unlikely that the authorities were insensitive to the needs and aspirations of the farmers[120] of the north west, however they were organised. Much land-tenure and usage was probably left without interference, as was perhaps the case with the complex of sites in the surviving ancient landscape of Leck Beck and Eller Beck;[121] by the middle of the first century A.D., it was generally held by Rome that local populations were easier to manage if left to pursue traditional activities and methods. Also, it will have been

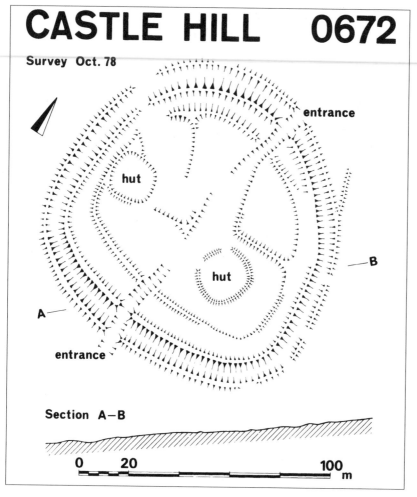

CASTLE HILL   0672

Survey Oct. 78

entrance

hut

hut

B

A

entrance

Section A–B

0   20   100 m

Figure 6.3: Romano-British rural site: Castle Hill, Leck; Reproduced by courtesy of Lancashire Sites and Monuments Record

Plate 6.34: Castle Hill, Leck: Romano-British rural settlement. Photograph by Lancashire Sites and Monuments Record

understood that native populations could advance themselves socially and politically if the profitability of their activities was encouraged. Although the period of Roman occupation may not have led to striking advances in agricultural technology, and although uncontrolled deforestation could obviously not be allowed for the damage it did to land-quality at upper levels, yet the clearance of some land will have greatly enhanced the opportunities for profit-making.

It is now clear that we have to reject the notion, so often advanced in the past, that apart from the areas of the Roman sites themselves, the population of the north west was thin;[122] even Tacitus disputed that. On the other hand, on present evidence it was not even; modern Lancashire was probably marginal by comparison with either Cumbria or Cheshire. It is clear, too, from the locations of agricultural sites that there was a strong economic interdependence between the Roman and native populations, a point emphasised by contents of 'stores-lists' contained amongst the writing-tablets from Vindolanda and Carlisle.[123]

The plotting of sites has proceeded much further in Cumbria than in Lancashire, where conditions do not lend themselves so readily to yielding results from aerial research.[124] Thus, whilst in some parts of the region the number of known sites is small, finds of Roman material suggest that the river-valleys and Roman roads, as well as the Roman sites themselves, provided the chief foci for settlement. Nonetheless, possible traces of the Romano-British landscape have been observed on the eastern flank of the West Lancashire mosses, and there are signs that the higher ground in the Fylde may have supported settlement.[125]

North of Lancashire, considerable settlement has been observed on the limestone of the Ribblehead area, as at Gauber High Pasture and Colt Park.[126] In north Lancashire and Cumbria, the principal areas of settlement are located in the valley floors and slopes of the communications corridors provided by the Lune and Eden rivers, and again on the Solway Plain and the northern slopes of the Lake District, as at Glencoyne Park on the shore of Ullswater, which, as now, may have been an area of 'rough pasture'.[127]

Although excavation of rural sites has been very limited, it would appear a reasonable assumption that a high proportion of them, even if multi-period, was active in the Roman period. It is similarly reasonable to suppose that many, if not most, of the sites, both arable and pastoral, enjoyed an 'economic relationship' with the Roman forts and extramural settlements. In other words, they were producing grain surplus to their taxation-requirement, and their animal husbandry was to an extent organised to take account of the Roman market for meat.[128]

Environmental characteristics were clearly the chief limiting factors to the farmer's activity; in particular, deforestation and soil erosion will have limited the use to which the higher terrain – that is, above approximately

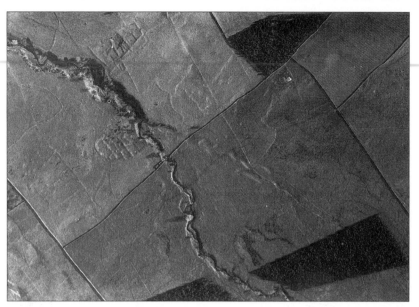

Plate 6.35: Eller Beck
Romano-British rural
settlement.
Photograph by
Lancashire Sites and
Monuments Record

300 metres – could be put. At the same time the very process of soil erosion from higher levels will have led to enhanced fertility in the valleys. During the Roman period, deforestation by environmental causes was intensified by the need for timber for building, though in a number of places excavation has revealed that Roman forts – as at Carlisle – were being built in areas already without forest cover, having been given over to grassland or occasionally to ploughing. Deforestation will have affected not only the local farmer's use of the land, but also the materials he used to provide housing for himself. Clearly, stone would have had to be used where timber was in short supply. Thus, for that reason, if for no other, the higher rural settlements would tend to be stone-built – and, incidentally, more resilient to the passage of time. Timber, wattle and thatch were generally used at lower levels, though a circular hut at Fingland appears to have been constructed of turves laid on a stone foundation.[129]

A total picture is, of course, beyond recovery; particularly on the valley floors and on the lower slopes subsequent agricultural activity has destroyed a good deal of the evidence. However, the density of sites located, particularly on the good land of the valley floors, suggests a picture of intense agricultural activity, based upon a mixed arable/pastoral economy. Evidence accumulated from the Eller Beck sites in the Lune Valley[130] suggests an extensive system of 'celtic' fields, spreading up the valley slopes and perhaps centred on the valley floor. The presence of 'mixed-farming' sites on the fells (for example, Waitby, Crosby Ravensworth and Crosby Garrett) perhaps indicates an attempt to utilise the slopes in a manner similar to that of the valleys themselves with cultivation carried probably to a higher altitude than nowadays.[131]

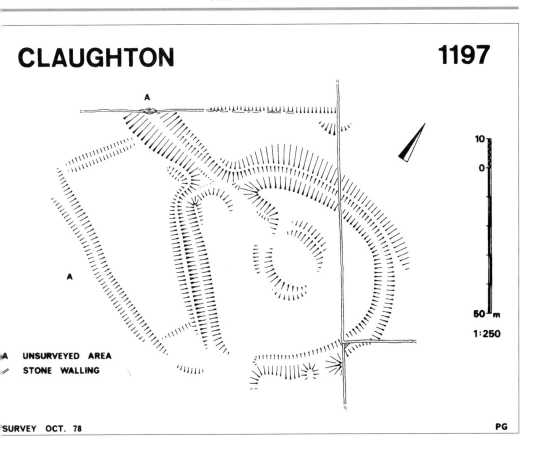

CLAUGHTON **1197**

A

A

10
0

50 m

1:250

A UNSURVEYED AREA
STONE WALLING

SURVEY OCT. 78 PG

Figure 6.4: Romano-British rural site: Claughton; reproduced by courtesy of Lancashire Sites and Monuments Record

On the whole, however, the higher-level sites (that is, above approximately 250 metres) carry, in the evidence of dykes and large 'fields', the indications of stock-management and pastoralism.[132] In the cases of Eller Beck and Waitby, it has been shown that in the later Roman period there is evidence of arable land giving way to pastoral use.[133] Such distinctions will obviously have been influenced by local environmental circumstances and by changing economic conditions.

As we have seen, rural settlement is identified in generally separate (if not isolated) farms – either rectilinear (as at Cantsfield near the confluence of the Lune and the Greta) or curvilinear (as at Wolsty Hall on the Solway Plain).[134] Most appear to be best described as single farmsteads rather than grouped as 'villages',[135] and generally display single entrances. Rectilinear and curvilinear forms appear to exist contemporaneously, although the rectilinear forms may be more commonly associated with field-systems. They are generally wholly enclosed, presumably to exclude marauders – human or animal – although some, as at Crosby Ravensworth, are partly unenclosed.

Whilst finds of artefacts (in addition to typological analysis) will permit relatively easy recognition of sites which belong to the Romano-

British period, the paucity of these artefacts usually precludes close dating. It is generally held that the more settled conditions which prevailed from the late-second/early-third centuries provided a major stimulus to settlement expansion, although some sites are undoubtedly earlier than this. Expansion includes not just the appearance of new sites, but also the development of existing ones, as happened at Cross Hill[136] (Penrith), where a circular house gave way to rectangular buildings; such a development could suggest the influence of the building-types in the extramural settlements, and thus carry chronological and cultural implications. Care needs, however, to be taken as change over a long period may be involved; for example, at Gauber High Pasture (in Upper Ribblesdale),[137] excavation demonstrated that a rectilinear building on a Romano-British site was, in fact, of ninth-century date. Conversely, excavations at Fingland showed clear evidence of a circular structure associated with late Roman pottery.[138] Whilst the huts might be placed anywhere within the enclosures, a striking phenomenon is found at Castle Folds on Orton Scar,[139] where a defensive stone wall circuit had circular and rectilinear buildings constructed against its interior face. It has also been shown that, over time, hut-sites might be moved and started anew a short distance away; without excavation, such sites might be seen as more complex than they really were.[140]

Plate 6.36:
Collingholme:
Romano-British rural
settlement.
Photograph by
Lancashire Sites and
Monuments Record

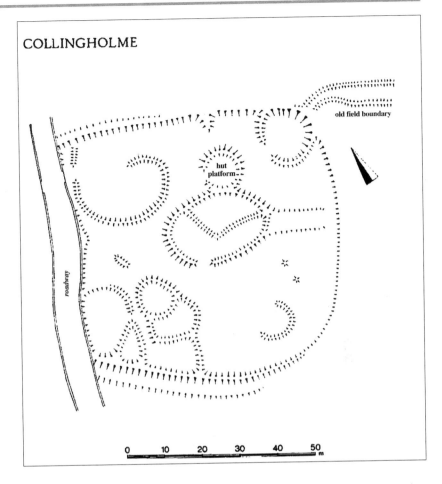

Figure 6.5: Romano-British rural site: Collingholme; reproduced by courtesy of Lancashire Sites and Monuments Record

The usage of rural sites has again to be generally inferred from the few examples which have been the subject of study. It is self-evident that economic advantage will have lain behind a great deal that was done; the realisation of such advantage might range from the position of a farm close to the Romano-British communications and site network to the co-operative management of land which may be visible in the larger field systems. The positioning of many sites tends to indicate that they were intended to take advantage of lower land for arable purposes and higher land for stock management. Such arable usage would presumably include the growing of crops for sale and for winter feed for the stock. The smaller fields intended for arable usage were probably demarcated with low stone banks, whilst larger fields associated with higher turf banks were presumably intended for stock management.

We can, therefore, see that in general cereal and hay cultivation took place in ploughed land in the valleys and the lower slopes, presumably utilising different areas according to season. It should also be noticed that land-use was not necessarily static; the Eller Beck complex has shown

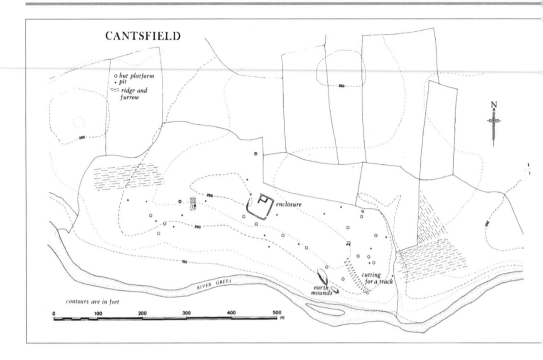

arable land given over to pastoral use in the later Roman period. Some field systems, however, may always have been intended for pastoralist use, as at Aughertree Fell on the northern slopes of the Lake District, or at Stone Carr (Penrith) where fields were bounded by deep ditches. Whilst much of the pastoralism was concerned with cattle and the many uses to which they could be put, we should not forget the role of sheep beyond the provision of food. Finds of textiles at Vindolanda demonstrate the potential significance of sheep farming and the local processing of the

Figure 6.6: Romano-British rural site: Cantsfield (after R. C. Turner)

Plate 6.37: Cantsfield: Romano-British rural settlement

wool. There is no reason to suppose that this may not have been carried out by local farmers, producing amongst other things the rather shapeless garments in which the 'cloaked deities' from Housesteads are depicted – possibly the *birrus britannicus* of Diocletian's Price Edict.

Whilst crop-growing and stock-management provided a living for a large section of the rural community, it should be noticed that for some hunting must have remained more of a living than a pastime. Areas of woodland will have provided a habitat for red deer and wild boar, which could clearly have made an economic contribution.

In short, whilst it has to be said that our knowledge is very selective, it is becoming possible to see a degree of integration between Roman and native in the north west, which exists on the economic, social and religious levels.[141] The evidence will be seen principally within the urban context, and in the rural environment in the close vicinity of fort/extramural settlement sites. The wider rural community will have generated what was required for taxation, and in some cases, a surplus for sale. However, that the volume of that surplus never reached major proportions in the north west is clear from the general inability of the extramural settlements to prosper without active support from a military presence. In this sense, Romanisation in the north west may have advanced – no doubt more for some than for others – but it did not attain the level of urbanisation and wealth-creation that we see further south. That is not, of course, to argue that the development of small towns outside Roman forts had no bearing on later urban development in the region; Lancaster, for example, is providing interesting evidence of possible long-term site-continuity.[142] Clearly, there is much research to be done, particularly on the detailed nature of the economic basis of the sites. Whilst aerial survey and field-work will continue to advance the picture, the excavation of more sites is clearly required. It is, however, possible with the present state of the evidence to see in part the relationship between the Roman troops and the native population – whether as craftsmen or farmers. To a degree, all were harmonised into a Romano-British economy; the native population was producing goods, manufactured or agricultural, on a commercial as well as a taxation basis, for this will explain the presence of items like Samian pottery on native sites, which must have been acquired in return for goods.

In short, therefore, it would appear to be far from the truth to argue for a 'conquerors and vanquished' model of relationship in the north west. The Romans were a stimulus; within limits the local population became Romanised. Whilst progress was less marked and dramatic than in lowland Britain, it would still be reasonable to assert that Roman and native lived together to mutual advantage, and that the north west of *Britannia* enjoyed and benefited from the *Pax Romana*.

Notes

1. Cicero *In Defence of Murena* 9. 22: 'Glory in war surpasses all other forms of success'.

2. Virgil *Aeneid* VI. 851ff.

3. Suetonius (*Life of the Deified Augustus* 23) dramatically shows the effect upon Augustus himself, as does Tacitus' account of legions visiting the 'fatal spot' in A.D. 15 (*Annals* I. 60–62).

4. Tacitus *Life of Agricola* 30–32.

5. Millett, 1990; this provides the most accessible treatment of the subject of Romanisation. See also Whittaker, 1994.

6. Dio Cassius *History of Rome* 56. 18, 2–3.

7. *Life of Agricola* 13, 1 and 21.

8. Mentioned on Claudius' triumphal arch in Rome (*ILS* 216).

9. Tacitus *Life of Agricola* 21, 1.

10. *Geographia* IV. 5, 2.

11. Nevell, 1999; Cowell and Philpott, 2000.

12. For example, Bewley, 1994; Higham and Jones, 1975; 1985; McCarthy, 2002.

13. Bowman and Thomas, 1983; Birley, Birley and Birley, 1993; Tomlin, 1998.

14. For early studies, see Richmond, 1958; Salway, 1965.

15. Holder, 1982; Breeze, 1988.

16. For tactics and fighting-methods, see Keppie, 1984, Peddie, 1994 and Gilliver, 1999.

17. Probably approximately 120 cavalry, and non-combatants, such as clerks, accountants, doctors, and priests.

18. For this subject, see, for example, a speech made in A.D. 48 by the emperor, Claudius (Tacitus *Annals* XI. 23–24 and *ILS* 212).

19. See Cheeseman, 1914; Holder, 1992.

20. 500– and 1000–strong units were termed 'quingenary' or 'milliary' respectively. In actual fact, the two figures were properly 480 and 960, though *Cohors I Tungrorum* (at Vindolanda), a quingenary unit, in fact, at one stage had 761 men on its strength (Gilliver, 1999, 25). Excavations at Wallsend have indicated that the *cohors equitata* there was made up of 600 men (480 infantry; 120 cavalry), and that mounts and men were barracked together.

21. See, for example, Birley, Birley and Birley, 1993, 23 for 337 men of *Cohors I Tungrorum* (based at Vindolanda) serving away, probably at Corbridge; also the seconding of 18 men to Vindolanda to work on the Bath-house (*Tab. Vindol.* 155; Birley Andrew, 2001, 15ff (esp. p.34)).

22. For evidence of this, see Tacitus *Life of Agricola* 29, 2 and 32, 1; also Birley, Birley and Birley, 1993, 37 (*Brittunculi*) and 59 (*Tab. Vindol.* 32B and 943). The point is illustrated by the tombstone of a Brigantian, Nectovelius, found at Mumrills on the Antonine Wall: Nectovelius died at the age of twenty-nine, after nine years' service with *Cohors II Thracum* (*RIB* 2142).

23. *RIB* 601 (also note on *RIB* 601 in *RIB* I2 (1995)); Shotter, 1973; *Not. Dign. Occ.* 40, 22. On *numeri* in general see Southern, 1989.

24. Dio Cassius *History of Rome* 72. 16. The Sarmatians at Ribchester had a number of titles (*ala, cuneus, numerus*), which may imply either a promotion to auxiliary status or suggests the possibility of Sarmatians having been sent to Ribchester on different

occasions (see Edwards, 2000, 39 and 49). The local settlement of discharged Sarmatians presumably gave Ribchester its name of *Bremetennacum Veteranorum* (Edwards, 2000, 7).

25. See Wilson, 1997, 67ff. These altars may now be seen at the Senhouse Roman Museum at Maryport.

26. See above on pp. 93 and 108.

27. Inscriptions on stone and other materials are collected in *Roman Inscriptions of Britain* (*RIB*), together with regular updates in *Journal of Roman Studies* (to 1969) and *Britannia* (since 1970). The writing tablets from northern sites have been published on an occasional basis (as in Bowman and Thomas, 1983 and Birley, Birley and Birley, 1993 for Vindolanda; Tomlin, 1998 for Carlisle). Military Diplomas are collected in *CIL* XVI and by Roxan, 1978 and 1985. The most recent such discovery in north-west England, was of a Diploma of a soldier of *Cohors I Aelia Classica* which was recovered on the beach at Ravenglass (Holder, 1997). See also Mann, 1988.

28. A good, recent, example of this is the discovery at Birdoswald of belt-buckles which are otherwise recorded only at Caerleon, the base of legion II *Augusta* (T. Wilmott, *pers. comm.* and forthcoming).

29. *RIB* 600.

30. Buxton and Howard-Davis, 2000, 419f; Olivier, 1987; Mann, 2002.

31. Mason, 2003.

32. Shotter, 2002a.

33. Rivet, 1970 (*Antonine Itinerary*); Ward, 1973 and Hassall, 1976 (*Notitia Dignitatum*); Richmond and Crawford, 1949 (*Ravenna Cosmography*); Strang, 1997 (Ptolemy's *Geographia*).

34. Hartley, 1972; Shotter, 1976; Swan, 1999; Abdy, 2002; Reece, 2002.

35. E.g. Higham and Jones, 1975; Richardson and Richardson, 1980; See also *Britannia* 27 (1996), 405 for the recent discovery of a substantial new fort at Cummersdale (near Carlisle), which has still to be 'fitted into' a chronological scheme. There is currently discussion on the nature of this site.

36. Juvenal *Satires* IV. 127.

37. *Journ. Rom. St.* 53 (1963), 160; Thorley, 2002; Shotter, 2003c.

38. Welsby, 1980.

39. Salway (1981, 590f) suggests the possible sharing of responsibility between fort-commanders and nearby civilian authorities, based upon a statement of Ulpian (*Digest* 50. 1, 30).

40. *RIB* 933.

41. *Journ. Rom. St.* 55 (1965), 224; this inscription, on a milestone found at Frenchfield, dates to the reign of the third-century rebel, Postumus, and may be seen in the museum at Brougham Castle.

42. For the Carvetii, see Higham and Jones, 1985 and McCarthy, 2002, 51ff.

43. McCarthy, 1990; 1993; 2002, 83–84.

44. *Britannia* 12 (1981), 325f and 13 (1982), 343f.

45. McCarthy, 2002, 69 and 77ff.

46. McCarthy, 2002, 76.

47. See *Britannia* 27 (1996), 405; the finding of Republican *denarii* suggests the presence of legionaries.

48. *RIB* 2283. See Birley E.B., 1953a; Potter, 1979, 195.

49. R.F.J. Jones (1981) has suggested that there may have been other *civitates* in the north, proposing Kirkby Thore as the location of another possible centre.

50. See Cowell and Philpott, 2000 for a discussion of sites in the south of the region.

51. Ptolemy *Geographia* II. 3, 2; Higham, 1986, 146–147; Shotter, 1995b.

52. McCarthy, 2002, 79.

53. See Dearne and Lord, 1998.

54. McCarthy, 1991 (Carlisle); Buxton and Howard-Davis, 2000 (Ribchester).

55. Shotter, 1990; 1995c; 2000c.

56. See Bidwell, Snape and Croom, 1999.

57. Mason, 1987; Mason, 2001, 101ff; Mason, 2002.

58. *Britannia* 16 (1985), 276.

59. Shotter, 1995b.

60. *RIB* 1700 (cf. *RIB* 899 from Old Carlisle).

61. Richmond and Steer, 1957.

62. See, for example, structures in the 'Southern Lanes' area of Carlisle (McCarthy, 2000; 2002, 77).

63. Potter, 1979, 187.

64. See the forthcoming report by Oxford Archaeology (North) on excavations at Mitchell's Brewery, Lancaster.

65. See Smith (1959) for the Palmyrene sculptor, Barates, at South Shields, who had married a British woman; cf. *RIB* 864 (Maryport) for the presence of a man from Galatia in Asia Minor.

66. For a small gold ring, possibly belonging to a child, see Buxton and Howard-Davis, 2000, 241.

67. Tylecote, 1962, 222ff.

68. Jones G.D.B., 1974; Bryant, Morris and Walker, 1986.

69. *RIB* 1700.

70. Holt (Grimes, 1930; Ward, 1998); Quernmore (Leather and Webster, 1988); Muncaster (Bellhouse, 1960b); Scalesceugh (Bellhouse, 1971); Brampton (Hogg, 1965).

71. See the fabric-analysis of Quernmore-material conducted by the late Professor A.R. Wellburn of Lancaster University (*Contrebis* 3 (1975), 50–52; Shotter, 1983).

72. McCarthy, 1986.

73. Birley A.R., 2002, 100ff; see, for example, *Tab. Vindol.* II. 186 (of A.D. 110).

74. Jones G.D.B., 1975.

75. Birley R., 1977.

76. Thompson, 1965, 88–97; Strickland, 2001; Evidently also a pre-Roman industry of importance (Matthews, 2001).

77. See Tacitus *Annals* IV. 72, 2 for the introduction of such a tax amongst the Frisii.

78. See Jones and Shotter, 1988, 61ff; Shotter and White, 1990, 23 (Note that the building at Vindolanda previously designated a *mansio* has now been re-interpreted as the residence of the commanding-officer of the fort of the Severan period).

79. This officer, named Lucius Vibenius, is recorded on *RIB* 602 (See *Contrebis* 26 (2001–02), 5).

80. Potter, 1979, 79ff.

81. Thompson, 1976; Mason, 2001 (Excavation of the Chester-amphitheatre is on-going at the time of writing); see also Jackson, 1983.

82. Thompson, 1965, 84.

83. Edwards, 1992; Jackson and Craddock, 1995.

84. As at Tomen-y-Mur in north Wales (Nash-Williams, 1969, 111–113).

85. *RIB* 583.

86. *Britannia* 16 (1985), 276; for Marsyas, see *Britannia* 14 (1983), 20 (Mosaic from Sherborne, Dorset).

87. For Roman religion in general, see Ogilvie, 1969; Ferguson, 1970; Green, 1976; Henig, 1984; Webster, 1986.

88. Ross and Robins, 1989.

89. Allason-Jones and McKay, 1985: a similar respect was clearly shown to Cocidius at Bewcastle.

90. These were collected over the years by the Senhouse-family, and are now on display in the Senhouse Roman Museum at Maryport.

91. *RIB* 1593.

92. *RIB* 2091; Joliffe, 1941.

93. This temple of Serapis was built under the auspices of Claudius Hieronymianus, *legatus* of legion VI (RIB 658).

94. Daniels, 1989b; Richmond and Gillam, 1951; the altars on site are modern replicas.

95. Shotter, 1990, 234–239. In general, see Petts, 2003; there is, of course, no evidence to allow us to determine how Roman material reached sites such as Furness Abbey.

96. *Britannia* 10 (1979), 353.

97. *RIB* 955 (Carlisle) and 787 (Brougham).

98. *RIB* 856; see Jarrett, 1954.

99. Penney and Shotter, 1996 and 2001; Shotter, forthcoming, in *Archaeology North-West*.

100. See Matthews, 2001, 21ff.

101. Edwards, 1971.

102. See Lambert *et al.*, 1996, 87ff.

103. For example, Higham and Jones, 1975.

104. Jones, 1974, 153.

105. Much remains unclear regarding the purpose and organisation of this site; post-excavation study continues.

106. Thompson, 1965, 97–100.

107. Thompson, 1965, 73–87; Grealey, 1976; Hinchliffe and Williams, 1992; Strickland, 1995.

108. Webster, P.V., 1975.

109. *Britannia* 15 (1984), 286.

110. Dearne and Lord, 1998.

111. T.C. Lord, *pers. comm.*

112. Percival, 1976.

113. Branigan, 1980.

114. For Kirk Sink, see *Britannia* 5 (1974), 416 and 6 (1975), 238; for Eaton-by-Tarporley, see *Britannia* 13 (1982), 353, and Mason, forthcoming.

115. King, 1978.

116. Middleton, Wells and Huckerby, 1995, 70f.

117. Richmond, 1945.

118. *RIB* 600; see also Mann, 2002.

119. See Richardson A. (1982) for discussion of an area around the fort at Old Penrith.

120. For a discussion of the Iron Age in the area, see Matthews, 2001, 4ff.

121. Lowndes, 1963 and 1964.

122. See, for example, distribution-maps as in Higham, 1980, 42; Potter, 1979, 355; Matthews, 2001, 2.

123. Bowman and Thomas, 1983; Birley, Birley and Birley, 1993; Tomlin, 1998.

124. Higham and Jones, 1975; Higham, 1986; Haselgrove, 1996; Cowell and Philpott, 2000. Note, for example, recent work on a curvilinear enclosure at Dutton's Farm (Lathom), though for a general assessment of west Lancashire, see Cowell and Philpott, 2000, 178ff. In contrast, recent work at Mellor (Stockport) suggests the likelihood of complex development of the site and its vicinity (N. Redhead and J. Roberts. *pers. comm.*)

125. Jones, 1979, 79ff; Cowell and Philpott, 2000; for a site at Salford, see *Britannia* 20 (1989), 281.

126. *Yorks. Arch. Journ.* 41 (1966), 559–560; King, 1978.

127. Higham and Jones, 1975; Higham, 1978; 1979; 1980; 1982. For Glencoyne Park, see Hoaen and Loney, 2003.

128. Jones G.D.B., 1975; Bowman and Thomas, 1983; Davies, 1971; Manning, 1975.

129. Richardson G.G.S., 1977, 57.

130. Lowndes, 1963 and 1964; Higham, 1979; Shotter and White, 1995, 58ff.

131. Pennington, 1970.

132. E.g. Aughertree Fell (Bellhouse, 1967).

133. Higham and Jones, 1975, 40ff; Higham, 1979, 34.

134. Blake, 1959, 7ff.

135. Higham, 1980, 41.

136. *Britannia* 8 (1977), 377; Also Higham and Jones, 1983.

137. King, 1978.

138. Richardson G.G.S., 1977.

139. Richmond, 1933; Higham, 1979.

140. Cowell and Philpott, 2000.

141. Manning, 1975.

142. For example, in the physical relationship between properties of Romano-British *vicus* and medieval burgage-plots (Rachel Newman *pers. comm.*).

CHAPTER SEVEN

The Later Years

At one time, it was customary to see 'the end of Roman Britain' as a relatively clear-cut event: faced by mounting crises in Europe, the Roman administration and army were pulled out of Britain early in the fifth century A.D. and the British formally abandoned by the emperor, Honorius, when he instructed them 'to look to their own defence'.[1] For their part, it was believed, the British were relieved to be free of the burden of Rome and resumed a lifestyle they had been persuaded to abandon nearly four centuries previously. This caricature has gradually crumbled, and in its place a very different picture has been emerging largely as a result of new archaeological evidence which has prompted major re-assessments.

******

We saw (in chapter 5) that, early in the third century, the emperor, Septimius Severus by armed force, and then his elder son, Caracalla, by 'diplomacy', achieved some measure of *détente* with the tribes of Caledonia. This seems to have brought about on the northern frontier, at least, a considerable period of peace which lasted for much of the third century. Our understanding of the effects of this on the military grip on northern Britain is, however, less straightforward. We lack literary source-material of any quality; the chronology of pottery is less precisely-known than it is for the first and second centuries; further, the coin-evidence is far less reliable in the third and fourth centuries, being complicated by deepening political and monetary crises and by the introduction in the late-third century of the *annona militaris* – the practice of paying troops, at least partly, in kind.

The coastal defences of Cumbria (with the exception of the forts) were probably not in general use in the third century, although a few sites have yielded coins of that period. Building-inscriptions and other evidence of building activity indicate that some forts were being kept in repair in the first half of the third century (for example, at Ribchester, Manchester, Lancaster, Watercrook, Old Carlisle, Old Penrith).[2] The second half of the century, however, presents a more confused picture.

The existence of a civilian authority, in the form of the *civitas Carvetiorum*, is certainly attested by the middle of the century,[3] and may, in fact, have been inaugurated in the Severan period, or soon after. Such an institution, which had its centre (*civitas*-capital) at Carlisle, implies internal peace in the north west and security from outside attack. It also indicates a desire to place more of the burden of local administration on to the local population, although it is likely that such a *civitas*, established in what was still, in part at least, within a military zone, shared the task with local military commanders. The establishment of the *civitas* is also an indication of the level of loyalty and of wealth to be found in the population of the north west, particularly at the upper end of the social ladder. This new tier of administration may have allowed some forts in the north to be demilitarised, or at least to be manned at reduced levels.

This appears to have happened at Hardknott[4] and Watercrook[5]: at the latter, a fresh coin of A.D. 320 in the top of the ditch-fill implies demilitarisation by the early-fourth century at the latest. Some forts on Hadrian's Wall (for example, Castlesteads and Birdoswald) and, indeed, parts of the Wall itself fell into a state of considerable disrepair, although it is possible that some forts were held by token-garrisons rather than being completely abandoned. It has been suggested that the new, smaller type of barrack-block shown to have been built at Housesteads, Birdoswald and other wall-forts in the early-fourth century implies a reduced or, perhaps, a less well-organised garrison – or perhaps even a population which comprised both military personnel and civilians.

In addition, the Severan period saw major changes in the nature and role of the army, as it became not just the supporter of the government, but its very backbone. These changes are echoed by the advice allegedly given to his sons by Severus: 'Look after the army .... and ignore the rest'.[6] The practical effect of this was an army whose command-structure comprised increasingly men who had risen through the army's own ranks rather than deriving, as previously, from men of superior social status. This change, which also acted to place senior administrative posts in the hands of men of equestrian, rather than senatorial, rank, may well have had an adverse effect upon military discipline. Further, regular legionary and auxiliary troops were now being increasingly supplemented by units of irregulars – a development of Hadrian's plan to bring in 'special skills' from men often recruited at or beyond the borders of the empire. In these circumstances, the more peaceful conditions evident in the north may have served to produce a relaxed, if not lax, holding of north-west England in the second half of the third century.

Thus, although the provinces of Britain were probably less troubled during this period by their external enemies, internal difficulties began to prove even more disruptive. The 'principle' of promotion through the ranks of the army led to heightened expectations on the part of many: anarchy began to become an endemic problem, leading in the middle of the century to a stream of 'pretenders' to imperial power. At the same time, such anarchic rivalry led to hyper-inflation through the 'printing of money' to support individuals' ambitious personal plans. Through the first half of the third century, the currency came close to collapse: many lower denominations of coin became useless and disappeared, whilst the *denarius* was progressively debased in terms of silver-content, falling to approximately 50% purity at the turn of the second and third centuries until its disappearance from circulation in the 240s. Its double and 'successor', the debased *antoninianus*, had itself by the 250s become a copper coin of variable size and quality. Inflation produced a situation where the mints could not keep up with the 'demand' for coins, leading to the large-scale local copying of these coins, often of execrable quality: the so-called 'barbarous radiates' were often very small, with blundered and illiterate legends and unrecognisable imperial portraits on their obverses and 'matchstick' figures of gods and personifications on their reverses. This, two-and-a-half centuries on, was the fate of the coin-system introduced by Augustus Caesar. The coinage, indeed, told the empire's story plainly enough.

In what looked like near-terminal collapse, the empire began to witness splits and breakaway-movements: Britain was involved in two of these – the *Imperium Galliarum* ('Independent Empire of the Gauls'), initiated by Postumus in A.D. 259, and, some years later (in A.D. 286), the rebellion of Carausius and Allectus.[7] Such splits were inevitably damaging, leading to the removal of troops from their 'proper' duties and general demoralisation; former friends and enemies probably found themselves on opposite sides of a battle between 'loyalists' (that is, supporters of the legitimate emperor) and rebels. Such battles perhaps led to physical violence: why, for example, did the bath-house and *basilica* at Lancaster require complete rebuilding in the 260s?[8] Who was the 'enemy' who killed the military clerk, Flavius Romanus, inside his fort at Ambleside?[9] When the Gallic rebellion was brought to an end in A.D. 273 by Aurelian, the bitterness of feeling is again evident in the crude removal of rebel-emperors' names from standing inscriptions.[10]

A slow recovery of order appears to have begun in the early-270s, although judging by the rarity of coins of legitimate emperors of the last quarter of the third century, Britain seems to have responded only slowly; indeed, Carausius' rebellion in A.D. 286 appears to demonstrate this. Diocletian, 'the greatest statesman of the Decline', came to power in A.D. 284; recognising that the anarchy of earlier years demonstrated the ungovernability of the Roman Empire as a single entity, he split the imperial rule between himself (in the east) and Maximian (in the west). Straightaway, Carausius, a naval commander in Britain, who had been appointed by Maximian to keep the English Channel and the North Sea free of pirates, issued coins with three heads on the obverse side – his own, Diocletian's and Maximian's – inside the legend, CARAVSIVS ET

FRATRES SVI ('Carausius and his brothers').[11] It was effectively a claim to be part of a kind of 'institutionalised anarchy'. Diocletian and Maximian, however, failed to accept Carausius as their 'brother', leaving him as *ipso facto* in a state of rebellion. Carausius, who seems to have presented himself as almost a Messianic figure, maintained his rebellion until his murder in A.D. 293 by his associate, Allectus, who survived until he was ousted three years later by the central government in the person of Constantius Chlorus (Constantius I).

The details of this rebellion do not concern us except in so far as to note that it was a period in which attention was paid to the problems of coastal defence.[12] Although not of uniform date, the Saxon-Shore fort system in the south east – from the Wash to Southampton Water – owed a good deal of its impetus to this period; Allectus' 'Galley' coin-reverses[13] stress a similar preoccupation. The new forts were architecturally very different from their predecessors, particularly with their artillery-bastions, and indicate a transition of the fort in Roman tactical thinking from the 'police-station' to the 'defended strong-point'.

At the empire's centre also, this was a time of great change: in A.D. 294, Diocletian inaugurated his tetrarchic system, in which the empire, now subdivided into four parts, would be ruled by four men; two of these, Diocletian himself and Maximian, were senior figures, entitled *Augustus*, and ruled respectively the eastern and western halves of the empire. These halves were subdivided again and quarters taken by two 'junior-emperors' with the title of *Caesar*; these posts were occupied by Galerius (in the east) and Constantius Chlorus (in the west). Diocletian and Maximian achieved a degree of lofty remoteness for themselves by assuming the titles respectively of *Jovius* ("Jupiter's Own") and *Herculius* ("Hercules' Own"). The tetrarchy was excessively bureaucratic with a system of retirements (of *Augusti*) and promotions (of *Caesares*), which did not pass its first 'test' in A.D. 306. Out of the ensuing chaos, Constantius' son, Constantine I, achieved undisputed control first of all (in A.D. 312) in the west, and later (in A.D. 324) over the whole reunited empire.

Diocletian's reforming zeal[14] also set about restoring the soundness of the coinage, the territorial integrity of the provinces as well as separating, for the first time in Rome's 1000–year history, the military and civilian command-structures. He and Constantine also initiated major reform of the Roman army.

Britain had been divided into two provinces by Septimius Severus; a further sub-division now took place, this time into four provinces – *Britannia Prima*, *Britannia Secunda*, *Maxima Caesariensis*, *Flavia Caesariensis*, each of them governed by an equestrian official, entitled *praeses*. Together, these four provinces made up a *diocese* under a *vicarius* who was responsible to the Praetorian Prefect of the Gauls; he, in his turn, was responsible to the western *Caesar*, Constantius Chlorus. It seems likely that the *vicarius* was based in London, as it is there that the *Notitia Dignitatum* places the officer who was presumably the fourth-century equivalent of the *Procurator Augusti* of earlier years.[15] The British provinces represented four out of a total which now reached 120. The *praesides* of the four provinces were in charge of civilian affairs, whilst new military commands were created: the *Dux Britanniarum* ('Duke of the Britains') had control of frontier troops, though this appears to have referred principally to the northern frontier; later, the forts of the Saxon Shore came under the *Comes Litoris Saxonici* ('Count of the Saxon Shore'); the post of *comes* was, however, a Constantinian creation, though it is thought by some that the Saxon Shore originally came under a *dux*. This swelling bureaucracy, augmented by political agents, imposed a considerable extra burden upon the tax-payers and probably made life particularly difficult for the elders of the *civitates*. For Diocletian, this fragmentation of power in the provinces was reassuring, as it will have made it much more difficult for potential rebels to gather support.

The changes to the organisation of the army were also far-reaching: the Augustan structure, which had remained broadly in place for three centuries, was now completely replaced. In future, there were two types of troops: the *Comitatenses* (or 'Mobile Field Armies') which were attached to each imperial personage, and detachments of which could be sent to emergencies in provinces in each emperor's area of responsibility. The *Limitanei* (or 'border-troops') were posted to the frontiers in relevant provinces. This reform meant the splitting up of units of the older type: the mobile field armies contained the better troops, whilst the *limitanei* consisted of remnants, often of only mediocre quality, of legions and auxiliaries, together with irregular units. Despite this, the *Notitia Dignitatum* in its sub-section, 'Also, Along the Line of the Wall',[16] seems to suggest that, in the fourth century, the Wall was manned by the same auxiliary units as indicated by the third-century inscriptions. This, however, probably tells us more about the method of compilation of the *Notitia* than it does about the manning of Hadrian's Wall in the fourth century.

The interpretation of the military situation in the late-third and early-fourth centuries on Hadrian's Wall and in the north in general gives rise to difficulties: it has been thought that an effect of Allectus' attempts to hold his rebel-island against the tetrarchs was the denuding of northern garrisons, leading to an attack on the frontier from the north. It is true that our accounts, mostly in contemporary *Panegyrics*[17] of Constantius, place most activity in the south, especially around London: this, for example, is the chief thrust of the gold medallion, found at Arras, which shows a kneeling personification of *Londinium* waiting to greet Constantius as he disembarked. Despite this, however, it would appear that the bulk of the work was done by Constantius' praetorian prefect, Asclepiodotus. There is certainly evidence for both demolition and dilapidation in the north in the late-third century, and for fire-damage at Ravenglass. An inscription records Constantius' involvement in rebuilding at Birdoswald,[18] and other forts of Hadrian's Wall and the hinterland certainly saw reconstruction in the early-fourth century.[19] But no evidence points unequivocally to coherent enemy-attack at that time.

Constantius was in Britain on at least two occasions – in 296, with Asclepiodotus, to crush the 'British rebellion' and again campaigning in the north in A.D. 305–306 against the Picts who now make their first appearance in the history of Roman Britain. It seems that the name, which means simply 'the Painted Ones', was a generic title given to a grouping of tribes who at one point had been referred to as the Caledonians and others,[20] whilst Ammianus Marcellinus indicates that they were made up of two peoples – the *Dicalydonae* and the *Verturiones*.[21] The situation recalls the relationship a century earlier between the *Caledones* and the *Maeatae*.

The dating of this rebuilding work is rather unclear, although it is generally seen as resulting from Constantius' supervision of Britain. However, as Frere has noted,[22] the coins which provide much of the dating-evidence may be misleading because of our problems in understanding the supply of new coins to Britain at the turn of the third and fourth centuries. Tetrarchic coins of good quality are not common as site-finds in northern Britain, and so the area may have been having to extend its use of earlier coins, at least until the second decade of the fourth century.

Plate 7.1:
Housesteads: Fourth century 'chalet'-barracks

At any rate, rebuilding, even if extending over a slightly longer period, touched sites on Hadrian's Wall, as well as Pennine forts, such as Brough-by-Bainbridge. Recent work at Housesteads has demonstrated that the third-century barrack-block in the fort's north-east corner had probably decayed, and was replaced by a far less 'formal' unit consisting of 'chalets' of variable size and internal arrangement, which were probably built of stone only to half-height. The new type of barracks is presumably to be taken as indicating a different kind of usage from that for which the building's predecessor was intended – perhaps a combination of civilians and military personnel,[23] although it has been observed that such 'domestic' artefacts as needles, which have sometimes been taken to indicate the presence of women in forts, should not in a military context necessarily be regarded as 'gender-specific'. Alternatively, the changes in buildings may reflect the use of military units rather different from earlier times;[24] in any case, these buildings do suggest that the size of garrisons in the forts may have been shrinking; this would not be surprising in the light of the likely effects upon provincial garrisons of the military reforms of Diocletian and Constantine.

Rebuilding also affected other internal buildings in forts: the residences of fort-commanders (*praetoria*) may suggest enhanced local status on the part of commanders, as at Binchester, Housesteads, Vindolanda and South Shields in the early-fourth century.[25] At Birdoswald, the early fourth-century *praetorium* appears to have replaced part of a barrack-block,[26] and a new aisled building may have been a drill-hall for cavalry (*basilica equestris exercitatoria*). Such activities appear to suggest changes not only within the army but also in the significance

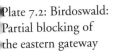

Plate 7.2: Birdoswald: Partial blocking of the eastern gateway

of individual forts: the notion of 'defence-in-depth' may have been coming to supersede the idea of the Wall as a 'curtain-barrier'. Indeed, the Wall itself, as distinct from its forts, may have been less important in the fourth-century arrangements.[27]

In A.D. 315, the emperor, Constantine I (son of Constantius Chlorus), took the title of *Britannicus Maximus*; a particular point of reference is not known, although it may have had some relation to the west coast,[28] or possibly to a continued attention to in-depth readiness, for which Constantine was, in fact, criticised in antiquity.[29] Behind the theory lay the assumption – easier perhaps to contemplate than to put into practice – that enemy-attacks would gradually be absorbed and eventually turned by the forts of the frontier and its hinterland.

As we have seen, the political, economic and military stability, which had been the principal objectives of Diocletian's reforms, did not long outlast him. Although Constantine did restore a unified authority over the empire, the evidence regarding the state of the British provinces in the fourth century is replete with inconsistencies:[30] many of the larger towns,[31] for example, appear somewhat 'run down', although this may be less a product of 'malicious neglect' than of an enforced 'desertion of responsibilities' on the part of some civic leaders, as increased taxes hit them hard, along with what must have been the crippling expense of providing their towns with defensive wall-circuits.

On the other hand, the major development of some villas in the south and south west – for example, at Lullingstone (Kent), Bignor (West Sussex), and Woodchester, Chedworth and Turkdean (Gloucestershire) – appears to point to a period of considerable, if localised, prosperity, especially in the earlier part of the fourth century; the evidence of the not-totally trustworthy *Panegyrici Latini*, together with the presence, possibly at Winchester, of a 'Procurator of Weaving', suggests that the basis of this prosperity may have been sheep-farming.[32] Such would also serve to explain the evidently growing prosperity of that major Cotswold town, Cirencester (*Corinium Dobunnorum*), which had been selected under the Diocletianic reforms as the capital of one of Britain's four provinces (*Britannia Prima*). A further sign of prosperity in Britain in the fourth century is to be seen in its ability to respond to a crisis in 359 on the Rhine-frontier by filling six hundred transport-ships with men and supplies.[33]

After the death in 337 of Constantine I, however, the overall picture again became less encouraging: there was renewed civil war, first in the 340s between Constantine's three sons and then in the 350s between Constantius II and Magnentius; both of these episodes affected Britain. Further, the visit to Britain of Constans in the *winter* of A.D. 342–343,[34] having in mind the antipathy of most Romans, even at the best of times, to sea-travel, surely points to the existence in Britain of an emergency of some kind.

Coming as it did so soon after the death of Constantine II and with the inevitability of a confrontation to come between Constans and Constantius II, it seems likely that the nature of the emergency on this occasion may have had more to do with disaffection amongst the troops in Britain. However, it seems that Constans' visit was in part, at least, concerned with the *areani* (or 'undercover-agents'); so we should also bear in mind that the 'Conspiracy of the Barbarians' of A.D. 367 was the climax to developing security-problems and that there were probably outbreaks of trouble in the years leading up to it. Since the 'Conspiracy' is known to have involved the Scotti (from Ireland), it is not inconceivable that Constans had to give attention to security in the west of Britain.

Thus, it is possible that we should date to this period the development of the west-coast 'Saxon-Shore' forts, although reliable dates are not to hand for Cardiff, Caernarfon or Caer Gybi. The new fort at Lancaster, however, would seem to date from the second quarter of the fourth century. It is difficult to say how far a *coherent* west-coast defence system existed;[35] however, the Bristol Channel appears to have taken on a naval significance, at least later in the century, as has been suggested on the basis of the letters PR REL (interpreted as an abbreviation of *Praefectus Reliquationis Classis* or 'Prefect of the Remainder of the Fleet'), which was found incorporated into a mosaic in the temple of Nodons at Lydney (Gloucestershire). This, together with the new forts, stresses the importance – and the vulnerability – of the Welsh coasts; it is further likely that it was the development of a fleet-base on the Bristol Channel which will have rendered redundant the legionary fortress at Caerleon,[36]

ate 7.3: Caer Gybi:
ourth-century fort

which does not appear to have outlasted the third century *as a legionary base*, at least. In any case, fourth-century evidence appears to connect legion II *Augusta* with the Saxon-Shore forts of the south east.

The Bristol Channel base will have linked to the still-maintained legionary fortress at Chester,[37] on the Dee-estuary, and thence to Lancaster on the Lune-estuary. It seems likely that, in the 330s/340s, an approximately nine-acre enclosure with polygonal corner bastions was built at Lancaster on an alignment totally different from that of earlier forts.[38] Excavations have also suggested[39] the abandonment at about this time of buildings in the extramural settlement at Lancaster. Another sign of the current naval pre-occupations may be seen in the discovery at Cockersands Moss, just south of Lancaster, of two statues (now lost) of the god, Nodons (Nodens).[40] This god provides a tentative link between Lancaster and Lydney and the Bristol Channel.

In what must have been an increasingly disturbed situation, it is unclear how long life could have been maintained at a reasonable standard in extramural settlements which were largely undefended. Obviously, the length of life of an extramural settlement will have represented a response to local conditions, thus precluding the establishment of a date of general application to the north west. At Ribchester, for example, changing environmental conditions, leading to flooding, may have forced the closure of parts, at least, of the extramural settlement as early as the late-second century; similar problems may have

Plate 7.4: Lancaster: 'Wery Wall': bastion of the fourth-centur fort (arrowed)

afflicted the site at Watercrook. As we have seen, recent excavations at Lancaster have suggested that buildings in the extramural settlement may have been in the process of abandonment in the mid-fourth century, leading to the possible relocation of inhabitants in the new fort on Castle Hill. Little is known of the interior of this fort, though its use by a mixed population of soldiers and civilians does not seem out of the question: in this way, social change may have been similar to what we have already seen was possibly occurring in the frontier-zone. The discovery of large numbers of fourth-century coins close to the *principia*-buildings in the forts at both Carlisle and Newcastle-upon-Tyne suggests their possible use, in part at least, as local commercial centres.

In a fast-changing situation, where most aspects of life were becoming dominated by instability, flexibility may well have been a key-concept. Vegetius,[41] for example, describes camouflaged scout-ships (*pictae*) which were used in the fourth century around Britain – presumably as a kind of 'early-warning system'. Lancaster and Morecambe Bay, too, may have seen novel use made of the soldiers of a *Numerus Barcariorum* – probably not those mentioned in the *Notitia Dignitatum* at South Shields (*Numerus Barcariorum Tigrisiensium*)[42] – whose normal function may be presumed to have been lighterage.

Arrangements further north on the coast are not easy to describe precisely: the coastal forts of Ravenglass, Moresby, Maryport and Beckfoot were all evidently occupied in the fourth century, although in the cases of Moresby and Beckfoot, it is not clear how long that occupation was sustained. Burrow Walls (Workington)[43] has produced little other than fourth-century pottery, and may well have been a new – or substantially re-modelled – fort of the period. There appears to have been fourth-century re-occupation of some of the presumably long-abandoned sites of the Hadrianic coastal-system; at Cardurnock (MF 5), for example, pottery suggested occupation both before and after A.D. 367; Blitterlees (MF 12) and Low Mire (MF 20) perhaps shared in it, although the absence of such material from Biglands (MF 1) and Swarthy Hill (MF 21) is sufficient to warn us that we cannot by any means assume a full-scale recommissioning. Similarly, re-occupation has been suggested for some of the towers also (for example, Wolsty North (T 13a) and Cote How (T 16b[44]).

Throughout the 340s and early-350s, internal troubles – that is, amongst army-personnel – will have been simmering. As we have seen, the deaths of Constantine II in 340 and of Constans (at the hands of Magnentius) in 350 highlight the constant rivalry for power, and the fact that the army in Britain was deeply involved in it. Because of the frequency of his coins, it appears that the rebel, Magnentius, had particular strength in Britain, and that he probably weakened the provinces' military potential by taking troops to Europe to assert his cause. Magnentius' eventual defeat in 353 at the hands of Constantius II will have brought further demoralisation to Britain in its wake and, in all probability, a witch-hunt in Britain as the uncongenial Constantius re-asserted his authority.[45]

In A.D. 355, Constantius appointed as western *Caesar* his cousin, Julian (the Apostate). Although Julian's period in Germany showed the underlying strength of Britain in its ability to provide the materials necessary to re-establish the Rhine-frontier, yet less than two years later the continuing insecurity manifested itself in trouble with the Picts and Scotti (from Ireland), which necessitated the posting to Britain of Lupicinus with a section of a 'field army'. The defining moment in the process of change appears to have been the so-called 'Conspiracy of the Barbarians' of A.D. 367,[46] in which Britain seems to have been hit by a coherent (and presumably collusive) attack mounted by all her current enemies, including those who were serving in the army in a 'frontier-security' role in the north (*areani* or *arcani*). Such an apparently unlikely event as a 'Conspiracy', the term used of it by Ammianus, is made perhaps less unlikely when it is appreciated how deep was the involvement of Romanised 'barbarians' in Roman political and military affairs. It is possible that 'leaked' information regarding the contemporary difficulties of the emperor, Valentinian I, was the trigger for this action:[47] the opportunity was evidently enhanced by the treacherous activities of the *areani*,[48] who were disbanded in the wake of the catastrophe, together with the closing of the 'outpost-forts' on the western end of the frontier.

 Valentinian's response was to send to Britain, again with a 'field army', Theodosius, the father of the later emperor of the same name. Ammianus makes it clear that the situation in Britain – military, urban and rural – was one of almost-total disarray. Some care, however, is required: we should beware of assuming that every archaeological sign of trouble relates to this particular year; as we have seen, the events of 367 were probably the climax of nearly two-and-a-half decades of uncertainty and raiding. Similarly, although Theodosius was undoubtedly responsible for rebuilding in the wake of the disaster, it should be borne in mind that, from the 360s, close-dating of archaeological material itself becomes more hazardous, particularly as supplies of pottery and coinage to sites became more erratic.

As we shall see, some of the work which is ascribed to Theodosius after 367 may have been the product of local initiatives over a somewhat longer period. Nonetheless, the work of recovery was probably considerable, although the absence of certain pottery-types may indicate that some sites – for example, Ribchester and Watercrook, as well as the 'outpost-forts' on the frontier – were not recovered. In addition, it has been stressed that many sites in the north west have not seen recent excavation, and statements about the chronology of their occupations lack the support of reliable evidence.

The hand of Theodosius may be detected in certain developments – for example, the construction of watchtowers on the north-east coast, perhaps from South Shields to Filey, although it is possible that the inception of some of these could have been earlier.[49] Forts in the north west, which were reconstructed in this period show no sign of the 'Saxon-Shore' architecture which had been employed in Wales and at Lancaster earlier in the century; there are, however, some features that are common to many of them. The blocking or narrowing of gateways, for example, which has been recognised at a number of northern forts – Birdoswald, for example – may have been 'learned' from the 'new architecture' of the Saxon-Shore forts. Similarly, Ravenglass and Bowness-on-Solway[50] have both shown that a changed constructional technique for internal buildings was employed in their final phase; instead of foundations consisting of horizontal 'sleeper-beams', buildings were apparently supported on a 'frame' of heavily-packed posts, a technique which has some similarities with buildings which have recently been closely studied at the fort of Birdoswald.[51] There is also evidence for new sites: two fortlets guard the road south from Carlisle – at Wreay Hall and Barrock Fell, though little is known of them;[52] recent research has indicated the possibility of another such site at Cummersdale.[53] Coin-finds may also suggest the possibility of further coastal sites of this type and period awaiting discovery at locations such as Barrow-in-Furness and Muncaster Castle.[54]

It is reasonable to suppose that the application of the honorific titles of *Augusta,* to London, and *Valentia,* perhaps to the British provinces as a whole, was intended to reflect official celebration of Britain's survival of the 'Conspiracy of the Barbarians'.[55] Indeed, the historian, Ammianus Marcellinus, appears to suggest that this interpretation of *Valentia* is to be preferred to the alternative, canvassed by more recent historians, involving the creation of an otherwise-unattested fifth British province.

As we have seen, the nature of the evidence of activity in the north west in the later-fourth century points away from the adoption of homogeneous explanations; indeed, the last *coherent* work may have been the extension of a 'Saxon-Shore' system on to the west coast. It is possible that the kind of very selective re-occupation that we have seen at certain sites of the Hadrianic coastal system could conceivably have been the work of local groups, who were in no way part of an overarching plan, but following their own initiatives to suit their own purposes and local circumstances. Although there may in the later years of the fourth century have been occasional reminders of the politics of earlier times – as when, in 382, Magnus Maximus took troops from Britain to assert a personal claim to power reminiscent of the *Imperium Galliarum,* or

when, in 398, Honorius evidently sent his general, Stilicho, to Britain[56] –
connections between Britain and the empire were becoming more
tenuous. The most recent interpretation of late-Roman evidence from
Birdoswald, however, presents a strong case for the emergence of groups
under the leadership of powerful individuals, reminiscent of pre-Roman
warlords; such local militias are perfectly comprehensible in the light of a
decision, made earlier in the fourth century, that military service should
become hereditary; a blurring of the distinction between soldiers and
civilians was an inevitable outcome of this.

The later years of the fourth century saw not a sudden withdrawal of
Roman administration, but rather its gradual withering, with a decline
and eventual loss of supplies of pottery and coinage as its most obvious
manifestation; army units went unpaid and taxes were no longer
collected. There will no doubt have been differing reactions to this crisis[57]
in the life and stability of Roman Britain: some, particularly perhaps the
civitas-leaders of the south, were probably looking for a re-emergence of
Roman control and, thereby, a resumption of their place in a familiar,
structured, world, – a hope which evidently some continued to entertain
into the middle years of the fifth century.[58] Others were more realistic:
perhaps influenced by the Pelagian heresy, which is known to have been
seen as a problem in the later years of Roman Britain, and which denied
the act of Divine Grace, arguing instead that 'man was the master of his
own salvation', they realised that the only way of defending their lifestyle
was by their own efforts; nor did they shrink from 'direct action' (as
suggested by Zosimus), if they thought that their cause demanded it. The
latest structural phases identified at Birdoswald seem to accord with the
presence there of men of such sentiments; in other words, despite the
failure of the administration, armed groups were still present in the forts,
and farmers in the hinterlands of the forts.

The internal re-modelling of Birdoswald during the second half of the
fourth century, involving the loss of granary-space, which was now
evidently considered to be redundant, suggests that the fort was
becoming more closely akin to a warlord's stronghold. Initially, on the
site of the south granary, refurbishment saw a structure with two
successive phases of hearths at the western end. Around these were found
various 'high-status' personal possessions, which pointed to the existence
at the site of the kind of social milieu that we might associate with a
warlord. Following the collapse of this building, the first phase of a new
and enlarged 'hall' was constructed at some time after *c.* A.D. 390; the
second, larger, phase of this sat astride the northern half of the north
granary and the southern side of the *via principalis*. This timber building,
the life of which must have extended well into the fifth century, occupied
the most prominent position in the fort: following the blocking of the
southern carriageway of the west gate, the narrowed access-road ran

adjacent to the 'hall', making it the first building to be encountered after entry into the fort. Today, the conserved outline marked by tree-trunks represents the second – Anglo-Saxon – phase of this building. Again, the appearance of a warrior-based society could hardly be more obvious, providing some justification for Higham's description of the events of this period as representing a 'return to tribalism'.[59]

In its own way, therefore, the fort at Birdoswald represents a Romano-British reaction to signs of a rapidly-failing Roman involvement. It is interesting that, although in different ways, later Roman military sites of the northern frontier and of the Saxon Shore were taking on characteristics that are more obviously recognisable as 'medieval'. The re-modelling of the fort's interior also points to the existence of a situation where the 'progression' of the fort-commander to local warlord was complete, as was that of the Roman auxiliary unit to a local militia, acting without reference to any overall plan or strategy imposed from above. It would, therefore, appear likely that the 'warlord' headed a militia (or community) which offered protection to local people in return for food and other goods; in other words, the taxation-system had lapsed, only to be replaced by a locally-operated 'protection-racket'. As already noted, it may be the case that fragmentary evidence from some other sites in the north west suggests the possibility of similar structural – and thus social – developments over a wider area, although still not working to any coherent plan.

late 7.5: Birdoswald: ater 'hall-building' narked by larger pright timbers), craddling the *Via rincipalis* and the orthern granary

2nd larger timber hall

Plate 7.6:
Birdoswald: Later
'hall-building' (as
seen from the fort's
interior). Reproduced
by courtesy of
Birdoswald Roman
Fort

The increasingly tenuous nature of contact between Roman Britain
and the Roman Empire is clear as we enter the fifth century A.D; no
further supplies of money to pay the army (or what was left of it) after
about A.D. 402, and evidence grows of an increasing sense of
independence within Britain – not just at sites such as Birdoswald, but
more widely. The latter years of the century's first decade saw a new series
of 'local' emperors elevated by the army, which we may assume to have
been the army's response to the failing support from the centre. To this
may be linked the action in 408 of independently-minded Britons,
perhaps followers of the Pelagian heresy, in expelling Roman officials and
organising the defence of Britain themselves. This was clearly not a
universal view, as others hoped for a renewal and strengthening of links
with the rest of the empire.

The 'independents', however, had been wise: there was to be no more
help from Rome, and Britain's formal place in the empire had now
lapsed. Although the emperor Honorius' famous rescript of A.D. 410 is
now thought not to have been directed towards Britain, the effect of
what was happening in Britain was much the same. The actions of the
'independents' should not, however, be taken as indicating a rejection of
everything Roman. The rejection was political; the inhabitants of Britain
after all, whether supporting or opposing Rome's current position, were
Romano-British. As many excavations,[60] particularly of the towns, have
shown, the people clearly remained for a considerable time, though
perhaps in varying degrees, within the Roman cultural orbit; as at
Birdoswald, Roman buildings were being re-used – as was the case with
the baths-*basilica* at Wroxeter – for current purposes. In general,
however, the physical fate of north-western sites can only be the subject

of guesswork, particularly since the means of dating within the fifth century are far from perfect: the repairing of chronologically-late vessels, worn coins of late fourth-century date and finds of Byzantine coins and vessels of African red-slip ware, all suggest a continuing attempt to retain in some degree the familiar way of life and the maintenance of contact with parts of what had been 'the Roman world'. Christianity, although not always a politically and militarily unifying force, will nonetheless have provided a link with Rome's cultural background, and perhaps, as has been shown recently in the case of the Cheshire salt-industry, some semblance of local organisation.[61]

In the north west, as elsewhere, we may reasonably imagine, therefore, that Roman fortifications continued to provide protection – particularly if we judge from sites like Lancaster, Brough and Brougham, where the medieval castles were erected in some kind of association with the presumably still-surviving Roman rampart-circuits.

For long-term survival, therefore, sites of the Roman period needed to have a significance that transcended their mere place in the Roman defensive network. Such will explain the survival of sites at crucial places on the road-system or adjacent to navigable waterways, as perhaps the fort at Low Borrow Bridge, which offered continued protection in remote and potentially dangerous places. Besides this, there were sites which offered a long-term hope of prosperity, as has been recently demonstrated by the discovery of a 'long-house' of the Viking period, situated on a Romano-British rural settlement at Gauber High Pasture in Upper Ribblesdale.[62] A striking view of how long-term this process might be is the recently-excavated site immediately to the south of the fort and

Plate 7.7: Gauber High Pasture: Viking-period 'long house' (entrances arrowed)

Plate 7.8: Muncaster Castle: *Solidus* of
Theodosius, A.D. 383–388

Plate 7.9: Carlisle (Scotch Street): *Solidus* of
Valentinian II, A.D. 388–392

extramural settlement at Maiden Castle-on-Stainmore, where the latest
structure on a site which shared both pre-Roman and Romano-British
activity was a cottage of the nineteenth century.[63]

Perhaps the north west's most significant signs of Romano-British
survival have come to light in recent excavations in Carlisle (particularly
at Blackfriars Street[64] and Scotch Street[65]). At the latter of these, a gold
solidus of Valentinian II (A.D. 388–392) was recovered from a bath-
building in a position which indicated that renovations on the site must
have continued well into the fifth century. At Blackfriars Street, a 'strip-
house' of Flavian origin demonstrated substantial repair-work, which was
dated by a worn, but stratified, copper coin of the 380s, and continued
usage until it was 'cut' by a timber-slot of seventh-century date on a
different alignment. Nor should we overlook the fact that, when St.
Cuthbert visited Carlisle in 685, he was shown elements of the town's
water supply-system, built in the Roman period and still functioning.[66]

Through the later-fourth and fifth centuries, therefore, we have
observed a decline in the degree of Roman military and administrative
commitment to the north west, and, with it, a declining ability on the
part of the population to continue in its established life-style. The people
of the north west, in both urban and rural contexts, must have been
thrown increasingly onto their own resources, with such elements of the
Roman army that remained probably disbanding and 'melting' in various
ways into the local community. The major preoccupation must now have
been self-provision; without the markets and protection which Roman
occupation had afforded, there was little else. Factionalism, no doubt, re-

emerged, directed principally at the ownership of resources; the 'Roman Interlude' was essentially over.

However, it seems likely that, as in other parts of Britain, the Romano-British of the north west continued to think of themselves as such, and retaining their culture in the best way that they could – until, that is, other pressures gradually caused them once again to 'become different without knowing it'.

Notes

1. Zosimus 6.10, 2; Salway, 1981, 442ff.

2. For the situation on Hadrian's Wall, see Breeze and Dobson, 2000, 216ff.

3. *Journ. Rom. St.* 55 (1965), 224.

4. Bidwell, Snape and Croom, 1999, 66.

5. Potter, 1979, 193.

6. Dio Cassius *History of Rome* 76.15, 2.

7. Casey, 1994.

8. *RIB* 605; see Shotter and White, 1990, 60–61. See also Welsby, 1980.

9. See *Journ. Rom. St.* 53 (1963), 160–164; Thorley, 2002; Shotter, 2003c.

10. For example, *RIB* 605 from Lancaster, showing the removal of the name of Postumus in two places; cf. *RIB* 949 from Carlisle showing the removal of the names (possibly) of Severus Alexander and his mother, Julia Mammaea.

11. *RIC* Vol. V (Carausius), p.550; note, for example, the almost Messianic EXPECTATE VENI ('O long-awaited one, come': *RIC* Vol. V (Carausius), p.483).

12. Maxfield, 1989; this book is a collection of essays by various authors deriving from a Conference held in 1989 at the University of Exeter. Also Mason, 2003, 149ff.

13. *RIC* Vol. V (Allectus), no.55ff.

14. Williams, 1985.

15. *Not. Dign. Occ.* 11. 37 (*Praepositus Thesaurorum Augustensium*).

16. Gillam, 1949.

17. Quoted in Casey, 1994, 192–197 (where the relevant passages are translated by R.S.O. Tomlin).

18. *RIB* 1912; Wilmott, 1996, 198ff.

19. Johnson, 1980, 83ff; Wilkes, 1965.

20. *Pan. Lat. Vet.* 6(7). 7, 2.

21. Ammianus Marcellinus 27.8, 5.

22. Frere, 1991, 334; Reece, 1991, 30f. Note that the large tetrarchic hoard from Kirksteads indicates that tetrarchic coins of good quality were not absent from the north (Shotter, 1990, 193–196).

23. Daniels, 1980; though see the comment, based upon evidence from Birdoswald, in Wilmott, 1997, 202; See also Wilmott, 2001, 115–116.

24. Holder, 1992, 96ff.

25. See Birley, Birley and Blake, 1999, 8f. At South Shields, the porch of the *praetorium* extended into the adjacent main street (Graeme Stobbs, *pers. comm.*).

26. Wilmott, 1996, 407.

27. Mann, 1974; Luttwak, 1976; Ferrill, 1991.

28. Eusebius *Life of Constantine* 1.8 and 25.

29. Zosimus 2.34.

30. For example, Ammianus Marcellinus 20.1, 1.

31. Esmonde Cleary, 1989, 66ff; Shotter, 2000d, 44–54; Hinton, 2000, 55–64.

32. Wild, 1970; Percival, 1976, 166ff; Salway, 1981, 656.

33. Salway, 1981, 359–360.

34. Julius Firmicus Maternus, *De Errore Profanarum Religionum* 28, 6. For the Roman view of when it was safe to sail, see Vegetius 4.39.

35. What was the relationship, for example, between the fort at Caer Gybi and the watchtower on Holyhead Mountain (Mason, 2003, 183)?

36. Boon, 1972, 62ff.

37. Mason, 2001, 193ff.

38. Shotter and White, 1990, 23ff; Shotter, 2001a, 23ff; the realignment of the fort may conceivably have related to a beaching-point in the area of what is now Damside Street.

39. Shotter and White, 1990, 36; Shotter, 2001a, 27.

40. *RIB* 616 and 617; Shotter, 1973; Shotter and White, 1995, 97f.

41. Vegetius 4.37: Vegetius' *Epitome of Military Science* is available in an annotated translation by N.P. Milner (Liverpool University Press, 1993).

42. *Not. Dign. Occ.* 40.22. At South Shields, the presence of bargemen from the Tigris presumably gave the site its fourth-century name (Arbeia, or 'Place of the Arabs').

43. Bellhouse, 1955; for a recently-reported late fourth-century coin-hoard from the area, see Caruana and Shotter, 2002.

44. Simpson and Hodgson, 1947; Bellhouse, 1989, 18ff.

45. Ammianus Marcellinus 14.5, 6–9; Hind, 1983, 1ff.

46. Ammianus Marcellinus 27.8 and 28.3; Hind, 1983.

47. Salway, 1981, 374f.

48. Ammianus Marcellinus 27.3, 8; Shotter, 1996, 121; Gillam, Jobey and Welsby, 1993; Austen, 1991.

49. Shotter, 1999c.

50. Potter, 1979.

51. Wilmott, 1996 and 2001. These recount and develop the important revisions of thinking that have emerged as a result of Wilmott's major excavations at Birdoswald in the 1980s and 1990s.

52. Wreay Hall (Bellhouse, 1953); Barrock Fell (Collingwood, 1931).

53. The late Professor Barri Jones, *pers comm*. A late site, adjacent to the earlier forts, could conceivably either have a military origin or be a Romano-British farm (*Britannia* 28 (1997), 415).

54. Shotter, 1990, 239ff.

55. Johnson, 1980, 98–99.

56. Johnson, 1980, 103; Miller, 1975.

57. Johnson, 1980, 104ff.

58. As is demonstrated by the plea to Aetius ('The Groans of the Britons') in *c.* A.D. 450 (Bede *History of the English Church and People* I.13).

59. Higham, 1986; for references to recent work, see footnote 51. Bede (*History of the English Church and People* I.12–14) describes in part the likely character of this 'warrior-society'.

60. For example, at Wroxeter (Barker, 1975).

61. See, for example, the case of the salt-proprietor, Flavius Viventius, at Shavington (Penney and Shotter, 1996 and 2001).

62. King, 1978.

63. Tom Clare, *pers. comm.*

64. McCarthy, 1990.

65. *Britannia* 20 (1989), 254f.

66. Bede *Life of St. Cuthbert* 27.

Dates, Emperors and Governors

Selective list of Romano-British dates

55–54 BC	Incursions of Julius Caesar
AD 43	Invasion of Britain; annexation of the south east
60–61	Rebellion of Boudica
c. 60–69	Increasing restlessness in the north; Roman intervention required
69	Roman civil war; breakdown of the treaty with Cartimandua
71–74	Annexation of the Brigantes by Cerialis and Agricola
77–83	Governorship of Agricola; annexation of Scotland
87	Withdrawal of a legion from Britain; evacuation of Scotland and development of Stanegate frontier; consolidation of occupation in north-west England
c. 110–120	Disturbances in northern Britain (?); further withdrawals of Roman troops (?)
118–119	Victories won under Pompeius Falco
121–122	Hadrian's visit to Britain; start of work on Hadrian's Wall and the coastal system
c. 125	Inception of 'fort phase' on Hadrian's Wall (completed by *c.* 138)
143	Renewed invasion of Scotland; building of the Antonine Wall
c. 157	Gradual reduction of occupation of the Antonine Wall
c. 160	Abandonment of the Antonine Wall; re-occupation of Hadrian's Wall and the coastal system. Evidence of instability in the north
180	Governorship of Ulpius Marcellus; disturbances in the north
192	Death of the emperor, Commodus; renewed political instability; eventual emergence of Septimius Severus (197)
209–211	Severus in Britain; campaigns in northern Scotland, leading to an 'accommodation' with the Scottish tribes
c. 250	Beginning of fortification of the east coast
259–273	'Independent Empire of the Gauls'; establishment of *civitas* of the Carvetii (?)
287–296	Rebellion in Britain of Carausius and Allectus

c. 306   Refurbishment of northern sites against hostilities from Scotland

c. 330–340 West-coast defences put in hand; increasing instability in the north

351–353   Rebellion of Magnentius

367   'Conspiracy of the barbarians'; followed by refurbishment of many northern sites and inception of watchtowers on the Yorkshire coast

383–388   Rebellion of Magnus Maximus; instability on all frontiers

c. 395   Stilicho in Britain

c. 400   Gradual fragmentation of order and administration

Selective list of Roman emperors

31 BC-AD 14	Augustus
AD 14–37	Tiberius
37–41	Gaius (Caligula)
41–54	Claudius
54–68	Nero
68–69 (Jan)	Galba
69 (Jan-April)	Otho
69 (April-Dec)	Vitellius
69–79	Vespasian
79–81	Titus
81–96	Domitian
96–98	Nerva
98–117	Trajan
117–138	Hadrian
138–161	Antoninus Pius
161–180	Marcus Aurelius (jointly with Lucius Verus, AD 161–169)
180–192	Commodus
192–193	Pertinax
193	Didius Julianus
193–194	Pescennius Niger
193–197	Clodius Albinus
193–211	Septimius Severus
198–217	Caracalla
209–212	Geta
218–222	Elagabalus
222–235	Severus Alexander
238–244	Gordian III
244–249	Philip I
249–251	Trajan Decius

253–259	Valerian
253–268	Gallienus
268–270	Claudius II
259–273	'Independent Empire of the Gauls'
	Postumus, 259–268
	Victorinus, 269–271
	Domitianus, 271
	Tetricus I and II, 271–273
270–275	Aurelian
284–305	Diocletian
286–308	Maximian
287–296	'British Rebellion'
	Carausius, 287–293
	Allectus, 293–296
293–306	Constantius I
306–337	Constantine I
337–340	Constantine II
337–350	Constans
337–361	Constantius II
351–353	Magnentius
360–363	Julian
364–375	Valentinian I
364–378	Valens
367–383	Gratian
375–392	Valentinian II
379–395	Theodosius I
383–388	Magnus Maximus
392–394	Eugenius
395–423	Honorius

Selective list of Roman governors of Britain (Undivided)

AD 43–47	Aulus Plautius
47–52	Ostorius Scapula
52–58	Didius Gallus
58–59	Quintus Veranius
59–61	Suetonius Paullinus
61–63	Petronius Turpilianus
63–69	Trebellius Maximus
69–71	Vettius Bolanus
71–74	Petillius Cerialis
74–77	Julius Frontinus
77–83	Julius Agricola
83–101	Sallustius Lucullus

	Metilius Nepos
	Avidius Quietus
101–?	Neratius Marcellus
115–118	Atilius Bradua
118–122	Pompeius Falco
122–125	Platorius Nepos
131–134	Julius Severus
134–138	Mummius Sisenna
138–145	Lollius Urbicus
155–158	Julius Verus
161–163	Statius Priscus
163–166	Calpurnius Agricola
175–178	Antistius Adventus
180–185	Ulpius Marcellus
185–187	Helvius Pertinax
191–196	Clodius Albinus
197–202	Virius Lupus
202–205	Valerius Pudens
205–207	Alfenus Senecio

Passages from Tacitus relating to the Early History of Rome's Relationship with the Brigantes

The Brigantes, Venutius and Cartimandua

The two fullest accounts of the Brigantes to have survived in classical writers are those of the historian, Cornelius Tacitus, in *Histories* III. 45 and *Annals* XII. 40. Some of the problems inherent in the passages have been discussed in the main body of the text (see above in Chapter 3).

The passage from the *Annals*, although written later (*c.* A.D. 115) describes the earlier of the two situations – that is, in the 50s and 60s. The passage from the *Histories* (written *c.* A.D. 102) covers events leading up to Roman intervention in the 70s. Whilst there are shades of difference between the two accounts, both stress that at least some of the squabbling between Venutius and Cartimandua remained internal to the Brigantes, although the former was able to call on help from outside – perhaps from what is now Scotland. It is also tolerably clear that the overall effect of the tensions was actually to maintain the *status quo*. The fact that Tacitus compares Venutius and Caratacus as warriors is itself of interest, and would certainly help to explain how the Brigantes were so formidable under him (that is, during Bolanus' and Cerialis' governorships), and so much easier when he had been removed (that is, when Agricola went through the area in a single season).

I: *Annals* XII. 40

'Following the Roman capture of Caratacus, the foremost military thinker left in Britain was Venutius who, as I have already recorded,* was a Brigantian. Whilst he was married to queen Cartimandua, he enjoyed

---

* This is a reference evidently to an earlier mention of Venutius in a portion of the *Annals* which is now lost (Presumably in books VII-X, which dealt with the reign of Gaius Caligula and Claudius' early years).

Roman protection and was a loyal ally; however, after they split up he attacked her and even became embroiled in hostilities against us. At first, the Brigantian leaders confined themselves to fighting each other, as Cartimandua cleverly trapped Venutius' brother and dependents. Before long, however, Cartimandua's enemies became angry at the disgrace which they perceived to be involved in being ruled by a woman, and they attacked her kingdom with a hand-picked band of strong, young, warriors. We were ready for this, and made a pre-emptive strike with a force of auxiliaries which we sent in to support Cartimandua. Although these support-troops achieved little to start with, they were eventually successful; a similar reward attended the efforts of the legion which was commanded by Caesius Nasica. Didius Gallus (i.e. the provincial governor), an elderly man who was by now resting on his laurels, was happy to keep the enemy at arm's length through the actions of his subordinates.'

II: *Histories* III. 45

'The persistent rumours of civil war encouraged British morale and Venutius capitalised upon this. He was a man with a naturally violent disposition who hated everything to do with Rome. At this time, his temper was made worse as a result of a bitter personal feud with queen Cartimandua. Her influence lay in the nobility of her birth, and she had ruled over the Brigantes for some time; her power had increased as the result of her treacherous capture of king Caratacus which, it was generally thought, was the crowning glory of the emperor Claudius' British triumph. So she became wealthy, and enjoyed the luxurious lifestyle associated with success. She tired of her husband, Venutius, and gave herself instead to Vellocatus, her husband's armour-bearer, and shared her kingdom with him. The immediate effect of this was a shock-wave which ran throughout the royal family.

'The Brigantian tribesmen retained their loyalty to Venutius, although the new husband prospered as a result of the queen's infatuation with him and the harsh control which she exercised over her people. So Venutius called up help from outside, and this prompted the Brigantes to defect from Cartimandua who was left in real danger of defeat. So she appealed for Roman assistance; in the event, our auxiliary cavalry and infantry units, after an uphill struggle, rescued the queen from her immediate peril. As a result, Venutius was left in control of the kingdom, whilst we had a full-scale war on our hands.'

The problems of relating these passages are considerable largely because of the vagueness of Tacitus' chronology; the only events which can be dated are the capture of Caratacus (A.D. 51) and the Roman civil war (A.D. 68–69). For discussions, see Hanson and Campbell, 1986;

Braund, 1984; Shotter, 1994 and 2002. The suggestion that the enigmatic 'Elliptical Building' in the fortress at Chester was put at the ousted queen's disposal is unlikely in view of what appears to have been the unsuitable nature of a building, which never reached completion.

Similarly vague in chronology and topography is Tacitus' account of Agricola's second campaign in which he appears formally to have added the Brigantes to the province.

III: *Life of Agricola* 20

'In early summer, Agricola prepared his army for the year's campaigning season. He was himself much in evidence on the march, praising those who were well-disciplined and chivvying the stragglers. Agricola chose the camp-sites himself and personally reconnoitred estuaries and woods. In all of this, the enemy was given little respite from the sudden raids which the Romans launched on them. When he had made sufficient use of such intimidatory tactics, he would take the heat off and show them the attraction of peace. As a result, many groups, which had up to that time, lived independently, gave hostages, laid aside their hostility and accepted being fenced in with forts and garrisons. This was all done with such attention to detail that no new area had ever become part of the province with as little trouble as this.'

Abbreviations

Arch. Ael.	:	Archaeologia Aeliana.
BAR	:	British Archaeological Reports.
BNJ	:	British Numismatic Journal.
CAJ	:	Chester Archaeological Journal.
CIL	:	*Corpus Inscriptionum Latinarum.*
Class. Phil.	:	Classical Philology.
CW2 / CW3	:	Transactions of the Cumberland and Westmorland Antiquarian and Archaeological Society (Second/Third Series).
GMAJ	:	Greater Manchester Archaeological Journal.
ILS	:	*Inscriptiones Latinae Selectae* (H. Dessau).
JRS	:	Journal of Roman Studies.
LCAS	:	Transactions of the Lancashire and Cheshire Antiquarian Society.
LCHS	:	Transactions of the Lancashire and Cheshire Historic Society.
PSAS	:	Proceedings of the Society of Antiquaries of Scotland.
RIB	:	Roman Inscriptions of Britain.
RIC	:	The Roman Imperial Coinage (ed. H. Mattingly *et al.*).
YAJ	:	Yorkshire Archaeological Journal.
ZPE	:	Zeitschrift für Papyrologie und Epigraphik.

Bibliography

Abdy, 2002: Abdy R., A Survey of the Coin Finds from the Antonine Wall, *Britannia* 33, 189–217.

Allan, 1994: Allan M., *The Roman Route across the Northern Lake District*, Lancaster.

Allason-Jones and McKay, 1985: Allason-Jones L. and McKay B., *Coventina's Well*, Gloucester.

Austen, 1991: Austen P., *Bewcastle and Old Penrith: A Roman Outpost Fort and a Frontier Vicus*, Kendal.

Barker, 1975: Barker P., Excavations at the Baths Basilica at Wroxeter, 1966–74, *Britannia* 6, 106–117.

Barrett, 1989: Barrett A.A., *Caligula: The Corruption of Power*, London.

Bellhouse, 1953: Bellhouse R.L., A Roman Fort at Wreay Hall, near Carlisle, *CW2* 53, 49–51.

Bellhouse, 1954a: Bellhouse R.L., A Newly-discovered Roman Fort at Park House, near Carlisle, *CW2* 54, 9–16.

Bellhouse, 1954b: Bellhouse R.L., Roman Sites on the Cumberland Coast, 1954, *CW2* 54, 28–55.

Bellhouse, 1955: Bellhouse R.L., The Roman Fort at Burrow Walls, near Workington, *CW2* 55, 30–45.

Bellhouse, 1956: Bellhouse R.L., The Roman Temporary Camps near Troutbeck, Cumberland, *CW2* 56, 28–36.

Bellhouse, 1960a: Bellhouse R.L., The Roman Forts near Caermote, *CW2* 60, 20–23.

Bellhouse, 1960b: Bellhouse R.L., Excavations in Eskdale: The Muncaster Roman Kilns, *CW2* 60, 1–12.

Bellhouse, 1962: Bellhouse R.L., *Moricambe* in Roman Times and Roman Sites on the Cumberland Coast, *CW2* 62, 56–72.

Bellhouse, 1967: Bellhouse R.L., The Aughertree Fell Enclosures, *CW2* 67, 26–30.

Bellhouse, 1971: Bellhouse R.L., Roman Tileries at Scalesceugh and Brampton, *CW2* 71, 35–44.

Bellhouse, 1989: Bellhouse R.L., *Roman Sites on the Cumberland Coast*, Kendal.

Bellhouse, 1992: Bellhouse R.L., *Joseph Robinson of Maryport*, Otley.

Bennett, 1997: Bennett J., *Trajan: Optimus Princeps*, London.

Bewley, 1994: Bewley R.H., *Prehistoric and Romano-British Settlement in the Solway Plain, Cumbria*, Oxford.

Bidwell, 1985: Bidwell P.T., *The Roman Fort at Vindolanda*, London.

Bidwell, 1997: Bidwell P.T., *Roman Forts in Britain*, London.

Bidwell, 1999: Bidwell P.T. (Ed.), *Hadrian's Wall, 1989–1999*, Carlisle.

Bidwell, Snape and Croom, 1999: Bidwell P.T., Snape M. and Croom A., *Hardknott Roman Fort, Cumbria*, Kendal.

Birley Andrew, 2001: Birley Andrew, *Vindolanda's Military Bath Houses: The Excavations of 1970 and 2000*, Hexham.

Birley A.R., 1973: Birley A.R., Petillius Cerialis and the Conquest of Brigantia, *Britannia* 4, 173–190.

Birley A.R., 1979: Birley A.R., *The People of Roman Britain*, London.

Birley A.R., 1981: Birley A.R., *The Fasti of Roman Britain*, Oxford.

Birley A.R., 1997: Birley A.R., *Hadrian: The Restless Emperor*, London.

Birley A.R., 1998: Birley A.R., A New Tombstone from Vindolanda, *Britannia* 29, 299–306.

Birley A.R., 1999: Birley A.R., (Editor and Translator), *Tacitus: Agricola and Germany*, Oxford.

Birley A.R., 2000: Birley A.R., The Life and Death of Cornelius Tacitus, *Historia* 49, 230–247.

Birley A.R., 2001: Birley A.R., The Anavionenses, pp. 15–24 in Higham N.J. (Ed.), 2001.

Birley A.R., 2002: Birley A.R., *Garrison Life at Vindolanda*, Stroud.

Birley E.B., 1932: Birley E.B., Materials for the History of Roman Brougham, *CW2* 32, 124–139.

Birley E.B., 1946: Birley E.B., The Roman Site at Burrow-in-Lonsdale, *CW2* 46, 126–156.

Birley E.B., 1947: Birley E.B., The Roman Fort at Low Borrow Bridge, *CW2* 47, 1–19.

Birley E.B., 1951: Birley E.B., The Roman Fort and Settlement at Old Carlisle, *CW2* 51, 16–39.

Birley E.B., 1953a: Birley E.B., The Roman Milestone at Middleton-in-Lonsdale, *CW2* 53, 52–62.

Birley E.B., 1953b: Birley E.B., *Roman Britain and the Roman Army*, Kendal.

Birley E.B., 1953c: Birley E.B., The Roman Fort at Netherby, *CW2* 53, 6–39.

Birley E.B., 1958: Birley E.B., The Roman Fort at Brough-under-Stainmore, *CW2* 58, 31–56.

Birley E.B., 1961: Birley E.B., *Research on Hadrian's Wall*, Kendal.

Birley E.B., 1963: Birley E.B., Roman Papcastle, *CW2* 63, 96–125.

Birley R., 1977: Birley R., *Vindolanda: A Roman Frontier Post on Hadrian's Wall*, London.

Birley R., 1994: Birley R., *Vindolanda: I. The Early Wooden Forts*, Hexham.

Birley, Birley and Birley, 1993: Birley E.B., Birley R. and Birley A.R., *Vindolanda: II. The Early Wooden Forts*, Hexham.

Birley, Birley and Blake, 1999: Birley R., Birley Andrew and Blake J., *The 1998 Excavations at Vindolanda: The Praetorium Site: Interim Report*, Carvoran.

Bishop and Dore, 1988: Bishop M.C. and Dore J. N., *Corbridge: Excavations of the Roman Fort and Town, 1947–80*, London.

Blake B., 1959: Blake B., Excavations of Native (Iron Age) sites in Cumberland, 1956–58, *CW2* 59, 1–14.

Blake J., 2001: Blake J., *Vindolanda Excavations 2000: The Southern Defences of Stone Fort Two*, Carvoran.

Boatwright, 1987: Boatwright M.T., *Hadrian and the City of Rome*, Princeton.

Boon, 1972: Boon G.C., *Isca*, Cardiff.

Booth, 2001: Booth K., *Roman Saddleworth*, Saddleworth.

Bowman, 1994: Bowman A.K., *Life and Letters on the Roman Frontier*, London.

Bowman and Thomas, 1983: Bowman A.K. and Thomas J.D., *Vindolanda: The Latin Writing-Tablets*, London.

Branigan, 1980: Branigan K. (Ed.), *Rome and the Brigantes*, Sheffield.

Braund, 1984: Braund D., Some Observations on Cartimandua, *Britannia* 15, 1–6.

Breeze, 1974: Breeze D.J., The Roman Fortlet at Barburgh Mill, Dumfriesshire, *Britannia* 5, 130–162.

Breeze, 1982: Breeze D.J., *The Northern Frontiers of Roman Britain*, London.

Breeze, 1988: Breeze D.J., The Roman Army in Cumbria, *CW2* 88, 9–22.

Breeze, 1996: Breeze D.J., *Roman Scotland*, London.

Breeze and Dobson, 2000: Breeze D.J. and Dobson B., *Hadrian's Wall* (Fourth Edition), London.

Bruton, 1908: Bruton F.A., *The Roman Forts at Castleshaw: First Interim Report*, Manchester.

Bruton, 1909: Bruton F.A., *The Roman Fort at Manchester*, Manchester.

Bruton, 1911: Bruton F.A., *The Roman Forts at Castleshaw: Second Interim Report*, Manchester.

Bryant, Morris and Walker, 1986: Bryant S., Morris M. and Walker J.S.F., *Roman Manchester: A Frontier Settlement*, Manchester.

Bushe-Fox, 1913: Bushe-Fox J.P., The Use of Samian Pottery in Dating the Early Roman Occupation of the North of Britain, *Archaeologia* 64, 295–314.

Buxton, 1996: Buxton K., Roman Ribchester, pp. 11–18 in Graystone P., 1996.

Buxton and Howard-Davis, 2000: Buxton K. and Howard-Davis C.L.E., *Bremetenacum: Excavations at Roman Ribchester, 1980, 1989–90*, Lancaster.

Campbell, 1986: Campbell D.B., The Consulship of Agricola, *ZPE* 63, 197–200.

Carrington, 1985: Carrington P., The Roman Advance into the North-west Midlands before A.D. 71, *CAJ* 68, 5–22.

Carrington, 1994: Carrington P., *Chester*, London.

Carrington, 2002: Carrington P. (Ed.), *Deva Victrix: Roman Chester Re-assessed*, Chester.

Caruana, 1992: Caruana I.D., Carlisle: Excavation of a Section of the Annexe Ditch of the First Flavian Fort, 1990, *Britannia* 23, 45–109.

Caruana, 1992: Caruana I.D., Maryport and the Flavian Conquest of North Britain, pp. 40–51 in Wilson R.J.A. (Ed.), 1997.

Caruana, 2000: Caruana I.D., Roman Bewcastle, pp. 17–21 in James I. (Ed.), *A Bewcastle Miscellany*, Bewcastle.

Caruana and Shotter, 2002: Caruana I.D. and Shotter D.C.A., A Hoard of Roman Coins of the Third and Fourth Centuries from Distington, Cumbria, *CW*3 2, 67–78.

Casey, 1994: Casey P.J., *Carausius and Allectus: The British Usurpers*, London.

Charlesworth, 1964: Charlesworth D., Recent Work at Kirkby Thore, *CW*2 64, 61–75.

Charlesworth, 1965: Charlesworth D., Excavations at Papcastle, 1961–62, *CW*2 65, 102–114.

Cheeseman, 1914: Cheeseman G.L., *The Auxilia of the Roman Imperial Army*, Oxford.

Coarelli, 1999: Coarelli F., *La Colonna Traiana*, Rome.

Collingwood, 1915: Collingwood R.G., The Exploration of the Roman Fort at Ambleside: Report on the Second Year's Work (1914), *CW*2 15, 1–62.

Collingwood, 1916: Collingwood R.G., The Exploration of the Roman Fort at Ambleside: Report on the Third Year's Work (1915), *CW*2 16, 57–90.

Collingwood, 1921: Collingwood R.G., Explorations in the Roman Fort at Ambleside (Fourth Year, 1920), *CW*2 21, 1–42.

Collingwood, 1931: Collingwood R.G., A Roman Fortlet on Barrock Fell, near Low Hesket, *CW*2 31, 111–118.

Collingwood, 1938: Collingwood R.G., The Hill-Fort on Carrock Fell, *CW*2 38, 32–41.

Cool, 2004: Cool H.E.M., *The Roman Cemetery at Brougham: Excavations 1966–67*, London

Cowell and Philpott, 2000: Cowell R.W. and Philpott R.A., *Prehistoric, Romano-British and Medieval Settlement in Lowland North-west England*, Liverpool.

Curle, 1911: Curle J., *A Roman Frontier Post and Its People*, Glasgow.

Daniels, 1978: Daniels C.M., *J. Collingwood Bruce's Handbook to the Roman Wall* (Thirteenth Edition), Newcastle-upon-Tyne.

Daniels, 1980: Daniels C.M., Excavation at Wallsend and the Fourth-century Barracks on Hadrian's Wall, pp. 173–200 in Hanson W.S. and Keppie L.J.F. (Eds.), *Roman Frontier Studies, 1979*, Oxford (*BAR* S71 (i)).

Daniels, 1989a: Daniels C.M., The Flavian and Trajanic Northern Frontier, pp. 31–35 in Todd M. (Ed.), *Research on Roman Britain, 1960–89*, London.

Daniels, 1989b: Daniels C.M., *Mithras and His Temples on the Wall*, Newcastle-upon-Tyne.

Davies, 1971: Davies R.W., The Roman Military Diet, *Britannia* 2, 122–142.

Dearne, 1993: Dearne M.J. (Ed.), *Navio: The Fort and Vicus at Brough-on-Noe, Derbyshire*, Oxford (*BAR* 234).

Dearne and Lord, 1998: Dearne M.J. and Lord T.C. (Eds.), *The Romano-British Archaeology of Victoria Cave, Settle*, Oxford (*BAR* 273).

De la Bédoyère, 1999: De la Bédoyère G., *Hadrian's Wall: A History and Guide*, Stroud.

Dodd and Woodward, 1921: Dodd P.W. and Woodward A.M., Excavations at Slack, 1913–1915, *YAJ* 26, 1–92.

Dore and Gillam, 1979: Dore J.N. and Gillam J.P., *The Roman Fort at South Shields*, Newcastle-upon-Tyne.

Edwards, 1969: Edwards B.J.N., Lancashire Archaeological Notes, *LCHS* 121, 99–108.

Edwards, 1971: Edwards B.J.N., Roman finds from Contrebis, *CW2* 71, 17–34.

Edwards, 1977: Edwards B.J.N., A Chester Mithraic Figure Recovered, *CAJ* 60, 56–60.

Edwards, 1992: Edwards B.J.N., *The Ribchester Hoard*, Preston.

Edwards, 1998: Edwards B.J.N., The Romans and Before, pp. 1–28 in Crosby A.G., *Leading the Way: A History of Lancashire's Roads*, Preston.

Edwards, 2000: Edwards B.J.N., *The Romans at Ribchester*, Lancaster.

Edwards and Webster, 1985–88: Edwards B.J.N. and Webster P.V. (Eds.), *Ribchester Excavations*, Cardiff.

Ellis, 1978: Ellis P.B., *Caesar's Invasion of Britain*, London.

Esmonde Cleary, 1989: Esmonde Cleary A.S., *The Ending of Roman Britain*, London.

Evans and Scull, 1990: Evans J. and Scull C., Fieldwork on the Roman Fort Site at Blennerhasset, *CW2* 90, 127–138.

Evans, Limbrey and Cleere, 1975: Evans J.G., Limbrey S. and Cleere H. (Eds.), *The Effect of Man on the Landscape: The Highland Zone*, London.

Ferguson, 1970: Ferguson J., *The Religions of the Roman Empire*, London.

Ferrill, 1986: Ferrill A., *The Fall of the Roman Empire: The Military Explanation*, London.

Ferrill, 1991: Ferrill A., *Roman Imperial Grand Strategy*, London.

Ferris, 2000: Ferris I.M., *Enemies of Rome: Barbarians Through Roman Eyes*, Stroud.

Forde-Johnston, 1962: Forde-Johnston J., Hill Forts of Lancashire and Cheshire, *LCAS* 72, 9–46.

Frere, 1987: Frere S.S., *Britannia* (Third Edition), London.

Frere, 2000: Frere S.S., M. Maenius Agrippa, the *Expeditio Britannica* and Maryport, *Britannia* 31, 23–28.

Gerrard and Mills, 2002: Gerrard J. and Mills S., Some Stray Finds from the Ravenglass area, Cumbria, and Their Implications, *CW3* 2, 59–66.

Gibbons, 1989: Gibbons P., Excavations and Observations at Kirkby Thore, *CW2* 89, 93–130.

Gillam, 1949: Gillam J.P., 'Also, Along the Line of the Wall', *CW2* 49, 38–58.

Gillam, 1958: Gillam J.P., Roman and Native, 122–197, pp. 60–90 in Richmond I.A. (Ed.), *Roman and Native in North Britain*, Edinburgh.

Gillam, Jobey and Welsby, 1993: Gillam J.P., Jobey I.M. and Welsby D.A., *The Roman Bath-house at Bewcastle, Cumbria*, Kendal.

Gilliver, 1993: Gilliver C.M., Hedgehogs, Caltrops and Palisade Stakes, *Journ. Of Roman Military St.* 4, 49–54.

Gilliver, 1999: Gilliver C.M., *The Roman Art of War*, Stroud.

Goodburn and Bartholomew, 1976: Goodburn R. and Bartholomew P. (Eds.), *Aspects of the Notitia Dignitatum*, Oxford (*BAR* 15).

Grainger, 2002: Grainger J.D., *Nerva and the Roman Succession Crisis of A.D. 96–99*, London

Graystone, 1992: Graystone P., *Walking Roman Roads in Bowland*, Lancaster.

Graystone, 1996: Graystone P., *Walking Roman Roads in the Fylde and the Ribble Valley*, Lancaster.

Graystone, 2002: Graystone P., *Walking Roman Roads in Lonsdale and the Eden Valley*, Lancaster.

Grealey, 1976: Grealey S., *The Archaeology of Warrington's Past*, Warrington.

Green, 1976: Green M., *The Religions of Civilian Roman Britain*, Oxford (*BAR* 24).

Grimes, 1930: Grimes W.F., *The Works Depot of the Twentieth Legion at Castle Lyons*, Y Cymrodor 41.

Hanson, 1987: Hanson W.S., *Agricola and the Conquest of the North*, London.

Hanson and Campbell, 1986: Hanson W.S. and Campbell D.B., The Brigantes: From Clientage to Conquest, *Britannia* 17, 73–89.

Hanson and Maxwell, 1983: Hanson W.S. and Maxwell G.S., *The Antonine Wall: Rome's North-west Frontier*, Edinburgh.

Hanson, Daniels *et al.*, 1979: Hanson W.S., with Daniels C.M., Dore J.N. and Gillam J.P., The Agricolan Supply-Base at Red House, Corbridge, *Arch. Ael.*[5] 7, 1–98.

Hartley, 1966: Hartley B.R., Some Problems of the Roman Military Occupation of Northern England, *Northern History* 1, 7–10.

Hartley, 1972: Hartley B.R., The Roman Occupations of Scotland: The Evidence of Samian Ware, *Britannia* 3, 1–55.

Hartley, 1980: Hartley B.R., The Brigantes and The Roman Army, pp. 2–7 in Branigan K. (Ed.), 1980.

Hartley, 1987: Hartley B.R., *Roman Ilkley*, Ilkley.

Hartley and Fitts, 1988: Hartley B.R. and Fitts L., *The Brigantes*, Stroud.

Hartley K.F. and Webster, 1973: Hartley K.F. and Webster P.V., Romano-British Pottery Kilns near Wilderspool, *Arch. Journ.* 130, 77–103.

Haselgrove, 1996: Haselgrove C., The Iron Age, pp. 61–73 in Newman R. (Ed.), 1996.

Hassall, 1976: Hassall M.W.C., Britain in the *Notitia*, pp. 103–117 in Goodburn R. and Bartholomew P. (Eds.), 1976.

Haverfield and Collingwood, 1914: Haverfield F.J. and Collingwood R.G., Report on the Exploration of the Roman Fort at Ambleside, 1903, *CW2* 14, 433–465.

Henderson, 1985: Henderson A.A.R., Agricola in Caledonia: The Sixth and Seventh Seasons, *Echos du Monde Classique* 29, 318–335.

Henig, 1984: Henig M., *Religion in Roman Britain*, London.

Higham, 1978: Higham N.J., Early Field Survival in North Cumbria, pp. 119–125 in Bowen H.C. and Fowler P.J. (Eds.), *Early Land Allotment in the British Isles*, Oxford (*BAR* 48).

Higham, 1979: Higham N.J., An Aerial Survey in the Upper Lune Valley, pp. 31–38 in Higham N.J. (Ed.), *The Changing Past*, Manchester.

Higham, 1980: Higham N.J., Native Settlements West of the Pennines, pp. 41–47 in Branigan K. (Ed.), 1980.

Higham, 1982: Higham N.J., 'Native' Settlements on the North Slopes of the Lake District, *CW*2 82, 29–33.

Higham, 1986: Higham N.J., *The Northern Counties to A.D. 1000*, London.

Higham, 2001: Higham N.J. (Ed.), *The Archaeology of the Roman Empire: A Tribute to the Life and Work of Professor Barri Jones*, Oxford (*BAR* Int. Series 940).

Higham and Jones, 1975: Higham N.J. and Jones G.D.B., Frontier, Forts and Farmers, *Arch. Journ.* 132, 16–53.

Higham and Jones, 1983: Higham N.J. and Jones G.D.B., Excavation of Two Romano-British Farm Sites in North Cumbria, *Britannia* 14, 45–72.

Higham and Jones, 1985: Higham N.J. and Jones G.D.B., *The Carvetii*, Stroud.

Hildyard, 1951: Hildyard E.J.W., Renewed Excavations at Low Borrow Bridge, *CW*2 51, 40–66.

Hildyard, 1954: Hildyard E.J.W., Excavations at Burrow-in-Lonsdale, *CW*2 54, 66–101.

Hill, 1970: Hill P.V., *The Dating and Arrangement of the Undated Coins of Rome, A.D. 98–148*, London.

Hinchliffe and Williams, 1992: Hinchliffe J. and Williams J.H., *Roman Warrington*, Manchester.

Hind, 1983: Hind J.G.F., Who Betrayed Britain to the Barbarians in A.D. 367?, *Northern History* 19, 1–7.

Hinton, 2000: Hinton D.A., Decay and Revival: Early Medieval Landscapes, pp. 55–73 in Waller P. (Ed.), 2000.

Hoaen and Loney, 2003: Hoaen A. and Loney H., Later Prehistoric Settlement in Matterdale and Hutton Parishes, *CW*3 3, 51–65.

Hobley, 1989: Hobley A.S., The Numismatic Evidence for the Post-Agricolan Abandonment of the Roman Frontier in Northern Scotland, *Britannia* 20, 69–74.

Hodgson, 1995: Hodgson N., Were there two Antonine Occupations of Scotland?, *Britannia* 26, 29–49.

Hodgson, 2000: Hodgson N., The Stanegate: A Frontier Rehabilitated, *Britannia* 31, 11–22.

Hogg, 1965: Hogg R., Excavations of the Roman Auxiliary Tilery, Brampton, *CW*2 65, 133–168.

Holder, 1992: Holder P.A., *The Roman Army in Britain*, London.

Holder, 1997: Holder P.A., A Roman Military Diploma from Ravenglass, Cumbria, *Bull. John Rylands Library* 79, 3–41.

Howard-Davis and Buxton, 2000: Howard-Davis C.L.E. and Buxton K., *Roman Forts in the Fylde: Excavations at Dowbridge, Kirkham, 1994*, Lancaster.

Hunter, Manby and Spaul, 1967: Hunter J.K.T., Manby T.G. and Spaul J.E.H., Recent Excavations at the Slack Roman Fort, Near Huddersfield, *YAJ* 42, 74–97.

Jackson, 1983: Jackson R.P.J., The Chester Gladiator Rediscovered, *Britannia* 14, 87–95.

Jackson and Craddock, 1995: Jackson R.P.J. and Craddock P.T., The Ribchester Hoard: A Descriptive and Technical Study, pp. 75–102 in Raftery B. (Ed.), *Sites and Sights of the Iron Age*, Oxford.

Jackson and Potter, 1996: Jackson R.P.J. and Potter T.W., *Excavations at Stonea, Cambridgeshire, 1980–1985*, London.

Jarrett, 1954: Jarrett M.G., A Christian Monogram from Maryport, *CW2* 54, 268–270.

Jarrett, 1976: Jarrett M.G., *Maryport, Cumbria: A Roman Fort and its Garrison*, Kendal.

Johnson, 1980: Johnson A.S., *Later Roman Britain*, London.

Johnson, 1988: Johnson A.S., *The English Heritage Book of Hadrian's Wall*, London.

Joliffe, 1941: Joliffe N., Dea Brigantia, *Arch. Journ.* 98, 36–61.

Jones and Price, 1985: Jones G.C. and Price J., Excavations at The Wiend, Wigan, 1982–84, *GMAJ* 1, 25–33.

Jones, 1968: Jones G.D.B., The Romans in the North-west, *Northern History* 3, 1–26.

Jones, 1970: Jones G.D.B., Roman Lancashire, *Arch. Journ.* 127, 237–245.

Jones, 1972: Jones G.D.B., Excavations at Northwich (Condate), *Arch. Journ.* 128, 31–77.

Jones, 1974: Jones G.D.B., *Roman Manchester*, Altrincham.

Jones, 1975: Jones G.D.B., The North-western Interface, pp. 93–106 in Fowler P.J. (Ed.), *Recent Work in Rural Archaeology*, Bradford-on-Avon.

Jones, 1979: Jones G.D.B., The Future of Aerial Photography in the North, pp. 75–87 in Higham N.J. (Ed.), *The Changing Past*, Manchester.

Jones, 1980: Jones G.D.B., Archaeology and Coastal Change in the North-west, pp. 87–102 in Thompson F.H. (Ed.), *Archaeology and Coastal Change*, London.

Jones, 1982: Jones G.D.B., The Solway Frontier: Interim Report, 1976–81, *Britannia* 13, 283–297.

Jones, 1990a: Jones G.D.B., Searching for Caradog, pp. 57–64 in Burnham B.C. and Davies J.L. (Eds.), *Conquest, Co-existence and Change: Recent Work in Roman Wales*, Lampeter.

Jones, 1990b: Jones G.D.B., The Emergence of the Tyne-Solway Frontier pp. 98–107 in Maxfield V.A. and Dobson M.J. (Eds.), *Roman Frontier Studies, 1989*, Exeter.

Jones, 1991: Jones G.D.B., Farndon: An Archaeological Opportunity, *Manch. Arch. Bull.* 6, 75–77.

Jones, 1993: Jones G.D.B., Excavations on a Coastal Tower, Hadrian's Wall: Campfield Tower 2B, Bowness-on-Solway, *Manch. Arch. Bull.* 8, 31–39.

Jones, 1994/5: Jones G.D.B., Farnhill: Excavation on the Solway Frontier, *Manch. Arch. Bull.* 9, 23–27.

Jones and Keillar, 2002: Jones G.D.B. and Keillar I., '*In Fines Borestorum*': Reconstructing the Archaeological Landscape of Prehistoric and Proto-Historic Moray, *North Scotland* 22, 1–25.

Jones, Keillar and Maude, 1993: Jones G.D.B., Keillar I. and Maude K., The Moray Aerial Survey, pp. 47–74 in Sellar W.D.H. (Ed.), *Moray: Province and People*, Edinburgh.

Jones and Mattingly, 1990: Jones G.D.B. and Mattingly D., *An Atlas of Roman Britain*, Oxford.

Jones and Shotter, 1988: Jones G.D.B. and Shotter D.C.A., *Roman Lancaster*, Manchester.

Jones and Webster, 1968: Jones G.D.B. and Webster P.V., Mediolanum: Excavations at Whitchurch, 1965–6, *Arch. Journ.* 125, 193–254.

Jones and Wild, 1970: Jones G.D.B. and Wild J.P., Manchester University Excavations at Brough-on-Noe (*Navio*), 1969, *Derbys. Arch. Journ.* 70, 99–106.

Jones and Woolliscroft, 2001: Jones G.D.B. and Woolliscroft D.J., *Hadrian's Wall from the Air*, Stroud.

Jones M.J., 1975: Jones M.J., *Roman Fort Defences to A.D. 117*, Oxford (*BAR* 21).

Jones M.J., 1977: Jones M.J., Archaeological Work at Brough-under-Stainmore, 1971–72: I. The Roman Discoveries, *CW2* 77, 35–50.

Jones R.F.J., 1981: Jones R.F.J., Change in the Frontier: Northern Britain in the Third Century, pp. 393–414 in King A. and Henig M. (Eds.), *The Roman West in the Third Century*, Oxford (*BAR(S)* 109).

Keppie, 1984: Keppie L.J.F., *The Making of a Roman Army from Republic to Empire*, London.

Kilbride-Jones, 1938: Kilbride-Jones H.E., Excavations of a Native Settlement at Milking Gap, High Shield, Northumberland, *Arch. Ael.*[4] 15, 303–350.

King, 1978: King A., Gauber High Pasture, Ribblehead – An Interim Report, pp. 21–25 in Hall R.A. (Ed.), *Viking Age York and the North*, London.

Lambert *et al.*, 1996: Lambert J., Hair N.J., Howard-Davis C.L.E., Newman R.M. and Oliver T.M., *A Transect Through Time*, Lancaster.

Leather and Webster, 1988: Leather G.M. and Webster P.V., The Quernmore Kilns, pp. 85–93 in Jones G.D.B. and Shotter D.C.A. (Eds.), 1988.

Leech, 1993: Leech R.H., The Roman Fort and Vicus at Ambleside: Archaeological Research in 1982, *CW2* 93, 51–74.

Lepper and Frere, 1988: Lepper F. and Frere S.S., *Trajan's Column*, Gloucester.

LeQuesne, 1999: LeQuesne C., *Excavations at Chester: The Roman and Later Defences*, Chester.

Levick, 1999: Levick B., *Vespasian*, London.

Lightbown, 1996: Lightbown E., *The Dane's Pad: A Roman Road to Nowhere?*, Blackpool.

Lowndes, 1963: Lowndes R.A.C., 'Celtic' Fields, Farms and Burial Mounds in the Lune Valley, *CW2* 63, 77–95.

Lowndes, 1964: Lowndes R.A.C., Excavation of a Romano-British Farmstead at Eller Beck, *CW2* 64, 1–13.

Luttwak, 1976: Luttwak E.N., *The Grand Strategy of the Roman Empire*, London.

Mack, 1975: Mack R.P., *The Coinage of Ancient Britain*, London.

MacReady and Thompson, 1984: MacReady S. and Thompson F.H. (Eds.), *Cross-Channel Trade between Gaul and Britain in the Pre-Roman Iron Age*, London.

Mann, 1974: Mann J.C., The Northern Frontier after A.D. 369, *Glasgow Arch. Journ.* 3, 34–42.

Mann, 1989: Mann J.C., Birdoswald to Ravenglass, *Britannia* 20, 75–79.

Mann, 2002: Mann J.C., The Settlement of Veterans discharged from Auxiliary Units in Britain, *Britannia* 33, 183–187.

Mann and Roxan, 1988: Mann J.C. and Roxan M.M., Discharge Certificates of the Roman Army, *Britannia* 19, 341–347.

Mann S. and Dunwell, 1995: Mann S. and Dunwell A., An Interim Note on Further Discoveries in the Roman Vicus at Ambleside, 1992–93, *CW2* 95, 79–83.

Manning, 1975: Manning W.H., Economic influences on land use in the military areas of the Highland zone during the Roman Period, pp. 112–116 in Evans, Limbrey and Cleere (Eds.), 1975.

Marsden, 1987: Marsden P., *The Roman Forum Site in London*, London.

Mason, 1987: Mason D.J.P., Chester: the *Canabae Legionis*, *Britannia* 18, 143–168.

Mason, 2000: Mason D.J.P., *Excavations at Chester: The Elliptical Building*, Chester.

Mason, 2001: Mason D.J.P., *Roman Chester: City of the Eagles*, Stroud.

Mason, 2002: Mason D.J.P., *The Heronbridge Research Project: First Interim Report*, Chester.

Mason, 2003: Mason D.J.P., *Roman Britain and the Roman Navy*, Stroud.

Matthews, 2001: Matthews K., The Iron Age of North-west England, *CAJ* 76, 1–51.

Maxfield, 1989: Maxfield V.A. (Ed.), *The Saxon Shore*, Exeter.

Maxwell, 1989: Maxwell G.S., *The Romans in Scotland*, Edinburgh.

Maxwell, 1990: Maxwell G.S., *A Battle Lost: Romans and Caledonians at Mons Graupius*, Edinburgh.

McCarthy, 1986: McCarthy M.R., Woodland and Roman Forts, *Britannia* 17, 339–343.

McCarthy, 1990: McCarthy M.R., *A Roman, Anglian and Medieval Site at Blackfriars Street, Carlisle*, Kendal.

McCarthy, 1991: McCarthy M.R., *Roman Waterlogged Remains at Castle Street, Carlisle*, Kendal.

McCarthy, 1993: McCarthy M.R., *Carlisle: History and Guide*, Stroud.

McCarthy, 2000: McCarthy M.R., *Roman and Medieval Carlisle: The Southern Lanes*, Bradford.

McCarthy, 2002: McCarthy M.R., *Roman Carlisle and the Lands of the Solway*, Stroud.

Meier, 1995: Meier C., *Caesar*, London.

Middleton, Wells and Huckerby, 1995: Middleton R., Wells C.E. and Huckerby E., *The Wetlands of North Lancashire*, Lancaster.

Miller, 1975: Miller M., Stilicho's Pictish War, *Britannia* 6, 141–145.

Millett, 1990: Millett M., *The Romanisation of Britain*, Cambridge.

Nash-Williams, 1969: Nash-Williams V.E. (rev. Jarrett M.G.), *The Roman Frontier in Wales*, Cardiff.

Nevell, 1999: Nevell M. (Ed.), *Living on the Edge of Empire*, Manchester.

Nevell, 2001: Nevell M., The Edge of Empire: Late Prehistoric and Romano-British Settlement in North-west England. A Study in Marginality, pp. 59–74 in Higham N.J. (Ed.), 2001.

Newman, 1996: Newman R. (Ed.), *The Archaeology of Lancashire*, Lancaster.

Ogilvie, 1969: Ogilvie R.M., *The Romans and Their Gods*, London.

Ogilvie and Richmond, 1967: Ogilvie R.M. and Richmond I.A., *Cornelii Taciti De Vita Agricolae*, Oxford.

Olivier, 1987: Olivier A.C.H., Postscript: The Nature of the Ribchester Civil Settlement, pp. 117–126 in Edwards B.J.N. and Webster P.V. (Eds.), *Ribchester Excavations, Part 2*, Cardiff.

Peddie, 1994: Peddie J., *The Roman War-Machine*, Stroud.

Penney and Shotter, 1996: Penney S.H. and Shotter D.C.A., An Inscribed Roman Salt-Pan from Shavington, Cheshire, *Britannia* 27, 360–365.

Penney and Shotter, 2001: Penney S.H. and Shotter D.C.A., Further Inscribed Salt-Pans from Shavington, Cheshire, *CAJ* 76, 53–61.

Pennington, 1970: Pennington W., Vegetation History in the North-west of England, pp. 41–79 in Walker D. and West R.G. (Eds.), *Studies in the Vegetational History of the British Isles*, Cambridge.

Percival, 1976: Percival J., *The Roman Villa*, London.

Petts, 2003: Petts D., *Christianity in Roman Britain*, Stroud.

Pitts and St. Joseph, 1985: Pitts L.F. and St. Joseph J.K., *Inchtuthil: The Roman Legionary Fortress*, Gloucester.

Potter, 1975: Potter T.W., Excavations at Bowness-on-Solway, 1973, *CW2* 75, 29–57.

Potter, 1977a: Potter T.W., Excavations at the Roman Fort at Watercrook, 1975: A Second Interim Report, *CW2* 77, 49–52.

Potter, 1977b: Potter T.W., The Biglands Milefortlet and the Cumberland Coast Defences, *Britannia* 8, 149–183.

Potter, 1979: Potter T.W., *Romans in North-west England*, Kendal.

Potter and Johns, 1992: Potter T.W. and Johns C.M., *Roman Britain*, London.

Poulter, 1982: Poulter A.G., Old Penrith: Excavations 1977 and 1979, *CW2* 82, 51–64.

Powell, 1963: Powell T.G.E., Excavation at Skelmore Heads, near Ulverston, 1957 and 1959, *CW2* 63, 1–30.

Pugmire, 2003: Pugmire M., The Roman Road from Ravenglass to Ambleside in Lower Langdale: A Suggested Surviving Fragment, *CW3* 3, 85–89.

Rae and Rae, 1974: Rae A. and V., The Roman Fort at Cramond, Edinburgh: Excavations 1954–66, *Britannia* 5, 163–224.

Raftery, 1994: Raftery B., *Pagan Celtic Ireland: The Enigma of the Irish Iron Age*, London.

Ramm, 1978: Ramm H., *The Parisi*, London.

Reece, 1991: Reece R., Money in Roman Britain: A Review, pp. 29–34 in Jones R.F.J. (Ed.), *Roman Britain: Recent Trends*, Sheffield.

Reece, 2002: Reece R., *The Coinage of Roman Britain*, Stroud.

Reed, 1971: Reed N., The Fifth Year of Agricola's Campaigns, *Britannia* 2, 143–148.

Reed, 1977: Reed N., Cartimandua at Chester? pp. 41–43 in Haupt D. and Horn H. (Eds.), *Studien zu den Militärgrenzen Roms*, Bonn.

Richardson G., 1977: Richardson G.G.S., A Romano-British Farmstead at Fingland, *CW2* 77, 53–59.

Richardson A., 1982: Richardson A., Evidence for Centuriation in the Inglewood Forest, *CW2* 82, 67–71.

Richardson and Richardson, 1980: Richardson G.G.S. and Richardson A., A Possible Roman Road in the Kirkstone Pass and Matterdale, *CW2* 80, 160–162.

Richmond, 1925: Richmond I.A., The Roman Road Across Blackstone Edge, *Trans. of the Rochdale Lit and Scientific Society* 15, 41–70.

Richmond, 1933: Richmond I.A., Castlefolds by Great Asby, *CW2* 33, 233–237.

Richmond, 1936: Richmond I.A., Roman Leaden Sealings from Brough-under-Stainmore, *CW2* 36, 104–125.

Richmond, 1945: Richmond I.A., The Sarmatae, Bremetennacum Veteranorum and the Regio Bremetennacensis, *JRS* 35, 15–29.

Richmond, 1949: Richmond I.A., The Roman Road from Ravenglass to Ambleside, *CW2* 49, 15–31.

Richmond, 1951: Richmond I.A., A Roman Arterial Signalling-System in the Stainmore Pass, pp. 293–302 in Grimes W.F. (Ed.), *Aspects of Archaeology in Britain and Beyond*, London.

Richmond, 1954: Richmond I.A., Queen Cartimandua, *JRS* 44, 43–52.

Richmond, 1958: Richmond I.A., *Roman and Native in North Britain*, Edinburgh.

Richmond (Ed. Hassall), 1982: Richmond I.A. (Ed. Hassall M.W.C.), *Trajan's Army on Trajan's Column*, London.

Richmond and Crawford, 1949: Richmond I.A. and Crawford O.G.S., The British Section of the Ravenna Cosmography, *Archaeologia* 93, 1–50.

Richmond and Gillam, 1951: Richmond I.A. and Gillam J.P., The Temple of Mithras at Carrawburgh, *Arch. Ael.*[4] 29, 1–92.

Richmond and McIntyre, 1934: Richmond I.A. and McIntyre J., The Roman Camps at Rey Cross and Crackenthorpe, *CW*2 34, 50–61.

Richmond and Steer, 1957: Richmond I.A. and Steer K.A., Castellum Veluniate and Civilians on a Roman Frontier, *PSAS* 90, 1–6.

Rivet, 1970: Rivet A.L.F., The British Section of the Antonine Itinerary, *Britannia* 1, 34–82.

Rivet and Smith, 1979: Rivet A.L.F. and Smith C., *The Place-names of Roman Britain*, London.

Robertson, 1990: Robertson A.S. (rev. Keppie L.J.F.), *The Antonine Wall*, Glasgow.

Robinson, 1999: Robinson D.J., The Romans and Ireland Again, *CAJ* 75, 19–31.

Rogers I., 1996: Rogers I., The Conquest of Brigantia and the Development of the Roman Road-system in the North-west, *Britannia* 27, 365–368.

Rogers R., 1960: Rogers R.S., A Group of Domitianic Treason Trials, *Class. Phil.* 55, 19–23.

Ross and Robins, 1989: Ross A. and Robins D., *The Life and Death of a Druid Prince*, London.

Roxan, 1978: Roxan M.M., *Roman Military Diplomas, (RMD I), 1954–1977*, London.

Roxan, 1985: Roxan M.M., *Roman Military Diplomas, (RMD II), 1978–1984*, London.

St. Joseph, 1951: St. Joseph J.K., Air Reconnaissance of Northern Britain, *JRS* 41, 51–65.

St. Joseph, 1958: St. Joseph J.K., Air Reconnaissance in Britain, 1955–7, *JRS* 48, 86–101.

Salway, 1965: Salway P., *The Frontier People of Roman Britain*, Cambridge.

Salway, 1981: Salway P., *Roman Britain*, London.

Schönberger, 1969: Schönberger H., The Roman Frontier in Germany: An Archaeological Survey, *JRS* 59, 144–197.

Sealey, 1977: Sealey P.R., *The Boudiccan Revolt against Rome*, Princes Risborough.

Shotter, 1973: Shotter D.C.A., *Numeri Barcariorum*: A Note on *RIB* 601, *Britannia* 4, 206–209.

Shotter, 1976: Shotter D.C.A., Coin Evidence and the Northern Frontier in the Second Century A.D., *PSAS* 107, 81–91.

Shotter, 1978a: Shotter D.C.A., Three Early Imperial Hoards from Lancashire, *Coin Hoards* 4, 44–45.

Shotter, 1979: Shotter D.C.A., The Evidence of Coin-loss and the Roman Occupation of North-west England, pp. 1–13 in Higham N.J. (Ed.), *The Changing Past*, Manchester.

Shotter, 1980: Shotter D.C.A., Roman Coins from Starling Castle, *CW*2 80, 163.

Shotter, 1983a: Shotter D.C.A., The Principate of Nerva: Some observations on the Coin-evidence, *Historia* 32, 215–226.

Shotter, 1983b: Shotter D.C.A., A Note on Tiles found on the Mitre Yard, Lancaster, in 1973, *Britannia* 14, 270–271.

Shotter, 1990: Shotter D.C.A., *Roman Coins from North-west England*, Lancaster.

Shotter, 1993: Shotter D.C.A., Coin-loss and the Roman Occupation of North-west England, *BNJ* 63, 1–19.

Shotter, 1994: Shotter D.C.A., Rome and the Brigantes: Early Hostilities, *CW2* 94, 21–34.

Shotter, 1995a: Shotter D.C.A., Roman Coins from Manchester: Casual Losses, *Manch. Arch. Bull.* 9, 47–59.

Shotter, 1995b: Shotter D.C.A., Romans in South Cumbria, *CW2* 95, 73–77.

Shotter, 1995c: Shotter D.C.A., *Roman Coins from North-west England: First Supplement*, Lancaster.

Shotter, 1996: Shotter D.C.A., *The Roman Frontier in Britain*, Preston.

Shotter, 1997a: Shotter D.C.A., *Romans and Britons in North-west England* (Second Edition), Lancaster.

Shotter, 1997b: Shotter D.C.A., Roman Coins from Maryport, pp. 132–140 in Wilson R.J.A. (Ed.), 1997.

Shotter, 1998a: Shotter D.C.A., Three Roman Forts in the Lake District, *Arch. Journ.* 155, 338–351.

Shotter, 1998b: Shotter D.C.A., Roman North-west England: The Process of Annexation, *LCHS* 148, 1–26.

Shotter, 1998c: Shotter D.C.A., Roman Coins from Holt, *Studia Celtica* 32, 68–72.

Shotter, 1998d: Shotter D.C.A., *Roman Britain*, London.

Shotter, 1999a: Shotter D.C.A., Middlewich: The Evidence of Roman Coin-loss, *CAJ* 75, 51–60.

Shotter, 1999b: Shotter D.C.A., Chester: The Evidence of Roman Coin-loss, *CAJ* 75, 33–50.

Shotter, 1999c: Shotter D.C.A., Roman Coins in Whitby Museum, *YAJ* 71, 65–71.

Shotter, 2000a: Shotter D.C.A., Petillius Cerialis in Northern Britain, *Northern History* 36, 189–198.

Shotter, 2000b: Shotter D.C.A., The Roman Conquest of the North-west. *CW2* 100, 33–53.

Shotter, 2000c: Shotter D.C.A., *Roman Coins from North-west England: Second Supplement*, Lancaster.

Shotter, 2000d: Shotter D.C.A., The Roman Contribution, pp. 32–54 in Waller P. (Ed.), 2000.

Shotter, 2001a: Shotter D.C.A., Roman Lancaster: Site and Settlement, pp. 3–31 in White A.J. (Ed.), *A History of Lancaster*, Edinburgh.

Shotter, 2001b: Shotter D.C.A., ' "Agricolan" is an overworked adjective', pp. 75–83 in Higham N.J. (Ed.), 2001.

Shotter, 2001c: Shotter D.C.A., Petillius Cerialis in Carlisle: A Numismatic Contribution, *CW3* 1, 21–29.

Shotter, 2002a: Shotter D.C.A., Chester: Early Roman Occupation, pp. 25–31 in Carrington P. (Ed.), 2002.

Shotter, 2002b: Shotter D.C.A., Roman Britain and the Year of the Four Emperors, *CW*3 2, 79–86.

Shotter, 2003a: Shotter D.C.A., *Rome and Her Empire*, London.

Shotter, 2003b: Shotter D.C.A., Roman Coins from Low Borrow Bridge, *CW*3 3, 222–225.

Shotter, 2003c: Shotter D.C.A., The Murder of Flavius Romanus at Ambleside: A Possible Context, *CW*3 3, 228–231.

Shotter, 2004: Shotter D.C.A., Vespasian, *Auctoritas* and Britain, *Britannia* 35 (forthcoming).

Shotter and White, 1990: Shotter D.C.A. and White A.J., *The Roman Fort and Town of Lancaster*, Lancaster.

Shotter and White, 1995: Shotter D.C.A. and White A.J., *The Romans in Lunesdale*, Lancaster.

Simpson and Hodgson, 1947: Simpson F.G. and Hodgson K.S., The Coastal Milefortlet at Cardurnock, *CW*2 47, 78–127.

Smith D., 1959: Smith D.J., A Palmyrene Sculptor from South Shields, *Arch. Ael.*⁴ 37, 203–210.

Smith I., 1987: Smith I.G., *The First Roman Invasion of Scotland*, Edinburgh.

Smith I., 1997: Smith I.G., Some Roman Place-Names in Lancashire and Cumbria, *Britannia* 28, 372–383.

Snape and Bidwell, 2002: Snape M. and Bidwell P.T., The Roman Fort at Newcastle-upon-Tyne, *Arch. Ael.*⁵ 31 (extra volume).

Soffe and Henig, 1999: Soffe G. and Henig M., Roman Marble and Bronze Sculpture in the Kingdom of Togidubnus, *Ara* 8, 8–10.

Southern, 1989: Southern P., The *Numeri* of the Roman Imperial Army, *Britannia* 20, 81–140.

Southern, 1997: Southern P., *Domitian: Tragic Tyrant*, London.

Speidel, 1987: Speidel M.P., The Chattan War, the Brigantian Revolt and the Loss of the Antonine Wall, *Britannia* 18, 233–237.

Start, 1985: Start D., Survey and Conservation Work at Castleshaw Roman Forts, 1984–5, *GMAJ* 1, 13–18.

Stead, 1986: Stead I., *Lindow Man: The Body in the Bog*, London.

Stevens, 1937: Stevens C.E., Gildas and the *Civitates* of Britain, *Eng. Hist. Rev.* 52, 193–203.

Strang, 1997: Strang A., Explaining Ptolemy's Roman Britain, *Britannia* 28, 1–30.

Strang, 1998: Strang A., Recreating a Possible Flavian Map of Roman Britain, with a detailed Map of Scotland, *PSAS* 128, 425–435.

Strickland, 1995: Strickland T.J., *The Romans at Wilderspool*, Warrington.

Strickland, 2001: Strickland T.J., *Roman Middlewich*, Middlewich.

Strickland and Davey, 1978: Strickland T.J. and Davey P.J. (Eds.), *New Evidence for Roman Chester*, Liverpool.

Strong, 1968: Strong D.E., The Monument, pp. 40–73 in Cunliffe B.W., *Report on the Excavations at the Roman Fort at Richborough, Kent, Vol.5*, London.

Summerson, Trueman and Harrison, 1998: Summerson H., Trueman M. and Harrison S., *Brougham Castle, Cumbria*, Kendal.

Sutherland, 1937: Sutherland C.H.V., *Coinage and Currency in Roman Britain*, Oxford.

Swan, 1999: Swan V., The Twentieth Legion and the Antonine Wall Reconsidered, *PSAS* 129, 399–480.

Syme, 1968: Syme R., *Ammianus and the Historia Augusta*, Oxford.

Thompson, 1965: Thompson F.H., *Roman Cheshire*, Chester.

Thompson, 1976: Thompson F.H., The Excavation of the Roman Amphitheatre at Chester, *Archaeologia* 105, 127–139.

Thompson, 1980: Thompson F.H. (Ed.), *Archaeology and Coastal Change*, London.

Thorley, 2002: Thorley J., The Ambleside Roman Gravestone, *CW3* 2, 51–58.

Tindall, 1985: Tindall A.S., Wigan: The Development of the Town, *GMAJ* 1, 19–23.

Tomlin, 1992: Tomlin R.S.O., The Twentieth Legion at Wroxeter and Carlisle, *Britannia* 23, 141–158.

Tomlin, 1998: Tomlin R.S.O., Roman Manuscripts from Carlisle: The Ink-Written Tablets, *Britannia* 29, 31–84.

Turnbull, 1984: Turnbull P., Stanwick in the Northern Iron Age, *Durham Arch. Journ.* 1, 41–49.

Turnbull, 1998: Turnbull P., Excavations at Milefortlet 21, *CW2* 98, 61–106.

Tylecote, 1962: Tylecote R.F., *Metallurgy in Archaeology*, London.

Van Arsdell, 1989: Van Arsdell R.D., *Celtic Coinage of Britain*, London.

Van Arsdell, 1994: Van Arsdell R.D., *The Coinage of the Dobunni*, Oxford.

Vyner, 2001: Vyner B., *Stainmore: The Archaeology of a North Pennine Pass*, London.

Waddelove, A., 1986: Waddelove A.C., *The Development of the Roman Road Network: The Lower Dee Valley before A.D. 138*, Unpublished M. Phil. Thesis, University of Manchester.

Waddelove and Waddelove, 1983: Waddelove A.C. and E., Watling Street, South of Chester, *CAJ* 66, 13–22.

Waddelove E, 2001: Waddelove E., The Location of Roman Coccium?, *Britannia* 32, 299–304.

Walker, 1989: Walker J.S.F., *Castleshaw: The Archaeology of a Roman Fortlet*, Manchester.

Waller, 2000: Waller P. (Ed.), *The English Urban Landscape*, Oxford.

Ward, 1973: Ward J.H., The British Sections of the *Notitia Dignitatum*: An Alternative Interpretation, *Britannia* 4, 253–263.

Ward, 1998: Ward M., Some Finds from the Roman Works-Depot at Holt, *Studia Celtica* 32, 43–84.

Watkin, 1883: Watkin W.T., *Roman Lancashire*, Liverpool.

Webster, 1969: Webster G., *The Roman Imperial Army*, London.

Webster, 1971: Webster G., The Military Situations in Britain between A.D. 43 and 71, *Britannia* 1, 179–197.

Webster, 1978: Webster G., *Boudica*, London.

Webster, 1980: Webster G., *The Roman Invasion of Britain*, London.

Webster, 1981: Webster G., *Rome Against Caratacus*, London.

Webster, 1986: Webster G., *The British Celts and Their Gods under Rome*, London,

Webster, 1991: Webster G., *The Cornovii*, Stroud.

Webster P.V., 1975: Webster P.V., The Late Roman Occupation at Wilderspool, *CAJ* 58, 91–92.

Welfare and Swan, 1995: Welfare H. and Swan V., *Roman Camps in England: The Field Archaeology*, London.

Wells, 2003: Wells C., Environmental Changes in Roman North-west England: a Synoptic View of Events north of the Ribble, *CW3* 3, 67–84.

Welsby, 1980: Welsby D.A., Roman Building Inscriptions, recording Buildings collapsed through Age or destroyed by the Enemy?, *Arch. Ael.*[5] 8, 89–94.

White, 2001: White A.J. (Ed.), *A History of Lancaster*, Edinburgh.

Whittaker, 1994: Whittaker C.R., *The Frontiers of the Roman Empire*, London.

Wild, 1970: Wild J.P., *Textile Manufacture in the Northern Roman Provinces*, Cambridge.

Wilkes, 1965: Wilkes J.J., Early Fourth-century Rebuilding in Hadrian's Wall Forts, pp. 114–138 in Jarrett M.G. and Dobson B. (Eds.), *Britain and Rome*, Kendal.

Williams, 1985: Williams S., *Diocletian and the Roman Recovery*, London.

Wilmott, 1995: Wilmott T., *Birdoswald Roman Fort: A History and Souvenir Guide*, Carlisle.

Wilmott, 1996: Wilmott T., *Birdoswald: Excavations of a Roman Fort on Hadrian's Wall*, London.

Wilmott, 2001: Wilmott T., *Birdoswald Roman Fort*, Stroud.

Wilmott and Wilson, 2000: Wilmott T. and Wilson P. (Eds.), *The Late Roman Transition in the North*, Oxford (*BAR* 299).

Wilson, 1997: Wilson R.J.A. (Ed.), *Roman Maryport and its Setting*, Kendal.

Woolliscroft, 1988: Woolliscroft D.J., The Outpost System of Hadrian's Wall, *CW2* 88, 23–28.

Woolliscroft, 1994: Woolliscroft D.J., Signalling and the Design of the Cumberland Coast System, *CW2* 94, 55–64.

Woolliscroft, 2001: Woolliscroft D.J., The Roman Gask Project: Interim Report, 1995–2000, pp. 85–93 in Higham N.J. (Ed.), 2001.

Woolliscroft, 2002: Woolliscroft D.J., *The Roman Frontier on the Gask Ridge, Perth and Kinross*, Oxford (*BAR* 335).

Woolliscroft and Swain, 1991: Woolliscroft D.J. and Swain S.A.M., The Roman 'Signal' Tower at Johnson's Plain, *CW2* 91, 19–29.

Index

Index of Places and Personal Names which appear in the text and endnotes (n)
(Names of Roman Emperors are cited in capital letters)